SAVING THE REPUBLIC

SAVING

—THE—

REPUBLIC

THE FATE OF FREEDOM IN THE AGE OF THE ADMINISTRATIVE STATE

FOREWORD BY
VICTOR DAVIS HANSON

EDITED BY
ROGER KIMBALL

ENCOUNTER BOOKS

NEW YORK · LONDON

First American edition published in 2018 by Encounter Books,
an activity of Encounter for Culture and Education, Inc.,
a nonprofit, tax exempt corporation.
Encounter Books website address: www.encounterbooks.com

Manufactured in the United States and printed on acid-free paper.
The paper used in this publication meets the minimum
requirements of ANSI/NISO z39.48–1992
(R 1997) (*Permanence of Paper*).

FIRST AMERICAN EDITION

LIBRARY OF CONGRESS CATALOGING-IN-PUBLICATION DATA

Names: Kimball, Roger, 1953– editor.
Title: Saving the republic : the fate of freedom in the age of the
administrative state / edited by Roger Kimball.
Description: New York : Encounter Books, 2018. | Includes index.
Identifiers: LCCN 2017049918 (print) | LCCN 2017051722 (ebook) |
ISBN 9781594039669 (ebook) | ISBN 9781594039652 (hardcover : alk. paper)
Subjects: LCSH: Political culture—United States. | Politics,
Practical—United States. | United States—Politics and government.
Classification: LCC JK (ebook) | LCC JK1726 .S328 2018 (print) |
DDC 323.440973—dc23
LC record available at https://lccn.loc.gov/2017049918

CONTENTS

FOREWORD

THESE FOURTEEN ESSAYS first appeared as short monographs as part of Encounter Books' Broadside series – during and after the heated 2016 presidential election campaign and victory of Donald Trump. They address a variety of contemporary dangers to the American republic under the general aegis that our government is becoming far too big, too powerful, and too dangerous. If the successful populist presidential campaign of Trump and his signature slogans of "Make America great again" and "Drain the swamp" make this collection especially timely, the authors in turn also remind us why people were justifiably infuriated by the status quo and felt pushed to the edge in 2016.

I

The warnings issued in *Saving the Republic* are diverse. The wide range of topics is justified by the multifaceted pathologies that are eroding constitutional government. That said, all the essays do share a common historical approach of charting the relentless and insidious explosive growth of the administrative state in the late twentieth century. They also ominously conclude with warnings that caution that the finite resources of the state are now nearing exhaustion as the demands put upon them continue to escalate or that the administrative state has made the current US government almost unrecognizable to what the Founders envisioned.

The irony of supposedly good intentions gone wrong is also thematic. One would expect naiveté from rigid bureaucracies, which, unlike individuals, do not react quickly to changing stimuli and unfamiliar conditions. It follows that gun violence grows as gun control spreads, almost as if our inability to deal with the felony is psychologically excused by focusing on the misdemeanor. The same state that once had the power to ensure race-based segregated houses naturally demands race-based remedies to many of its own self-inflicted disasters. Left-wing free speech movements on campus turn totalitarian as unpopular speech is libeled as being hate filled – and thus by definition are not free. Government-mandated redistribution to alleviate inequality usually leads to greater impoverishment. Equality is achieved only in the sense of making richer people poorer, rather than making poorer people richer. The United Nations is neither united nor in most cases even nations, as we understand that word.

These essays, however, are not pessimistic, despite detailing the existential dangers posed by the expanding administrative state. They offer recognizable antidotes that are as time tried as they are simple: Trust the individual to make better decisions than unelected bureaucrats. Seek solutions by empowering grassroots democratic bodies rather than distant, centralized, and unelected agencies. Understand the fated cycle of higher taxes leading to larger government, to less freedom, and to greater impoverishment. Accommodate and react to predictable and unchanging human nature rather than empowering the state to try to change or deny it. Place confidence in human ingenuity and inventiveness as collective assets rather than demonizing them as selfish and disruptive traits deserving of fear and punishment.

II

The huge and still-growing permanent bureaucracy and deathless administrative state have become unaccountable to the voters by outliving elected officials, outlasting reform movements, and counting on revolving-door elected officials to stay dependent on stationary and tenured entrenched "experts." One natural result, according to Jay Cost's initial essay, is that the pragmatic attitude of "if you cannot beat them, join them" leads to the permanence of crony capitalists, both liberal and conservative. These insiders stifle competition. They redirect economic activity away from market rationalism and private-sector profit and loss. And they drive up consumer costs. Crony capitalism ensures that regulations are aimed at perceived innovative competitors who play by new rules while government and private-sector managers switch occupations so frequently that they become almost indistinguishable.

Philip Hamburger emphasizes how the growing tentacles of the government octopus are nourished by the full assets of the state. In comparison, the targeted individual citizen usually has neither the time nor the money to fight back, whether in the courts, against imposed regulations, or when hounded by vindictive civil servants who are legally and financially exempt from the consequences of their overreach. The local midlevel bureaucrat can draw on his resources to make a regulatory case that his targeted offender cannot match — a fact known to a state auditor that only further encourages his sense of unchecked ambition and vindictiveness. The psychosocial landscape assumes that the state is working on behalf of the people; the individual solely for himself.

It is difficult to know, in this chicken-and-egg dilemma, whether such an administrative state restricted our freedoms or those opposed to free expression naturally created the administrative state. It is perhaps easier to appreciate just how compatible bureaucracies are with censorship and a servile press. As Mollie Ziegler Hemingway goes on to show in a prescient essay on the new twenty-first-century media – written during and right after the release of the WikiLeaks trove revealing journalists' collusion with the 2016 Hillary Clinton campaign – cronyism is not just confined to business. It infects and has nearly destroyed a once-independent media as well.

Like their corporate counterparts, journalists go in and out of government. Indeed, one reason that they are overwhelmingly liberal is perhaps because the administrative state offers them so many revolving doors for profitable sinecures. The administrative state's bicoastal culture mimics the tastes and values of the big media. But, far more importantly, modern journalism accepts the presumptions of both the administrative state and elitist crony capitalism: the shared notion that one can afford to be utopian and adopt ideological principles on the assurance that the real-life consequences can be avoided as they fall on the less well connected. As it translated to the 2016 election, that meant the pitchfork-bearing outsiders were largely in the red-state swath between the two coastal corridors, and furious over the hypocrisy and arrogance of the ruling class. So it is no accident that the media despised Donald Trump, not just as yet another conservative but as a reckless and uncouth conservative outsider who won through mesmerizing what Senator John McCain once dismissed as the "crazies." It was also no surprise that this media disdain was joined by the animosity of deep-state employees and insider corporations.

This insidious rise of the state, however, does not just involve the loss of an independent and self-critical media or our daily habits and traditions – as we saw during the Obama administration, when reporters were temperamentally unable to expose government crimes and misdemeanors that jeopardized the progressive idea of an always more intrusive bureaucracy.

David B. Kopel reminds us that the zeal for federal gun control and emasculation of the Second Amendment is not fueled necessarily by a desire for less gun violence. Indeed, if the aim of gun control was just less murdering on the streets, the carnage of Chicago and Baltimore would have been reduced by the strict gun control laws of both Illinois and Maryland and even-tougher municipal statutes. Nor is the effort to deny citizens the right to bear arms just the effort of a tyrannical state that believes it can violate the Constitution more easily amid a docile and unarmed populace. It is far worse than that. Once the modern citizen is denied the ability to protect his own person and property, he becomes entirely reliant on the state for security. The disarmed and dependent citizen must become an unwitting ally in the tyranny of the paternal government. Disarming the citizen does not reduce crime; indeed, armed citizens create a general sense of deterrence that discourages criminal activity. Instead, massive federal gun control ensures that a once-autonomous citizen will need to be docile if he wants reliable state protection for his family and property – and servile in the face of the government growth and policies deemed necessary to provide it.

The protocols of the administrative state are not natural to the individual. They have to be inculcated. That challenge means the veritable end to the ancient idea of a university as a safe space where induction and empiricism are prized, and eccentricity and dissent even more so. But if the individual is taught to think – and given the curricula, resources, and instruction to practice independent and critical inquiry – what happens should he oppose the administrative state, and, by inference, the university-progressive doctrines that fuel large government? As Greg Lukianoff laments, the result is a veritable American Animal Farm in which anti-Constitutional rules and a mob mentality stifle free expression. The previously unsubstantiated notion of minorities, females, and the poor without power, who once counted on the right to free speech, personal protection, and equitable integration, has now become a surreal landscape in which censorship, gun control, and segregation are pushed on campuses to perpetuate self-serving dogmas – protected by the very state apparatus that once was seen as antithetical to the aspirations of the outsider. Once an equality of opportunity was ensured, the university saw its next duty as mandating an equality of result – and doing so by whatever means were necessary to achieve that impossible goal. Segregation has become safe spaces; free speech is now hate speech; censorship is renamed trigger warnings; and mandated racial discrimination is praised as affirmative action.

In this new symbiotic relationship between the progressive university and administrative state, Andrew C. McCarthy demonstrates how abstract ideas soon have deadly consequences when institutionalized by government. To address the evil that manifested itself on September 11, 2001, and has led to hundreds of Islamic-inspired terrorist attacks in the West since, modern society must remain empirical and inductive to identify and define its existential enemies – in this case, radical Islamists who have scapegoated Western society for their own self-inflicted ills. But honest discussion of the dangers and pathologies of radical Islam had revealed two fault lines. One, popular multiculturalism of the campus and state held that no particular culture, religion, or tribe is inferior to its Western counterpart – and more often that only Western paradigms and traditions are blameworthy. Second, because Islamists are illiberal and inherently violently intolerant of their critics, it has become dangerous to disagree with them. The result throughout the West has been base cowardice in failing to call out the prejudices and hatred of Islamists – albeit dressed up as multicultural deference and sensitivity. Progressive outreach has usually been interpreted by radical Muslims as a weakness to be exploited rather than a magnanimity to be reciprocated, on the strong-horse theory of bin Laden that any civilization that does not defend its values has lost it Darwinian right to exist.

The dangers posed by the progressive administrative state are not just confined to government, culture, universities, free speech, and national security. The very economic vitality of a society hinges on free-market economics, the sanctity of private property, and the freedom to succeed or fail in the marketplace. Yet these are precisely the values that the administrative state sees as dangerous and antithetical to its own monopoly of ensuring that mandated equality is far more important than general prosperity. The ensuing damage to the economy is manifested in lots of ways.

Jared Meyer points out the ironies of progressive cities enacting regulations that hurt the working classes and poor. Union requirements, strict environmental regulations, and no-growth policies tend to ossify a shared economy and discourage fluidity between the classes and thwart upward mobility. Efforts to ban Uber, for example, in deference to limousine and taxi interests, limit choice and opportunity – both for those who are finally afforded the ability to drive without first having to find capital for licenses and for the poor who cannot afford access to specialized and tailored transportation. The same thinking seeks to restrict Airbnb – the online hospitality brokerage service that matches tourists with a vast of array of inexpensive lodging choices – which faces state discouragement driven by well-funded hotel interests. To empower such new online businesses, which most effectively serve the poor and middle class, would require the administrative state to concede the superiority of private enterprise over state regulators in addressing the practical needs of citizens – and thus it becomes nearly impossible to conceive of it actually happening.

In two related essays, James Piereson demonstrates why state efforts to mandate equality through redistributive taxes and entitlements usually not only fail but often can depress economic activity to such an extent that they widen inequality. The rich either invest huge amounts of resources in avoiding high taxes, often in ways that hurt the larger economy, or retrench, reasoning that any meager after-tax profits are not worth the extra effort.

More deleterious is the boomerang effect of mandated redistribution. The state often taxes the lower classes to pay the Social Security and Medicare costs of those who are far wealthier – along with the vast overhead of administrate-state employees. Piereson, in dissecting Thomas Piketty's new book *Capital in the Twenty-First Century* and the liberal hagiography that followed it (what he calls the "Piketty Bubble"), notes that CEOs and the new mega-wealthy are richer than ever before, but largely because everyone is as well. The principles of free-market capitalism, in varying degrees, have united the world and brought into the workplace billions of people who were for a variety of reasons not engaged in mutually profitable pursuits for a globalized shared economy. Implicit in Piereson's dismantling of the theories of state redistributionists is exposing the doctrine that evidence and results do not matter for the administrative state. Big government always believes that its own ideas of mandatory equality should be excused from rigorous cross-examination.

Speaking of a globalized economy, world markets are quite different from world governance, and freer markets do not always equate with more open and freer societies. The internationalist project of the United Nations is a good case in point. Claudia Rosett asks why the United States still participates fully in a supposedly democratically organized supranational body whose members are so often nondemocratic and quite bloodthirsty – not surprising when less than 50 percent of the world's population live under constitutional and consensual governments. Few of the U.N.'s postwar promises were ever met. The United States and NATO won the Cold War despite, not because of, the U.N. Its peacekeeping forces rarely keep the calm, and often manage to corrupt it. For Americans, the U.N. has had a bad habit of relying on American funding, military supremacy, and liberal governance to play global sheriff, even as it hectors and ankle-bites its patron – apparently on the premise that America would never ask it to leave New York, much less cut its funding. Rosett warns that the compromised ethics, inefficiency, lack of accountability, and moral equivalency of the U.N. reflect the unaccountable administrative state taken to its logical global conclusion – and therefore that it is something to be avoided at all costs.

What is the ideological and political fuel for the administrative state at home and sympathy for statism abroad? Progressive politics and the Democratic Party largely explain the ceaseless effort to cede the autonomy of the individual to an unelected bureaucracy beholden to politicians who, in practical terms, promise income redistribution, government employment, and state entitlements in exchange for votes. Avik Roy demonstrates why Medicaid – the federal government's program to ensure medical coverage for the impoverished – is not just cost ineffective but actually does not deliver real care to those who are "insured." The chief fallacy of Medicaid, as is also true of Obamacare, is a notion "that health insurance equals health care." It does not. When government does not reimburse health care providers at market rates, there are fewer doctors willing to take on Medicaid patients. And for those doctors who do, there is an incentive to bill the government for often-unnecessary and more expensive specialized treatments, to order superfluous procedures and tests, and to up the number of patients in order to seek compensation through the quantity rather than quality of care offered. The downward spiral is fueled by the subsidized patient who has little incentive to investigate doctors and hospitals to ensure that his coverage will provide cost-effective care.

In policing sex discrimination in education, the administrative state has ignored individual rights. The result has not just been inefficiency and waste but, as in the case of Medicaid, an outcome that is antithetical to the government's own original intent. Title IX refers to the 1972 federal law that was originally sold as a means to prevent sex discrimination in all education programs that receive federal funds. Forty-five years later, Title IX has expanded into something unimaginable at its birth: a lawless government that has reengineered and often eliminated college athletic programs and denied students both their First and Fifth Amendment rights to free expression and due process under the law. Title IX, as Robert L. Shibley relates, embraced all the familiar administrative state themes. Bureaucratic theories of sex equity and disparate impact supersede any need to prove gender discrimination. Critics that cite constitutional abuses are silenced on the implication that their expression must be sexist and discriminatory. Title IX Justice Department officials and campus bureaucrats can exercise such unconstitutional powers because their targets do not have the legal resources to resist effectively. And the more supposed sex discrimination that can be found and punished, the more incentives to justify an expansion of Title IX adjudication. Ultimately almost every US campus receives some sort of federal financial aid, and thus the fear of cash cutoffs makes it cost effective for targets simply to concede and plea bargain.

Michael Walsh and Kevin D. Williamson conclude the volume by narrowing the focus of culpability for the administrative state to the Democratic Party. Walsh reminds us that, in a classic case of "Who will police the police?" many of the sins that the administrative state has claimed to address – from slavery to racism – were originally embedded deeply within the Democratic Party. The Democrats' administrative state might have originally been concerned with ensuring an equality of opportunity, but once that goal was legally achieved, Democrats, like the university, moved on to the next and far greater challenge of ensuring an equality of result. Their premise has been that the individual characteristics and conditions that govern success or failure are not as critical as the collective immutable constants of race, class, and gender. In more practical terms, the Democratic Party has been able to grow the administrative state, despite bouts of popular and legislative pushback, through its tripartite sources of unelected power in the courts, the campuses, and the media. The thrust of Walsh's essay is that the Democratic Party appreciates the power of government because it has so often used it to perpetuate what in its latest incarnation it ostensibly opposes.

Kevin D. Williamson finishes and summarizes the volume with the tragic case of Detroit – once the most successful and indeed affluent of American cities. Its florescence is synonymous with America's technological and industrial miracles that won World War II. Subsequently, the policies that the coming Detroit mayors enacted – higher taxes and fees, larger budgets, greater deficits, mandated race-based hiring, government housing, and generous welfare entitlements – ostensibly sought equality and racial harmony. But they had the opposite effect of driving out the working classes, spiking crime, fomenting riot and unrest, ensuring white flight, and institutionalizing a large nonwhite underclass almost wholly dependent on the quid pro quo generosity of the administrative state and its legions of federal, state, and local clerks. What happened when the money ran out? Williamson's summary of Detroit's sad plight might just as well apply to the impending fate of the country at large: "Detroit is a case of the parasite having outgrown the host."

III

For all the diverse and deleterious symptoms, the medicine for the common disease is familiar in all these contributions: Always trust the individual over the state. Assume that human nature is neither malleable nor can be recalibrated by elite minders in education, health, and the media. Ensure that state administrators are accountable to the people and stop hounding their individual targets. Equate government bureaucracies, more regulations, and larger entitlements with the Democratic Party, which must win over new voters by promises of hiring, paying, and giving always more. Government programs can be judged only by the degree of incentives and self-reliance they offer the individual. And treat the loud cynic and bothersome critic as invaluable in modifying, changing, and ending a program – not as the near treasonous dissenter who acts out of material and psychological selfishness.

One way or the other, the administrative state will come to an end – either with the bang of insolvency or through the whimper of reform and restraint. *Saving the Republic* warns us of the former even as it offers the remedy of the latter. In our eleventh hour of $20 trillion of national debt, a bureaucracy whose chief aim is its own growth, and an irate and restless populace, the choice is ours alone.

JAY COST

WHAT'S SO BAD ABOUT CRONYISM?

C RONYISM IS a relatively new issue for the conservative
movement. While long worried about burdensome
regulations and taxes, the right has only recently grown
concerned about the improper networks connecting the
government and special interests. Of course, conservatives have opposed cronyism in specific instances over the
decades. For instance, they complained about farm subsidies as early as the 1950s, and they celebrated the 1986
Tax Reform Act because it eliminated tax breaks for many
special interests. Still, thinking about cronyism as a general issue is of recent vintage.

The first conservative critiques of cronyism began
around 2006. In *The K Street Gang,* Matt Continetti attacked
the relationship between congressional Republicans and
lobbyists, and in *The Big Ripoff,* Timothy P. Carney detailed
how the government favors special interests. Combined,
they signaled growing conservative frustration that the
"Republican revolution" had facilitated bigger government
and more corruption. The Troubled Asset Relief Program
of 2008 exacerbated these worries. While many believed
this program to be necessary, conservatives of all stripes
thought it a bitter pill to swallow. Government favoritism

toward the housing and financial-services industries had precipitated an economic collapse, and here was Uncle Sam bailing out its own cronies.

Then came the Barack Obama administration. For the two years that Obama, Nancy Pelosi, and Harry Reid ran the government, it was as if Tammany Hall had descended upon the Potomac River. Suddenly, cronyism was everywhere. From the stimulus to Obamacare to Dodd-Frank to the IRS scandal, it seemed as if Obama's cronies had taken complete control over public policy. That is when cronyism emerged as a major issue on the right, generating an explosion of serious work. Carney, Peter Schweizer, Michelle Malkin, and David Freddoso all wrote accounts detailing the pernicious links between the government and special interests. The *Washington Examiner* and the *Washington Free Beacon* started tracking down bad actors on a daily basis. The Tea Party waves of 2010 and 2014 produced senators like Mike Lee and Tom Cotton, who made cronyism a centerpiece of their political campaigns.

This hardly marks the start of the fight against cronyism. Ralph Nader and his allies have been railing against "corporate welfare" for a half century. Before him, Teddy Roosevelt's Progressive Party bemoaned the "invisible government" of "corrupt interests ... owing no allegiance and acknowledging no responsibility to the people." Nearly a century before T. R., Andrew Jackson had denounced the capacity of government "to grant titles, gratuities, and exclusive privileges, to make the rich richer and the potent more powerful." Before Old Hickory, Thomas Jefferson and James Madison had been deeply worried about corruption in the Bank of the United States.

In other words, cronyism is an old issue, even if conservatives are relatively new to it. As a public-policy problem, it should not be taken lightly. Jefferson, Madison, Jackson, and Roosevelt all fought cronyism, yet it still vexes the body politic. So if we hope to deal with it, we need to understand it better.

* * *

A sensible starting point is Aristotle. In *The Politics,* he categorizes a *polis* (civic body) by answering two questions: First, is the sovereign a single person, a few elite, or the people at large? Second, on whose behalf does this sovereign rule?

> *On this basis we may say that when the One, or the Few, or the Many rule with a view to the common interest, the constitutions under which they do so must necessarily be right constitutions. On the other hand the constitutions directed to the personal interest of the One, or the Few, or the Masses, must necessarily be perversions.*

By this reckoning, cronyism is a perversion of good government. *Merriam-Webster* defines *cronyism* as "the unfair practice by a powerful person (such as a politician) of giving jobs and other favors to friends." When politicians use their authority to benefit their associates rather than the people at large, that is cronyism. Because you usually have to have money to make friends with politicians, cronyism is typically a type of oligarchy, which Aristotle defines as the rule of the wealthy.

The question of what to do about cronyism has long troubled political philosophers. The framers of our Constitution did not use the word *cronyism,* but they understood how government could be perverted in such ways. Madison in particular was worried about factions distorting policy for their own ends. Factionalism, he argues in *Federalist*

No. 10, is "sown into the nature of man," which means that the promotion of public virtue is only of limited efficacy. The best way to deal with this problem is a "well-constructed Union," which may "break and control the violence of faction." In other words, all people are self-interested and will try to pervert government toward their interests; what we need, therefore, are rules that keep this from happening.

Prior to Madison's age, cronyism had been a common problem in monarchies. The king's favorites often established a court faction that could rule against the common good. England's Glorious Revolution strongly cut down on the sovereignty of the king, but new problems soon emerged, thanks to the development of international trade and the market economy. This was a boon for Europe, and many governments adopted a mercantilistic model to direct the economy. Britain, for instance, kept tight control over her American colonies with the Navigation Acts and directed the flow of trade via royally chartered organizations like the East India Company, which was enormously profitable for Britain and created many a fortune for those who invested in it. This in turn gave it enormous political power, as these wealthy nabobs entered the House of Commons with an eye to protecting the company.

This mixing of public and private interests led to cronyism. By the 1760s the company was struggling, so the nabobs lobbied for a bailout, which the government supplied. The Tea Act of 1773 allowed the company to dump its surplus directly into North America, rather than through secondary merchants. Moreover, the Tea Act retained the Townshend duties on tea sold in the colonies. Lord North, the British Prime Minister, thought he had killed two birds with one stone: the company could unload its surplus, and the American colonists would implicitly accept Parliament's right to tax them (as the company's tea would still be cheaper than that of its competitors, even with the tax). Yet North had gravely miscalculated. Boston merchants and the Sons of Liberty sneaked into Boston Harbor in December 1773 and dumped more than 300 crates of tea into the water. This event, later named the Boston Tea Party, would be a milestone in America's path to independence. It was also one of the nation's first experiences with cronyism.

As an independent nation, the United States would similarly bestow government charters upon corporations, and cronyism was a predictable result. In 1790, Treasury Secretary Alexander Hamilton proposed the Bank of the United States, an ingenious institution that would secure the nation's perilous finances by linking the financial and commercial elite to the new government. Yet it was a breeding ground for cronyism, as those with insider knowledge of the bank's activities enriched themselves. Jefferson and Madison were outraged and hotly opposed the bank during the 1790s, but the demands of modernization were too pressing for them to dismantle it. As president, Jefferson kept the bank in place, and Madison even chartered the Second Bank in 1816. This, too, was prone to cronyism, as bank managers rewarded their political friends at the expense of the nation's financial well-being. Meanwhile, state governments chartered corporations left and right – not only banks, but also new companies to build canals, bridges, and railroads. Insiders made vast fortunes on their political connections, making state-based cronyism even more pernicious than the federal variety.

The problem was that the government's new economic ventures typically supported public ends through private means. In such undertakings, the distinction between the two often becomes blurry. Those who make a private fortune from a public undertaking are compelled to invest a portion of their subsidies into the political process to protect their benefits. For instance, the First Bank secured the nation's finances via the Northeastern elite, who used their profits to influence the government. Jefferson warned George Washington that Hamilton's Treasury was distributing bank shares to create "an influence of his department over the members of the legislature" in order to keep the bank's charter from being altered or revoked. Meanwhile, Madison predicted, "the stock-jobbers will become the pretorian band of the Government, at once its tool and its tyrant; bribed by its largesses, and overawing it by clamours and combinations."

Jefferson and Madison were striking at an essential aspect of modern cronyism. It is a *conflict of interest*, which directly relates to the scope of the government's purpose. In his veto message for the Second Bank, Jackson praised a government that would "confine itself to equal protection, and, as Heaven does its rains, shower its favors alike on the high and the low, the rich and the poor." Such a night-watchman state would likely not fall prey to cronyism, but it also would not do many tasks we take for granted, including developing the economy. When the government does that – by chartering corporations, imposing protective tariffs, subsidizing exports, or whatever – it inevitably distributes benefits unequally. These may be public-spirited measures to grow the economy, but they use some faction for that purpose. In theory, everybody benefits at least a little bit from such initiatives, but those whom the government directly employs benefit more. They are naturally prone to become cronies to protect their subsidy.

Another lesson from the early republic is that mass-based democracy facilitates cronyism. If government activism creates a supply of cronies, democracy creates a demand for them among politicians. The modern campaign poses enormous logistical and financial challenges to office seekers, in an example of what economists call the collective-action dilemma. The money and manpower required to win an elective office are simply staggering, and have been for a long time. This problem became particularly acute in the 1820s, when the presidency became fully democratized. Jackson generated the effort needed to wage his successful campaign by developing the spoils system, which distributed government jobs to campaign loyalists. Faced with a raucously democratic electoral process, politicians from all across the country embraced Jackson's program. Pretty soon, all manner of jobs and contracts were distributed based on how much somebody had helped the campaign. After the Civil War, patronage birthed massive statewide political machines, where party bosses ruled with an iron fist.

This was cronyism on a massive, *systemic* level, the likes of which the world had never seen before. The effect on public administration was enormously detrimental. For starters, the heavy turnover at government agencies meant that the workload had to be left to a clique of low-level, permanent staffers. In addition to that, the party expected a lot in return from its workers. They had to kick a portion of their salary back to the party and set their public duties aside during campaign season. And then there was the graft. To appreciate the scale of embezzlement during this period, consider the New York Customs House, which collected much of the nation's tax revenues. By subjecting public administration to partisan politics, the spoils system legitimized fraud at the customs house on a massive scale. Customs agents would intentionally undervalue imports, then make "official" discoveries of the error. They received a cut of the bounty, with the expectation that they kick some back to the party. The customs house kept Republican boss Roscoe Conkling atop New York politics for 15 years, and it made all the top party brass rich.

And then, in an instant, the whole thing fell apart. The spoils system had been a cause of outrage from the moment it started, but nobody had been able to stop it. The Whigs complained about Jackson in the 1830s, the Republicans complained about James Buchanan in the 1850s, the Liberal Republicans complained about Ulysses S. Grant in the 1870s. But the regime endured – until a crazy person assassinated President James Garfield in 1881. The assassin claimed to have been a member of the pro-patronage faction of the Republican Party, though in truth he was simply insane. Public outrage boiled over, and Congress passed the Pendleton Civil Service Reform Act, which eventually eliminated most federal patronage jobs. States followed suit, and by the middle of the 20th century, the bureaucracy was mostly professionalized and insulated from politics.

While Pendleton was a victory for good government, the success was short-lived. It remained a stark reality that politicians had to fund their campaigns, and the need for campaign cash only increased as the population grew and new communication technologies proliferated. Without access to patronage, politicians began aggressively courting those looking to profit from the government's economic activism. Today, millions of dollars are required to saturate television with campaign messages, finely tuned by professional consultants who charge top dollar. For such expansive financing, politicians inevitably rely heavily on interest groups.

Meanwhile, the Industrial Revolution made business more dependent upon government. Businesses became vast conglomerates that spanned the nation, which meant they inevitably fell under the Interstate Commerce Clause. They also needed favorable tax rates, beneficial monetary policy, and heavy infrastructure investment. Thus, they developed powerful lobbying operations to pressure the federal government. These outfits were informal at first, usually depending upon personal relations between executives and politicians, but over the past 80 years, these networks have been largely supplanted by sophisticated, highly specialized lobbying organizations that acquire as much from the government as possible.

Moreover, the scope of federal authority began to increase. Hamilton's proposal for the national government to develop the domestic economy was controversial in the 1790s, but a century later it was widely accepted. The progressive movement substantially broadened the government's regulatory power, and the New Deal expanded this authority even more. The government also began dispensing social-welfare benefits via minimum-wage guarantees, union protections, Social Security, and the like. As federal power grew, more groups faced the same incentives as businesses: their well-being depended directly upon the policymakers in Washington, so they had to become "friends" with politicians.

These factors – expensive campaigns without patronage, the rise of big business, and the expansion of government power – generated the current variant of cronyism. Modern cronyism combines the oligarchy of mercantilism with the spoils system's subjugation of public administration to electoral politics. Desperate to secure their well-being and re-election, today's politicians sell public policy to the highest bidders. This institutionalized conflict of interest touches almost every policy domain: taxes, regulation, infrastructure grants, science and technology spending, support for businesses, farm subsidies, social-welfare programs, and even military appropriations. There are hundreds of special interests, employing thousands of lobbyists, constantly clamoring for favors from the government. And Uncle Sam happily obliges. To borrow that line from Madison, modern interest groups are the new "pretorian band of the Government, at once its tool and its tyrant; bribed by its largesses, and overawing it by clamours and combinations."

Far from being illegal, this practice is widely accepted, with the informal norm being that the benefits politicians reap from special interests must be removed by several degrees from themselves. For instance, politicians cannot accept personal checks from interest groups, but groups may donate to their campaigns, which indirectly benefit politicians and are sometimes even run by their families and friends. Politicians may not accept gratuities beyond a very small amount from lobbyists, but after they leave office, they can collect multimillion-dollar paydays by working for lobbyists. Politicians cannot knowingly profit from government appropriations or regulations, but in practice such violations are common, because only the most egregious are provable.

Congress is the locus of cronyism, with the committee system being a particular problem. Congressional committees have substantial power over their policy domains. Their members have more knowledge than the average legislator, so they provide important cues on how to vote. Committees also determine the specifics of policy: while amendments on the floor of the House and Senate can alter committee products, committees usually have the final say over the details. What's more, committee leaders typically helm the conference committees that the two chambers use to finalize legislation. This combination of specialization and authority generally helps Congress do its business, but it facilitates cronyism in two ways. First, it enables interest groups to concentrate their lobbying efforts and campaign cash. Thus, banks focus on the Financial Services Committee and ignore the Agriculture Committee, while agribusinesses do the opposite. Second, it enables "high demanders" in the government to squeeze the most out of policies. A union-backed congressman from eastern Ohio goes to the Energy and Commerce Committee, while a Southern California member with defense-industry cronies joins the Armed Services Committee. All told, the committee system helps interest groups pinpoint their resources and ensures that the politicians they target are eager partners.

Cronyism is a bipartisan phenomenon. Democrats mostly controlled Congress from the 1930s until 1994, and they brought modern cronyism into being. Republicans have usually held Congress since 1994 and have entrenched the practice, often at the expense of their public commitment to limited government. For instance, the farm-subsidy program is one example of cronyism that Republicans successfully reformed in 1996 – only to undo it within a few years. In 2014, they passed the most wasteful farm bill in recent memory.

Meanwhile, Washington journalists are usually establishment liberals who do not believe the government needs to be reformed and who want to encourage public faith in it, so they are disinclined to highlight the issue. Compounding this, cronyism usually happens within fine-grained policies, which require technical knowledge that journalists lack. To top it off, journalists depend upon access to politicians, and writing unflattering exposés of cronyism is not a good strategy for career advancement.

Thus the grandees of the media are happy to chalk up cronyism to "the way things work."

* * *

Maybe the powers that be are right. Maybe cronyism is just the price of political business. A philosopher like Plato might have had the luxury of sketching out an ideal Republic, but we must deal with the world as it is and try to make the best of it. Hamilton held such a pragmatic view of cronyism, judging it to be necessary for the proper functioning of government. He once told Jefferson and John Adams in a private conversation that the British king's patronage was essential to good government. It was the means by which the monarch could induce narrow-minded legislators to do what was truly in the national interest. In theory, they should not have needed such inducements, but in practice they did. According to this perspective, cronyism is a necessary evil that an actual republic must accept. Similarly, contemporary commentators like Joe Klein and Thomas Edsall have suggested that earmarks (a form of congressional pork-barrel spending) are necessary to get big pieces of legislation passed.

Yet pragmatism can be overdone, just like idealism. If it is unwise to judge our government against a model that cannot actually exist, it is equally imprudent to apply no standard whatsoever. For his part, Aristotle occupied a middle ground, acknowledging the practical necessities of governance while retaining normative standards by which to judge them. Importantly, Hamilton was not an apologist for cronyism, per se. His defense was predicated upon its necessity to good government, which implicitly assumes that it has not perverted the ends of the *polis*. Similarly, we can acknowledge that some self-interested transactions are necessary for any republic and ask whether cronyism has transgressed this limit. Has it gone on to endanger the republic itself?

There are three reasons to worry that cronyism has indeed gone too far. First, cronyism costs a lot of money, too much for this age of low economic growth and high budget deficits. A precise figure is difficult to estimate, but some examples illustrate just how substantial the premium for cronyism is. Take Medicare, for starters. It is a delegated welfare program that reimburses providers for their expenses in treating patients. Until the 1980s, the program basically paid providers whatever they deemed reasonable, which is why costs went up so much in the 15 years after the program was passed. Then Congress implemented a cost-control system to pay providers based on an estimate of the value of each procedure. This approach has yielded two problems, both of which relate to cronyism. First, the government pays roughly $40 billion per year for improper claims. Second, the providers themselves basically set their own rates, which is an enormous conflict of interest that inflates the costs of the program and medicine in general.

The government could, in theory, take control of the process, developing its own payment schedules and hiring auditors to recover improper claims. But it does not do that – because the medical-services industry is one of the most powerful lobbyists in the country. It provided about $140 million in campaign contributions in the 2014 cycle – more than those of labor, natural resources, or agricultural businesses. It also spent about $1 billion in lobbying in 2013–14, second only to the financial-services industry. This points to the extraordinary nature of cronyism: for only $1 billion, the health-services industry can secure tens of billions in government rents. The return on this political investment is hundreds, if not thousands, of times better than what the stock market offers, where annual returns rarely exceed 10 percent.

The cost of cronyism often does not even show up in the federal budget. Corporate tax giveaways cost upwards of $100 billion per year, but they are not considered spending. For instance, in 2014 the Tax Foundation estimated that the corporate tax code contains about $45 billion worth of corporate welfare, which is of dubious economic utility. This is not money that is "spent" in a budgetary sense, but it still provides an enormous benefit to recipients. Relatedly, the government looks the other way as U.S.-based corporations aggressively hide domestic profits overseas. This is why profits booked in the Cayman Islands amount to 1,600 percent of its gross domestic product. The money is not earned there, just hidden from the tax man. This is cronyism by inaction. Under pressure from multinational firms, the government leaves tax shelters alone.

The real costs of Obamacare's cronyism are also off budget. Obama cut deals with all manner of interest groups to secure the passage of the Affordable Care Act. The insurers, the hospitals, the AARP, and drug manufacturers won favorable policies in exchange for their political support of and participation in the new program. At the time the bill was passed, the Congressional Budget Office estimated that the law would cost less than $1 trillion in its first 10 years. That figure, high as it is, was actually a gross underestimate of the true cost. Much of it was pushed off the federal books – in the form of higher premiums, deductibles, and co-payments on the individual marketplace. Moreover, a 2014 study by the American Health Policy Institute found that Obamacare was increasing costs for the largest employers by about $5,000 per employee.

The burdens of cronyism can ripple throughout the

economy at large. The average citizen overpays on all manner of products – whether it be a gallon of milk, a pair of jeans, an airline ticket, or even a home – because of cronyism. Farm subsidies alter the economic incentives in the agricultural industry, pushing farmers to grow crops and raise livestock that are subsidized by the federal government and increasing the price of many foods. Similarly, the consumer pays a premium for tariffs that prop up a handful of politically connected industries like textiles. Additionally, the Export-Import Bank supposedly helps domestic exporters by providing loans to overseas borrowers, but these can have perverse downstream effects. Ex-Im does a lot of business on behalf of Boeing, which means it helps foreign airlines in competition with domestic carriers like Delta. Finally, Fannie Mae and Freddie Mac aligned with affordable-housing groups, mortgage brokers, and home builders in the late 1990s and early 2000s to encourage the federal government to reduce underwriting standards. This misguided policy inflated home prices, fueled a housing bubble, and ultimately contributed to the Great Recession of 2008–09.

In general, cronyism creates enormous *waste*. The government misallocates scarce resources for political purposes, while interest groups spend heavily on politics rather than on improving their businesses. We all bear this burden, even if we are unaware of it. It is impossible to estimate precisely just how much this costs, but it easily costs hundreds of billions of dollars per year. Ours is an extremely wealthy country, but it is still hard to wave off such waste – especially in an era of persistently weak economic growth, structural deficits, and income stagnation for the middle class.

Cronyism also limits the political debate. In our pluralistic system of government, participation is open to all.

Cronyism corrupts this process by giving disproportionate influence to those with the greatest, most personal stake in policies. The result is a constricted public space for discussing our options. When a policy is in need of reform, the only solutions that may be practically considered are those that the dominant interest groups deem acceptable. In plenty of cases, this is not a problem; after all, interest groups can offer perfectly reasonable solutions in many circumstances. But in other instances, this means common-sense fixes are never even mentioned, let alone considered.

Scholars have long understood that the ability to determine the range of options is a very important power. In *The Semisovereign People*, political scientist E. E. Schattschneider termed this the mobilization of bias. He wrote that "the definition of the alternatives is the supreme instrument of power.... He who determines what politics is about runs the country." Cronyism mobilizes bias on a whole host of issues to ensure that certain options are off the table before debate even begins. It therefore diminishes democratic accountability over public policy.

Consider again the example of Medicare. The program is enormously expensive, and the two parties fight endlessly over its price tag, which is projected to balloon over the next half century. Yet neither party complains about the glaring conflict of interest at the heart of the program, which is highly relevant to the problem of cost containment: medical-service providers basically set their own reimbursement rates. This is what $1 billion buys the medical-services industry – bipartisan silence. Medicare is not the only such example. For instance, the nation has lousy policies dealing with food stamps and agriculture because of cronyism. These two distinctive domains have been joined for 50 years in a massive logroll, whereby rural farmers and the urban poor limit the range of reforms that the country may enact in either area, despite their manifest problems. Similarly, the political influence of the financial-services industry ensured that the country did not have a robust debate about the causes and consequences of the Great Recession. Instead, the original version of what became the Dodd-Frank law was likely drafted by a Wall Street law firm. Little wonder that it enshrined "too big to fail" for the largest institutions, which not coincidentally spend lavishly on the political process.

Third, cronyism exacerbates economic, social, and political inequality. This is usually not an issue that troubles conservatives, who accept that a dynamic, market-based economy is going to make some men wealthier than others. In the long run – so this argument goes – everybody is better off. Yet this logic has little bearing on cronyism. Political power is of a fixed and finite quantity, which distinguishes it from economic growth. Thus, the conservative apology for economic inequality has no force when it comes to cronyism. What one group gains in power, another *must* lose. Moreover, the inequality of cronyism often works against the dynamic forces of the marketplace. If a man has made his fortune selling widgets and prevails upon the government to keep others from competing against him, he has actually *destroyed* the market, to create a monopoly for himself. Thus, all the dynamism that would have occurred because of competition among widgetmakers disappears. Widgets do not get any better, cheaper, or more reliable. They stay the same, and in that small way, society stagnates because of cronyism, even though the original innovator prospers greatly.

Granted, cronyism need not produce inequality. For instance, while the spoils system had many faults, it generally was a leveling force in which average citizens could participate. But modern cronyism, which derives in part from the old system of mercantilism, is quite different. To be a politician's crony, you must have something he wants. To be precise about it, you must *bid* for his friendship amid intense competition, which means your final bid will have to be quite high. Lobbying shops do not come cheap, after all. So today's cronyism usually reinforces the wealth, power, and status of those who already possess all three. Political scientists have long noted this problem. In *The Semisovereign People,* Schattschneider claimed that "the flaw in the pluralist heaven is that the heavenly chorus sings with a strong upper-class accent." In *The End of Liberalism,* Theodore Lowi argued that our system of government tends to maintain old "structures of privilege" and create new ones, even when the program's ostensible purpose is to help the poor. Inequality may be tolerable for the sake of economic dynamism, but it is an insufferable consequence of cronyism.

* * *

Cronyism is not only a public-policy problem; it is the *essential* problem. Cronyism infests every corner of our government, so in any policy domain where conservatives have an interest – from health care and taxes to education and energy – cronyism is an impediment to sensible reforms. There is no ignoring it.

To date, conservative reformers have notched victories against the excesses of cronyism, in the hopes that they would lead to later successes. In particular, they have invested enormous energy in trying to eliminate the Export-Import Bank. This is a highly vulnerable institution because its benefits go mostly to Boeing. Ex-Im is an egregious form of corporate welfare that has bred rampant cronyism, and it should be gotten rid of. Yet the problem with this strategy is that it is like going after low-hanging fruit: after that has been plucked, there is little else to do. Indeed, other forms of cronyism – like conflicts of interest in Medicare, the logrolling that connects food stamps to farm subsidies, or federal housing policy – have survived because politically they are much more powerful than Ex-Im. Such programs benefit a large number of groups, which coordinate a vigorous defense against any threats. The fight against Ex-Im succeeded because it pitted determined reformers against (mostly) just Boeing. But to eliminate Medicare overpayments, reformers would have to defeat a vast, interconnected array of interest groups that annually pour a billion dollars into politics.

It is better to view big government programs not as the underlying disease but rather as its symptoms. If we are looking for a cure, we must dig deeper – beneath the programs, to the politicians who create and sustain them. They are the problem, and as already noted, they come from both parties. It is not enough to simply elect more Republicans to Congress. The country has been doing that for the past 20 years, to little effect. So we must examine the incentive structures of the political class itself and think about how to induce politicians to reduce cronyism. Our focus should not be the great statesmen, those who readily sacrifice their interests for the sake of the public good. Meanwhile, the worst politicians are beyond hope, and many should be prosecuted by the Department of Justice. So we must ponder the average member of Congress, for he is the critical case.

No doubt he has some selfless impulses, but the average politician cares mostly about himself and wants three things above all else: first, money to fund his campaign; second, information, to ensure that he does not vote against his constituents on important matters; and third, personal income that is commensurate with his social standing. Those are the main reasons he collects cronies. They help him achieve these goals, and he gives them public policy in return. On each item, reformers must find ways to restrict his access to cronies and otherwise supply the goods and services he collects from them.

A century of campaign-finance reform has failed to do this, and for good reason. Reformers are often motivated by the highest ideals, but too often they wrongly think the best strategy is simply to limit a candidate's access to funds. This tactic often runs afoul of the First Amendment, and the Supreme Court regularly guts campaign-finance legislation, leaving behind an incoherent hodgepodge that fails to do any good. Moreover, the restrictions themselves inevitably generate loopholes that favor cronyism. In fact, today's campaign-finance regime is a kind of incumbent-protection cartel. By capping the dollar amount of total contributions at a low level, current law forces candidates to collect money from a wide array of donors. Congressmen can easily make such contacts via their committees, but challengers struggle mightily. This is one reason cronyism has gotten worse over the past half century, despite several major campaign-finance reforms. The solutions have exacerbated the problem.

A better approach would be to create alternative sources of campaign funds, under the assumption that if politicians do not have to develop cronyistic relationships to build their war chests, they are less likely to do so. Why not have a refundable tax credit for small donors, capped at $300 per individual, with a federal matching fund to bolster the political power of average citizens? This would impose only a modest burden on the Treasury, and it could scramble the current campaign-finance calculus altogether. Ideally, it would be great for small donors to provide the bulk of a candidate's funds. Their investment in politics is too small to purchase some special favor, so they are typically motivated by a public interest. Moreover, a tax credit would publicly finance campaigns, based on the preferences of taxpayers. This would be an improvement over the patronage system, which lent itself to fraud because politicians controlled the funds, as well as over the presidential financing system, which collapsed because bureaucratic rules and governmental stinginess could not keep up with the rising cost of the modern campaign.

A key job of interest groups is providing information to members of Congress. Our legislature has the authority to weigh in on just about any public-policy problem one can imagine, but doing so in an intelligent fashion requires expertise that the average member of Congress simply lacks. Unfortunately, the legislature does not provide members with those resources: the staff of Congress was only 21,000 as of 2009, less than it was in 1979. This is simply not enough manpower for a member to get timely and accurate answers to policy questions, so he relies inevitably upon interest groups to fill the gaps. The problem is that such information often favors the interests of the group that provides it. On top of this, Congress does not pay its senior staffers a salary that is commensurate with what they could command in the private market, which gives them an incentive to curry favor with interest groups before they leave the public sector. Accordingly, Congress needs a larger staff, and it should pay them more. Expanding congressional staff does not violate conservative norms about limited government; the legislative branch is the closest to the people, and adding legislative staffers would not transfer power from the people to an unelected bureaucracy but would help elected members serve their constituents better. Plus, doubling the legislative staff would still leave it at a fraction of the executive branch's staff. The Agriculture Department alone has over 100,000 employees.

Finally, reformers must deal realistically with members' personal finances, taking politicians not as we would like them to be but as they are. While most do not intend to become rich from public service, they want an income commensurate with their social status. Right now, members make $174,000 per year. Considering that they must maintain two homes (one in the expensive Washington, D.C., metro area), this leaves many feeling pinched. The squeeze provides an opportunity for cronies, who can win favors by providing for politicians' personal well-being.

In response, reformers should demand a strict ethos of public service. The place to start is with the revolving door. Social scientists have found that before members leave Congress, they often change their behavior to court prospective employers, like lobbyists. Reformers should therefore impose a lifetime lobbying ban upon former members, with an exemption for public-interest groups like Heritage and Brookings. Moreover, the definition of *lobbyist* must be amended to account for the various loopholes that enable former members to lobby without technically being registered. And while in office, members whose assets rise above a certain threshold should be obligated to place them in a blind trust. This is commonplace for presidents, and the same logic applies as forcefully for members of Congress. Finally, the Federal Election Commission should have more staff and resources to audit political committees to prevent members from siphoning money from their campaigns into their bank accounts. Relatedly, its six-member panel should be reduced to five members, so it can be an effective regulatory agency (with a permanent spot for two Democrats, two Republicans, and one independent).

These suggestions are meant to be illustrative, not comprehensive. Above all, reformers must think carefully about these pathways of corruption – campaign finance, information, and personal enrichment – to develop innovative ways to alter the incentives that the average member faces. Only then will we get a handle on cronyism.

* * *

These reforms are sensible, but are they salable? After all, going after cronyism is to strike at the foundation of modern politics itself. That may be in the public interest, but politicians like the status quo, which is why they will not reform it. How do we get them to accept change?

This is a very old question. In surveying the disastrous state of public affairs in the 1780s, Madison noted that politicians are motivated by "1. Ambition 2. Personal interest. 3. Public good. Unhappily the two first are proved by experience to be most prevalent." But he did not despair; instead, he designed a system whereby the ambitions and personal interests of politicians would promote the public good. He argues in *Federalist* No. 51, "Ambition must be made to counteract ambition," so our system divides power to give politicians competing incentives, thereby "supplying, by opposite and rival interests, the defect of better motives." This is what reformers must now do: adjust the rules of the game so that self-interested politicians actually want to reform the system.

Madison has more to teach. He hoped this system would be self-correcting, but he judged the Federalist Party of the 1790s an existential threat to republican government. He thought it unconstitutionally expanded government authority, passed laws suppressing political opposition, and created a standing army to impose its will on a recalcitrant people. In *The Federalist,* he argues that the recourse against such minorities is the "republican principle" of majority rule. But how to bring that ideal to life? How to rally the people at large to vindicate the public interest? The answer that Madison and Jefferson devised was a *political party.* Their Republican Party (often known by the neologism "Democratic-Republican Party") transformed widespread public dissatisfaction into a forceful political movement.

Opponents of cronyism would do well to heed Madison's counsel. For all intents and purposes, lasting reform will not come until one of the parties makes cronyism a top issue. The parties are the principal way – perhaps the only way – to defend the public interest in the face of rampant factionalism. Conservatives should focus on the Republican Party, whose growing reformist wing led the assault on Ex-Im. Supporting these good-government Republicans would be helpful to the party as a whole. After all, cronyism – as we have noted – tends to favor the wealthy and well connected, whom voters often think of as partial to the Republicans. Standing up to cronyism would help the GOP play against type and maybe win over voters who think the party is too elitist.

Of course, the GOP has been an unreliable supporter of good government over the past 20 years. There are quarters of the party that are interested in reform, but too much of its establishment goes along to get along. What to do about this? Return to Madison's three motives: ambition, personal interest, and the public good. Conservative reformers need to link the ambitions and personal interests of Republican politicians to the public good, and the best way to do that is through *primary elections.* These are powerful yet underused tools to clean house in a party. Lately, reformers have been trying to topple Republican senators who are too comfortable with cronyism, but this may be biting off more than they can chew. The best place to start is with primaries for the House and the state legislatures. These incumbents cannot collect as much money to defend themselves as United States senators can, so it is easier to cashier the lackluster ones. This is not to say that the task would be easy. Conservatives would have to educate themselves about which officeholders are true reformers and which are phonies. They would have to recruit quality challengers, and they would have to commit time and money to securing victory. None of this is easy work, but it is essential in remaking the Republican Party. Total victory would not be required – rather, just enough victories to make those average Republican politicians sensitive to the serious mood of their constituents.

This might strike some conservatives as unappealing. Many are ready to write off the GOP altogether, after 20 years of disappointment. Yet this would be a mistake. We would do well to take our cue from Madison. Reform inevitably requires a political party that is committed to bringing it about, which means that conservatives must work within the Republican Party. This starts with an effort to clean our own house. Then and only then can we clean up the halls of the government, finally striking a blow against the cronyism that has so damaged our republic.

PHILIP HAMBURGER

THE ADMINISTRATIVE THREAT

Some of the constitutional problems with administrative power – such as federalism and the separation of powers – are familiar. Less well understood is that administrative power threatens constitutional freedoms. It weakens the freedom secured by the Constitution's structures; it denies procedural rights such as juries and due process; it erodes substantive rights such as free speech; it even undercuts equal voting rights. Standing alone, any one of these constitutional violations would be appalling. Taken together, they reveal that administrative power is a profound threat to civil liberties. It is difficult to think of a more serious civil liberties problem for the twenty-first century.

ALTHOUGH THE UNITED STATES remains a republic, administrative power creates within it a very different sort of government. The result is a state within the state – an administrative state within the Constitution's United States. The state within is sometimes called the "regulatory state" to emphasize its burdens on economic and personal freedom, and is sometimes called the "deep state" because of its tendency to interfere with our elected government. This book focuses on the legal side of the problem – on the power claimed by the administrative state and how it slices through basic civil liberties.

NOT JUST ECONOMICS

Over the past century, most complaints about administrative power have come from an economic perspective. It is said that administrative power is inefficient, dangerously centralized, burdensome on business, destructive of jobs, and stifling for innovation and growth. All of this is painfully true, but these are largely economic complaints, and economic complaints are not the entire critique of administrative power.

Although this power began as an exceptional method of regulation, and was applied mostly to corporations, it has become the dominant reality of American governance, which intrudes into the full range of American life, including not only economic endeavors but also political participation and personal decisions.

The economic critique does not address the breadth of this danger. Indeed, it tends to protest merely the degree of administrative regulation, and it thereby usually accepts the legitimacy of administrative power – as long as it is not too heavy-handed on business. No wonder the economic criticism has not stopped the growth of administrative power.

THE CENTRALITY OF THE LEGAL CHALLENGE

For a better understanding of the administrative threat, one must turn to law. The legal critique more fully addresses the problem than does the economic protest, for although much administrative power is economically inefficient, all of it is unconstitutional. And this legal objection is central, because it confronts administrative power on its own terms – on its pretension to bind Americans in the manner of law.

In saying that administrative power is unconstitutional, this is not to deny that executive power is extensive. Executive power is often portrayed as merely the power to execute the laws, but more accurately (as recognized by Alexander Hamilton) it amounts to the power to execute all of the nation's lawful force. It thus includes the power to prosecute offenders in court, to exercise discretion in distributing benefits, to determine the status of immigrants, and so forth.

In contrast, administrative power involves not force but legal obligation, and this is why the legal challenge matters so much. Contemporary theorists sometimes suggest that law is a sovereign's command backed by coercion. But traditionally in America, notably when the Constitution was adopted, law was something that came with legal obligation – the obligation to obey. Working from underlying ideas about consent, eighteenth-century Americans assumed that a rule could have the obligation of law only if it came from the constitutionally established legislature elected by the people, and that a judicial decision could have such obligation only if it came from a constitutionally appointed judge exercising independent judgment. On the basis of such principles, the US Constitution placed lawmaking power in Congress and judicial power in the courts. The power to bind – that is, to create legal obligation – was thus in these departments, not the executive.

Nonetheless, through administrative power, the executive purports to create legal obligation. It binds Americans and deprives them of their liberty, not through acts of Congress and acts of the courts but through other mechanisms. And this evasion of the Constitution's pathways for law is what makes the legal objection to administrative power so central.

Adding to the problem, administrative power also evades many of the Constitution's procedures, including both its legislative and judicial processes. Administrative power thereby sidesteps most of the Constitution's procedural freedoms.

Administrative power is thus all about the evasion of governance through law, including an evasion of constitutional processes and procedural rights. These legal problems are forceful reasons to reject all administrative power and, indeed, to consider it the civil liberties issue of our time.

ABSOLUTE POWER, THEN AND NOW

An initial step toward understanding the danger and unconstitutionality of administrative power is to examine some examples, past and present. Although our republic may seem too American and contemporary to bear comparison with England's old absolute monarchy, the similarities are therefore all the more disturbing.

English absolutism was epitomized by King James I, who ruled from 1603 to 1625. Rather than being content with the government's regular power to make statutes in Parliament and to have cases adjudicated in the courts, he tried to exercise versions of legislative and judicial powers in his "prerogative" commissions or tribunals – his equivalent of administrative agencies. And his capacity in these bodies to bind his subjects was a significant part of what was called his "absolute power."

His prerogative tribunals most famously included the Star Chamber and the High Commission. The one had statutory authorization for some of its jurisdiction, and the other was entirely founded on statute. With or without legislative authorization, these bodies exercised absolute power.

Such tribunals are often assumed to have been blood-soaked torture chambers, but they were more bureaucratic than bloody. They were efficient prerogative agencies, and they exercised absolute power in ways that have come back to life in America.

LAWMAKING. Instead of legislating through acts of Parliament, King James personally issued proclamations in the Star Chamber that served as binding regulations on trade, manufacturing, and urban development. He even had these proclamations published in a volume that looked like a statute book – an early equivalent of the *Federal Register*.

James undoubtedly had the power to issue proclamations, but proclamations that bound in the manner of law were another matter. In 1610, after James used proclamations to create regulatory offenses, Chief Justice Edward Coke and the other chief judges declared such proclamations unlawful and void, saying that the king "by his proclamation cannot create any offense which was not an offense before." The judges recognized that lawmaking outside of the legislature was unlawful.

James, however, had other means of legislating outside of Parliament – most notably, Star Chamber regulations, which were issued more bureaucratically than his personal proclamations. Acting through its adjudicatory proceedings, the Star Chamber could issue regulations in the form of judicial decrees. In other words, judicial-style process was used for lawmaking, and this practice came to an end only when Parliament in 1641 abolished the Star Chamber.

In the twentieth century, the sort of power exercised by King James was revived in the United States. With remarkable fidelity to the old absolutism, some federal agencies used adjudicatory-style proceedings as a basis for issuing binding rules – a process known as "formal rule making." Because such proceedings came to seem cumbersome, agencies nowadays issue binding rules with little more ceremony than giving notice and soliciting public comments – this being called "informal rule making." Either way, like their seventeenth-century precursors, federal agencies are engaged in lawmaking.

The Affordable Care Act, for example, authorizes Health and Human Services to issue binding rules on health care. Indeed, many federal agencies make binding rules with express authorization. This sort of administrative rule making is justified on the fiction that when Congress states an "intelligible principle," agencies that follow the principle are merely specifying what Congress has enacted. But this is a fantasy. The crude reality, as recognized long ago by James Landis (a prominent advocate of administrative power) is that the agencies are exercising legislative power.

INTERPRETATION. Not content with overt prerogative lawmaking, James also used his prerogative tribunals to make law through what he called the "interpretation" of statutes. Where statutes seemed ambiguous or indefinite, the Star Chamber and the High Commission used interpretation to make law. And to ensure that these prerogative interpretations had legal effect, James demanded judicial deference to them.

The judges, however, stood their ground; they generally refused to defer. As Chief Justice Coke explained to James in 1610, although the king appointed judges, he lacked judicial office. In contrast, the judges had the office of judging and interpreting. The judges therefore could not defer to the king's interpretations.

Of course, what really was at stake was not James's personal interpretations of statutes but the interpretations put forth by his prerogative tribunals. Correspondingly, Coke's point was that although the members of these bodies acted as the king's agents, even the king himself could not make authoritative interpretations of law.

The king and his minions obviously had to interpret statutes every day to decide the lawfulness of their own conduct – just as any individual regularly had to interpret statutes to avoid violating the law. And in making such decisions, all such persons could rely on the judgment of their lawyers. But authoritative interpretations came only from the judges, for only they had an office of independent judgment in deciding cases. Because of their office or duty to exercise independent judgment, and because the king's interpretations were without such authority, the judges could not defer to the interpretations that came from the king's agents or agencies.

The lawmaking interpretation that James desired for his prerogative bodies has become a reality for American administrative agencies. Federal judges show varying degrees of deference to agency interpretations, and the agencies therefore can use their interpretations to create law.

Most famously, under the 1984 Supreme Court case *Chevron v. Natural Resources Defense Council*, judges must defer to administrative interpretations of ambiguities in statutes. Such interpretations must be among the "permissible" possible interpretations, but within this standard, agencies generally enjoy much freedom to choose their interpretations and thus to make law wherever they can find a plausible statutory ambiguity. As a result, even where

Congress has not expressly authorized administrative rule making, agencies often can use interpretation to make binding rules – that is, to make law.

This can be illustrated by the Clean Power Plan – an Environmental Protection Agency (EPA) rule designed to reduce greenhouse gas emissions by establishing emission standards for existing power plants. Most commentators protest its substance (for example, its destruction of jobs), but the point here is how the agency made the rule. According to the EPA, it can issue the rule because it is merely interpreting an ambiguous section of the Clean Air Act (§111d). Similarly, the EPA relies on interpretation to make its rule on the waters of the United States – a rule that potentially regulates almost all waters in the nation (admittedly not puddles, but nearly everything else).

Even where an agency does not interpret a statute with the formality required for *Chevron* deference, it can issue less formal statutory interpretation. Although such interpretation does not get as much deference from the courts as the formally issued sort, it receives what the courts call "respect" under the so-called *Mead-Skidmore* doctrine, and this is enough for agencies to use informal interpretation as a means of legislating.

Topping it off, agencies make law not only by interpreting statutes but also by interpreting their own rules, often in the form of guidance. And this sort of interpretation gets great judicial deference under *Auer v. Robbins*. An agency can thus both issue a binding rule and interpret it, and at each stage it is making law.

These methods of lawmaking through agency interpretation are disturbing. They are pathways for agencies to do what Congress itself did not do, or even expressly authorize. And they revive a mode of lawmaking that once flourished under James I.

ADJUDICATION AND PROCEDURAL RIGHTS. In addition to using the Star Chamber and High Commission for lawmaking, King James also used them for adjudication. These prerogative tribunals employed civilian-style inquisitorial proceedings. Accordingly, in relying on these tribunals, James escaped not only the courts and their judges but also their juries and the full range of their procedural rights.

Medieval kings had already tried to evade the courts and their processes by summoning, trying, and punishing subjects in prerogative proceedings. In response, fourteenth-century statutes confined kings to acting through the "due process of law." As put by a medieval summary of the most comprehensive of these statutes, "None shall be put to answer without due process of law." Sixteenth- and seventeenth-century kings, however, used the Star Chamber and High Commission to bind subjects, and King James and his son Charles I took this so far as to provoke profound opposition. Many lawyers complained that prerogative adjudication violated the due process of law, and their protests concluded in 1641 with the abolition of both the Star Chamber and the High Commission.

Like the old prerogative courts, contemporary administrative tribunals evade the courts, their judges, their juries, and the due process of law. Administrative tribunals sometimes apply inquisitorial methods, but even where their proceedings are adversarial, they do not live up to the Constitution's procedural guarantees. The Securities Exchange Commission (SEC), for example, can bring civil insider-trading cases in federal courts, or it can refer insider-trading cases to the Justice Department for it to prosecute criminally in such courts, and either way, defendants get judges and juries and the full range of the Constitution's applicable procedural rights. But the SEC can also pursue insider-trading cases before administrative law judges, who work for the commission, are not really judges, do not offer juries, and do not even allow equal discovery.

Like their prerogative predecessors, moreover, administrative adjudicators cannot question the lawfulness of the regulations they enforce. It often is said that administrative law judges are independent because they are protected in their tenure and salary. But actually they can be demoted or have their salary docked if they reject administrative regulations as unlawful. This is especially problematic because an underlying question in all administrative proceedings concerns the unlawfulness of the applicable regulations, not least under the Constitution. It thus becomes apparent that administrative law judges are precommitted to upholding the government's position on the most persistent and serious legal questions. And this means that they usually are systematically biased in favor of one of the parties before them, in violation of the due process of law. Once again, administrative adjudication echoes the past.

WAIVERS. Finally, James I and most other sixteenth- and seventeenth-century English kings claimed a power to suspend the law or at least dispense with it. The suspending power allowed the king to suspend a statute's obligation for all persons; the dispensing power enabled him to dispense with its obligation for particular named persons. In both ways, a king could evade the need to persuade Parliament to repeal or amend a statute and, instead, could simply relieve some or all subjects of their duty to comply.

This waiver power was widely criticized. It was open to corruption and political favoritism, and it left subjects unequal under the law and in the courts. Eventually, in 1689, the English Declaration of Rights declared the suspending and dispensing powers unlawful unless exercised with Parliamentary consent. And in the next century, at least some Englishmen considered any use of these powers incompatible with the division of executive and legislative power between the Crown and Parliament. As to the suspending power, for example, it was said that "the constitution has entrusted the crown with no power to suspend any act of Parliament, under any circumstances whatever." In other words, royal or executive power could never include the power to unmake law.

Nowadays, the prerogative to suspend and dispense with the law has been revived in administrative waivers. The waivers sometimes are authorized by statute and sometimes are not – as with the so-called mini-med waivers issued under the Affordable Care Act. Either way, waivers are agency letters that tell persons they are excused from complying with a statute or a regulation under it, thus placing them above the law. Although usually issued, like the old dispensations, to particular persons, waivers can be given to all affected parties, so as to create the effect of the old suspending power.

*   *   *

In one instance after another, contemporary administrative power echoes the old absolutism. In place of prerogative lawmaking, we have administrative lawmaking. Instead of prerogative adjudication, we have administrative adjudication. Rather than the prerogative evasion of procedural rights, we have the administrative evasion of such rights. And instead of royal dispensations and suspensions, we have administrative waivers.

The old absolutism thus seems to have crawled out the grave and come back to life. Of course, the contemporary version is only "soft absolutism," exercised not for a monarch but for the masses. Nonetheless, as Alexis de Tocqueville recognized, this is more than dangerous enough.

What Is Absolute Power?

In exactly what sense does administrative power revive absolute power? Put more broadly, what could explain the remarkable parallels between the old and the contemporary – between the prerogative and the administrative?

The answer rests ultimately on human nature. Ever tempted to exert more power with less effort, rulers are rarely content to govern merely through the law, and in their restless desire to escape its pathways, many of them try to work through other mechanisms. These other modes of binding subjects are absolute power, and once one understands this, it is not altogether surprising that absolute power is a recurring problem and that American administrative power revives it.

Some commentators in the first half of the twentieth century denounced administrative power as "absolute" without really understanding what absolutism was. They used the word loosely to condemn discretion and anything they did not like. But the term "absolute power" traditionally had very specific meanings, one of which is especially important for understanding administrative power – namely, that absolute power is extralegal power. From this perspective, absolute power includes all efforts to bind (or impose legal obligation) not merely through law and the courts but through other pathways.

Put more instrumentally, absolute power can be understood as an evasion of law. It has been a means by which rulers, whether in a monarchy or a republic, avoid the trouble of binding persons merely through acts of the legislature and of the courts, and instead impose legal obligation through other sorts of edicts. In this sense, absolute power is an evasion of the regular paths of governance, and this is why it has been a repeated problem across the centuries.

The evasion, moreover, is why administrative power has continually expanded. There has been (as Gary Lawson observes) a continual "rise and rise" of the administrative state, and this is no coincidence. Being not law but a mode of evasion, which flows around law and law-like things, administrative power has flowed around the Constitution's pathways of power and even around formal administrative pathways, thus creating a cascade of evasions.

Of course, extralegal power has sometimes been expressly authorized by statute, and sometimes not (as evident nowadays from most administrative interpretations and some waivers). But with or without statutory authorization, when government imposes legal obligation through acts other than those of the legislature and the courts, it is not acting merely through the law. Its power is therefore extralegal and, in this sense, absolute.

Incidentally, although absolute power was most centrally understood as extralegal power, the phrase "absolute power" had other possible meanings, one of them being unlimited power. English kings thus had some "absolute" powers that did not bind or unbind their subjects, but were considered absolute in the sense that they were entirely, and thus without limitation, in the hands of the monarch – indeed, inherent in him. For example, he alone could pardon offenders and enter agreements with foreign rulers. But such powers did not purport to create or displace legal obligation and were soon brought under law, and they therefore were considered lawful and unproblematic elements of royal or executive power. Indeed, the US Constitution treats pardons and foreign agreements as part of the president's lawful executive power. Tellingly, however, if a foreign agreement is to be binding as domestic law, the president must get the Senate to ratify it as a treaty.

Power thus can be considered absolute for different reasons, but the absolutism that matters here is extralegal power – the power that binds not merely through acts of the legislature or the courts but through other sorts of edicts. This was the key problem with much of the king's old prerogative power, and it remains the central problem with contemporary American administrative power. Put another way, under the US Constitution, legislative and judicial acts are the only ways for the federal government, at the national level, to create domestic legal obligation. Accordingly, when the government binds persons through other paths, its acts are extralegal and, in this sense, absolute.

The extralegal or absolute character of administrative power is very revealing. At the very least, it shows that absolute power is a recurring danger. In addition, as now will be seen, it allows one to understand that constitutional law developed in response to this threat.

The Constitutional Rejection of Absolute Power

In justifying federal administrative power as constitutional, its apologists often suggest that administrative power is a modern development, which therefore could not have been anticipated by the US Constitution. Early Americans, however, were familiar with English constitutional history, and they therefore were well aware of the danger from absolute power and its extralegal paths.

The English in the seventeenth century largely repudiated the absolute powers with which monarchs bound their subjects extralegally. James I seriously abused absolute power, but it was left to his son Charles I to take it to the limit and thereby provoke open resistance and eventually a civil war. In 1641, just before the conflict, Parliament abolished the two primary prerogative tribunals, the Star Chamber and the High Commission, which carried out most of the king's extralegal lawmaking, interpretation, and adjudication. Later, one of Charles I's sons, James II, would live up to his namesake's failings and thereby prompt the English Revolution of 1688; and one result was that Parliament the next year, in the Declaration of Rights, began what would become a repudiation of the suspending and dispensing powers.

Underlying these events were English constitutional ideas. The very notion of constitutional law developed in England to defeat the extralegal aspects of absolutism, and constitutional law was therefore inextricably intertwined with the question of absolute power. Some notable English lawyers expounded the ideal that kings had to rule through acts of Parliament and the courts, not through other edicts. Some added that, under the English constitution, legislative power was in Parliament, judicial power in the judges, and executive power in the Crown. On this understanding, the English constitution left no room for the Crown to bind subjects extralegally. Of course, the English constitution was merely unwritten custom, and it thus was open to multiple and often conflicting ideals. But the English constitutional vision that rejected absolutism and its extralegal power would appeal to Americans.

Early Americans tended to understand that constitutional law had developed in England as a means of barring absolute power. They therefore were determined in their constitutions to be even more systematic than the English in precluding a revival of the absolute prerogative or anything like it.

Just how much Americans viewed such power with

horror is apparent from John Adams. In 1776, he observed that his countrymen aimed to establish governments in which a governor or president had "the whole executive power, after divesting it of those badges of domination called prerogatives" – by which Adams meant, of course, the absolute prerogatives. Similarly, when James Madison in *Federalist* 48 worried about legislative tyranny, he noted that the "founders of our republics ... never for a moment ... turned their eyes from the danger to liberty from the overgrown and all-grasping prerogative of an hereditary magistrate." Indeed, he worried that Americans went so far in worrying about the prerogative that they were paying insufficient attention the danger from the legislature.

Americans thus were fully aware of the threat from absolute power and its extralegal paths, and they feared that this dangerous mode of governance might come back to life. To be sure, the term "administrative power" was not yet ordinarily used in England or America. But absolute power was a familiar problem and much on the minds of Americans. It therefore should be no surprise that, in the US Constitution, they adopted structures and rights that systematically barred this danger.

The Constitution's Structures

How exactly does the US Constitution bar administrative power? Most basically, the Constitution's broad structures systematically preclude extralegal or absolute power. The revival of such power, whether called "prerogative" or "administrative," is therefore unconstitutional.

Incidentally, the argument here about the unconstitutionality of administrative power (whether in this section on structure or the next section on rights) relies on the Constitution's early history and may therefore prompt anxieties about originalism and attempts to return to the past. Such concerns, however, have little application here, for administrative power has already returned America to the past – not to the constitutionalism of 1789 but to something more like the absolutism of about 1610. Although administrative power is a softer absolutism than that of James I, it nonetheless is a preconstitutional mode of governance – the very sort of power that constitutions were most clearly expected to prevent. A great lurch backward has thus already occurred, and the underlying constitutional questions are not about refinements of interpretation but about things as basic as whether Americans will be governed solely through law and whether they will enjoy the Constitution's procedural rights.

ARTICLES I AND III. The Constitution establishes only regular avenues of power, and thereby blocks irregular or extralegal power. To be precise, it blocks extralegal lawmaking by placing legislative power exclusively in Congress, and it prevents extralegal adjudication by placing judicial power exclusively in the courts.

It thus authorizes only two pathways for government to bind Americans, in the sense of imposing legal obligation on them. Although a few exceptions will be noted later, the government generally can impose binding rules only through acts of Congress (or treaties ratified by the Senate), and can impose binding adjudications only through acts of the courts. These are its lawful options. Other attempts to bind Americans, whether with rules or adjudications, are unconstitutional.

Rather than merely arcana of government structure, these are core civil liberties issues. Binding agency rules deny Americans their right under Article I to be subject to only such federal legislation as is enacted by an elected

Congress, and such rules thereby dilute the constitutional right to vote. Moreover, binding agency adjudications deprive Americans of their right under Article III to be subject only to such federal judicial decisions as come from a court, with a real judge, a jury, and the full due process of law. Thus, even before one gets to the violations of enumerated constitutional rights, it should be apparent that the administrative evasions of the Constitution's pathways for binding power come with severe consequences for constitutional freedom.

DELEGATION. Administrative lawmaking is often justified as delegated power – as if Congress could divest itself of the power that the people had delegated to it. The Constitution, however, expressly bars any such subdelegation.

This conclusion may initially seem odd, for the Constitution contains no nondelegation clause. How, then, does the Constitution bar congressional subdelegation? The answer comes in the Constitution's first substantive word. The document begins: "All legislative powers herein granted shall be vested in a Congress ..." If all legislative powers are to be in Congress, they cannot be elsewhere. If the grant were merely permissive, not exclusive, there would be no reason for the word *All*. That word bars subdelegation.

When it came to the judicial power, the Constitution in Article III established only the Supreme Court and left Congress free to establish other courts. The Constitution therefore could not say that "all judicial power" shall be vested in any particular court or courts. All the same, Article III does not allow the judges to subdelegate their power, for it was well understood at the time that judicial power, by its nature, could not be delegated. As it happens, the civil law, drawing on Roman law, allowed judges to subdelegate their judicial power. But the common-law vision of a judge precluded any such subdelegation. For example, although judges could rely on clerks and special masters for many purposes, they could not rely on them to exercise judgment in a case.

The Constitution's barriers to any subdelegation of legislative or judicial power may sound merely technical, but they were expressions of an old and crucial principle against subdelegation, which underlay the efficacy of constitutions. The logic was that once the people had delegated different powers to the different branches of government, any subdelegation of such powers would allow the government to evade the structure of government chosen by the people. Alas, this has happened.

Significantly, however, the Supreme Court has not openly embraced delegation. At least when discussing expressly authorized rule making, the Court claims that binding agency rules are not delegated lawmaking but rather are merely specifications of the law – this being the theory of how agencies give effect to congressional expressions of "intelligible principles." Although this theory is a mere fig leaf, which does not really cover agencies' naked exercise of subdelegated legislative power, it is revealing that the Supreme Court remains committed to the idea that administrative lawmaking does not involve delegated lawmaking. Although the Court is deluding no one but itself, it thereby makes clear its understanding that the Constitution bars any subdelegation.

WAIVERS. Not only in making law but also in unmaking it through waivers, administrative power is unconstitutional. And courts cannot constitutionally give waivers any effect.

When the Constitution places all legislative powers in Congress, it gives Congress not only the power to make law but also the power to unmake it. And it thereby bars the executive from suspending or dispensing with the law. When the Constitution, moreover, places the judicial power in the courts and guarantees the due process of law, it precludes the executive from telling the courts not to apply the law, and prevents the courts from abandoning their own judgment about what the law requires.

Note that some state constitutions carefully preserved a limited executive suspending power, and the US Constitution authorized a legislative suspension of habeas corpus in narrow circumstances. It thus becomes all the more apparent that the Constitution generally does not permit administrative waivers. Nonetheless, waivers are now commonplace.

Although waivers reduce regulatory burdens for the well connected, they increase the burdens for others. Anticipating the availability of waivers, the government often feels free to impose overly constraining rules. As a result, those who do not get waivers usually suffer under especially restrictive regulations.

NECESSARY AND PROPER. The Necessary and Proper Clause authorizes Congress to make all laws that are "necessary and proper" for carrying out the government's other powers, and the clause is therefore usually said to allow Congress to create administrative power. But the clause needs to be read more carefully.

The usual argument from the Necessary and Proper Clause takes for granted that Congress is authorized to do what is necessary and proper for carrying out the government's powers in the abstract. From this perspective, Congress can give effect to the legislative and judicial powers by shifting them partly to administrative agencies.

But the Necessary and Proper Clause actually gives Congress only the power to carry out the government's other powers as they are "vested" by the Constitution in various departments and persons. This focus on vested powers precludes Congress from using the clause to rearrange or otherwise unvest any such powers. Of particular significance here, the clause does not allow Congress to shift the powers vested in Congress or the courts to administrative agencies.

And even if one were to imagine that the Necessary and Proper Clause says more than it does, it cannot authorize any administrative violation of an enumerated right. The Bill of Rights and other constitutionally enumerated rights are limits on the government's power, and thus even the most expansive power cannot justify administrative violations of constitutional rights. All the same, it will be seen that this has happened.

FEDERALISM. A further problem with federal administrative power is its interference with state law. Under the Constitution's Supremacy Clause, federal laws defeat state laws. But (as recognized by Bradford Clark) the clause specifies that only federal laws "made in pursuance" of the Constitution have this trumping effect. Thus, under the Constitution, although statutes enacted by Congress render contrary state laws void, mere agency rules and interpretations do not.

Nonetheless, agency rules and interpretations defeat state laws – including the states' constitutions, statutes, and common law – all on the theory that Congress authorized the agencies and that the agencies are merely specifying what Congress said in its enactments. The Constitution, however, reserves the trumping authority of federal law for acts of Congress, and thus not for the acts of agencies authorized by Congress. And in many instances – notably, when agencies interpret statutes – they are acting only under the authority of congressional ambiguity or silence, thus rendering any congressional authority utterly fictitious.

The effect is to deprive Americans of their freedom under the US Constitution to govern themselves through their elected state governments. Rather than enjoy self-government in layers of local and state elections, subject to the supremacy of federal laws, Americans now find that their state choices get crushed by unconstitutional assertions of the supremacy of administrative power.

*   *   *

By now it should be evident that the US Constitution systematically precludes administrative power. Extralegal governance is a type of absolute power, and regardless of whether it is called "prerogative" or "administrative," the Constitution bars it. In particular, the Constitution carefully authorizes the government to bind Americans and the states only through acts of Congress and the courts. It thereby forbids the government from evading these avenues of power by going down other pathways. Accordingly, when agencies issue binding rules or adjudications, or when they issue waivers, they are violating the Constitution.

The Constitution's Procedural Rights

The Constitution repudiates extralegal or absolute power not only with its structures but also with its guarantees of procedural rights. The administrative violation of these rights makes it especially clear that administrative power is a serious assault on civil liberties.

Due Process. The Fifth Amendment guarantees "the due process of law" and thereby bars the government from working outside the courts to issue orders to particular persons – whether to testify or even make an appearance. In defense of administrative adjudication, it often is suggested that due process is centrally a limit on the courts, not so much on the other parts of government.

As already evident, however, from the English history of due process, guarantees of due process of law developed precisely to bar extralegal adjudications. Rather than merely set a standard for the courts, they evolved primarily to preclude any binding adjudication outside the courts – a meaning summarized in the principle "None shall be put to answer without due process of law." This is why the English asserted the due process of law against the High Commission and the Star Chamber. And this is a large part of what the Fifth Amendment accomplished by guaranteeing due process.

The implication for adjudication outside the courts was recognized by one of the earliest academic commentators on the Bill of Rights. When lecturing on the Constitution at William & Mary, the Virginia judge St. George Tucker quoted the Fifth Amendment's Due Process Clause and concluded: "Due process of law must then be had before a judicial court, or a judicial magistrate." Similarly, Chancellor James Kent explained that the due process of law "means law, in its regular course of administration, through courts of law." And Justice Joseph Story echoed both Tucker and Kent. So much for administrative adjudication!

On behalf of the administrative evasion of due process, it may be said that due process has been expanded, and this has some truth. Ever since *Goldberg v. Kelly* in 1970 and *Mathews v. Eldridge* in 1976, there has been a due process right to a hearing before the government cuts off some welfare benefits, and the result has been to expand the availability of some process. This, however, is only part of the story.

Goldberg and *Mathews* offer only a smidgeon of administrative process for denials of some *benefits*, and are part of a broader jurisprudence that accepts a profound denial of due process for administrative *constraints*. There once was a constitutional right to the full due process of law in the courts of law for binding adjudications – adjudications that impose legal obligation – whether in cutting off life or restricting liberty or property. This essential right, however, has been reduced to a mere administrative "hearing" (often where one cannot be heard) and more typically "something less."

The familiar result is that federal agencies can demand testimony and private records and can impose fines without even going to court, let alone offering much administrative process. Most dramatically, the United States can now simply detain some Americans without trial – as evident from *Hamdi v. Rumsfeld*. Yaser Esam Hamdi was a US citizen who was captured as an enemy combatant, and as he apparently remained a citizen, he traditionally would have had a due process right to a trial in court with a jury and the full due process of a criminal prosecution. But the Supreme Court relied on *Mathews* to conclude that the government owed Hamdi nothing more than an administrative decision about his status by a neutral adjudicator.

The sort of doctrine evident in *Goldberg* and *Mathews* thus strains at a gnat and swallows the proverbial camel. It secures negligible administrative process in some benefit cases while accepting ruinous denials of due process in constraint cases. The overall effect is to expand due process very marginally at the edges and to eviscerate the right at its core.

JURY RIGHTS. Like due process, the right to a jury bars administrative and other extralegal adjudication. Juries are available only in the courts, and the right to a jury, in both civil and criminal cases, thus precludes binding adjudication in other tribunals.

Early Americans understood this. For example, in the decade after American independence, the legislatures of New Jersey and New Hampshire authorized judicial proceedings before justices of the peace – in the one state, qui tam forfeiture proceedings with a six-man jury, and in the other, small claims actions without a jury. Rather than accept these evasions of regular judicial proceedings, the courts of these states (New Jersey in 1780 and New Hampshire in 1786) held the statutes void for violating the right to a jury.

Although the US Constitution in 1789 guaranteed juries only in criminal cases, this prompted an outcry that juries also needed to be guaranteed in civil cases. The Seventh Amendment therefore secured the right to a jury in "Suits at common law." If, instead, the amendment had provided for juries "in common-law actions," it would have allowed the government to avoid juries in statutory actions. And if it had provided for juries "in existing common-law actions," it would have allowed the government to avoid juries in newly created actions. But the phrase "Suits at common law" meant civil suits brought in the common-law system, as opposed to those brought in equity or admiralty. Thus, in addition to the debates leading up to the Bill of Rights, the Seventh Amendment's very words make clear that the Amendment does not exclude statutory actions, least of all statutory actions in administrative proceedings. Instead, it secures juries in all civil cases other than those in equity and admiralty.

Nowadays, however, the Supreme Court says that the government's interest in congressionally authorized administrative adjudication trumps the right to a jury. In the Court's strange locution, where the government is acting administratively under newly created statutory "public rights," its public rights defeat the private assertion of the constitutional right to a jury trial.

The Court traditionally had used the term "public rights" merely as a label for the lawful spheres of executive action. In a series of cases, however – notably in 1977 in *Atlas Roofing v. Occupational Safety and Health Review Commission* – the Court unmoored the phrase from its traditional usage and used it to displace the Seventh Amendment right to a jury in civil cases. As it happens, binding agency adjudication, including fact-finding, is not within the scope of the Constitution's grant of executive power; even if it were, it would not defeat the Seventh Amendment, for the Constitution's rights are limits on government power. In other words, rights trump power. Understanding this obstacle, the Supreme Court in *Atlas Roofing* recast administrative power as a right – indeed, as a "public right." It thereby, in effect, denigrated the constitutional right to a jury as a mere private right and allowed the government's "public" right to defeat the private constitutional right.

This public-rights reasoning is a disgraceful assault on the Bill of Rights. On such reasoning, all rights are at risk.

Even where agencies are resolving disputes between merely private parties, the Supreme Court justifies the jury-less proceedings with the public-rights theory. The public right that eviscerates the Seventh Amendment is therefore not the government's legal claim in any particular administrative proceeding but merely the government's interest in administrative adjudication.

The Court thus sweepingly applies its generalization about "public rights" to all administrative adjudications, without pausing to consider whether the Constitution's right to a jury might, at least occasionally, prevail against the government's public rights. Administrative agencies can therefore, as a matter of course, violate the Constitution's jury rights without worrying about the strength of their claim of public rights.

OTHER PROCEDURAL RIGHTS. The antiadministrative implications of jury and due process rights are merely the beginning. In fact, almost all of the Constitution's procedural rights – including most provisions of the Bill of Rights – were designed not only to set standards in court but also to defeat extralegal adjudication.

Of course, different types of administrative proceedings violate different procedural guarantees. Where administrative adjudication is civil in nature, it evades the Constitution's procedures for civil cases; where it is criminal in nature, it evades the Constitution's procedures for criminal prosecutions.

Consider, for example, warrants for search and seizure. When the Fourth Amendment established its requirements for warrants, it was understood that a legally binding warrant for a search or seizure was an exercise of judicial power. Thus, both the Fourth Amendment and Article III (which grants judicial power to the courts) require a legally binding warrant to come from a judge or a justice of the peace. These provisions preclude administrative warrants. Nonetheless, binding administrative warrants have become commonplace.

More broadly, the phrasing of almost all the procedural rights discloses that they bar administrative power. Rather than actively state that the courts cannot violate various procedures, the procedural rights are typically stated in the passive voice, and they thereby limit government in general, including Congress and the executive.

Also revealing is the placement of most procedural rights after the main body of the Constitution. To bar adjudication outside the courts, the procedural amendments could not simply modify Article III of the Constitution, for then they would have limited only the courts. They also had to limit the executive, established in Article II. They even had to limit Congress, established in Article I, lest Congress authorize adjudication outside the courts.

The drafters of the Bill of Rights therefore changed how they wrote it. They originally framed amendments that would have rewritten particular articles of the Constitution – altering their wording, article by article, section by section. Ultimately, however, the drafters added their amendments at the end of the whole Constitution. This was crucial, for it allowed the procedural amendments to limit all parts of government.

These two drafting techniques – the passive voice and amendments at the end – give the procedural rights their breadth. Had the drafters merely made adjustments to Article III, or otherwise focused exclusively on the courts, they would have left the barn door open for administrative evasions of procedural rights. With the passive voice and amendments at the end, however, the procedural rights make clear that they limit all parts of government. They thereby bar all binding adjudication outside the courts, including administrative adjudication.

Nonetheless, agencies impose binding adjudication outside the courts, without judges and juries. They issue summons, subpoenas, warrants, and fines without the due process of law of the courts. They deny equal discovery, as required by due process, where agency actions are civil in nature. And they impose prosecutorial discovery, which is forbidden by due process, in cases that are criminal in nature. They even reverse the burdens of proof and persuasion required by due process. Agencies thereby repeatedly deprive Americans of their procedural rights.

REDUCTION OF CONSTITUTIONAL GUARANTEES TO MERE OPTIONS. The seriousness of the administrative evasion of procedural rights has not been sufficiently recognized. It becomes apparent, however, when one realizes that the government now enjoys ambidextrous enforcement.

The government once could engage in binding adjudication against Americans only through the courts and their judges. Now, it can choose administrative adjudication. In some instances, Congress alone makes this choice; in others, it authorizes an agency, such as the SEC, to make the selection. One way or another, the government can act ambidextrously – either through the courts and their judges, juries, and due process or through administrative adjudication and its faux process.

The evasion thereby changes the very nature of procedural rights. Such rights traditionally were assurances against the government. Now they are but one of the choices for government in its exercise of power. Though the government must respect these rights when it proceeds against Americans in court, it has the freedom to escape them by taking an administrative path. Procedural rights have thereby been transformed. No longer guarantees for the people, they now are merely options for the government.

SUBSTANTIVE RIGHTS. The administrative evasion of procedural rights is especially worrisome because it facilitates violations of substantive rights. Although this is a danger for many such rights, including religious liberty and the right to assemble, the threat is clearest for the freedoms of speech and the press, as they traditionally were understood in procedural terms.

The central historical understanding of speech and press rights was as a freedom from licensing – from the requirement of having to get prior administrative permission. And when such rights were threatened by postpublication prosecutions, they were recognized to be dependent on the right to a jury trial.

It therefore is shocking that the federal government uses administrative proceedings, including administrative licensing, to regulate words and speakers. The Federal Election Commission regulates political participation, and to avoid the fines it imposes through administrative adjudication, political speakers often ask the commission for advisory opinions – thus enabling the commission to license their political speech. The Federal Communications Commission imposes administrative licensing on broadcasters and thereby limits what they say. The SEC uses this sort of licensing to regulate some financial disclosures. Least well known but perhaps most dangerous, Health and Human Services establishes licensing, conducted by institutional review boards, for what is said in much empirical academic research and even for what can be published about it. (This last type of licensing is especially egregious because it limits the production and publication of medical knowledge. In thus limiting the ability of doctors to save lives, Institutional Review Boards leave a body count larger than that of Vietnam.) To be sure, the government needs to regulate some of the things it licenses; most clearly, it needs to allocate airwaves among broadcasters. But this does not mean it needs to regulate through administrative proceedings, let alone the prior administrative licensing of words.

The underlying constitutional danger is a wholesale mode of control. Traditionally, the government could engage in only retail suppression. It had to prove its case before a judge and jury in the course of prosecuting a particular person for his particular words. Nowadays, the government can employ administrative proceedings against words and even speakers, thereby avoiding the difficulty of persuading judges and juries. And by using licensing against speech or speakers – that is, by forcing potential speakers to seek prior administrative permission – the government can go further than is usual even in most administrative proceedings in reversing the usual burdens of proof and persuasion. The administrative evasion of procedural rights thus enables the government to avoid the difficulties of retail prosecutions. Indeed, it allows the government to engage in the sort of wholesale control of words and speakers that, unsurprisingly, last flourished in common-law nations in the seventeenth century.

* * *

Reflecting their origins as obstacles to extralegal pathways, the Constitution's procedural rights preclude administrative adjudication. Not merely the Constitution's structures but even its procedural rights bar administrative power.

Administrative power, however, ignores all of this. It even reduces procedural rights to mere options for government, and reintroduces prior licensing and its wholesale control of speech. It is difficult to think of a more serious civil liberties problem for the twenty-first century.

Procedural Deprivations in Court

Sadly, the loss of procedural rights in administrative tribunals is not the end of the matter. When hearing appeals from administrative adjudications, judges protect these proceedings in ways that further violate of procedural rights. The result is a double violation of rights, initially by agencies and then by the courts themselves.

Judicial Bias in Deference to Agency Interpretation. When agencies make law in the guise of interpreting statutes, they rely on the courts to defer to their interpretations. But this judicial deference is unconstitutional.

One problem is the judicial abandonment of independent judgment. When judges defer to agency interpretations, they depart from their judicial office or duty, under Article III of the Constitution, to exercise their own independent judgment. Recognizing this duty, Chief Justice John Marshall wrote in *Marbury v. Madison*: "It is emphatically the province and duty of the judicial department to say what the law is. Those who apply the rule to particular cases, must of necessity expound and interpret that rule." The judges therefore cannot defer to an agency's interpretation without abandoning their duty – indeed, their very office – as judges.

But this is not all; it gets worse. When the government is a party to a case, the doctrines that require judicial deference to agency interpretation are precommitments in favor of the government's legal position, and the effect is systematic judicial bias. Of course, this is an institutional rather than a personal predisposition, but it is therefore all the more systematic in favoring the most powerful of parties. One might object that the judges are said to defer in other areas of law. Such other "deference," however, is usually little more than deference to the law itself and its allocation of power. It never is deference to a single party. The doctrines that require judicial deference to agency interpretation thus stand out as dangerous violations of the Fifth Amendment's due process of law.

Put bluntly, what ordinarily is called "*Chevron* deference" (to agency interpretations of statutes) is really *Chevron* bias. Similarly, "*Auer* deference" (to agency interpretations of rules, often in the form of guidance) is really *Auer* bias. And although "*Mead-Skidmore* respect" (for informal agency interpretation of statutes) is not as predictable, it also is a form of bias. All such deference grossly violates the most basic due process right to be judged without any judicial precommitment to the other party.

Incidentally, the judges do not need to use any such deference. They sometimes say they need to rely on agency interpretation to fill statutory gaps because they otherwise would have to create law in such spaces. But judges should neither make law nor defer to agency interpretations. If, after the judges apply their usual tools of interpretation, they can find no further meaning in a statute, they should simply declare that the ambiguous provision has no discernable meaning – thereby leaving the ambiguity to be cured by Congress. The judges therefore do not need to defer to the government's legal position. The bias is unnecessary.

Just how severe is the bias problem? The first canon of judicial conduct declares: "An independent and honorable judiciary is indispensable to justice in our society." And the third canon states that a judge "shall disqualify himself or herself in a proceeding in which the judge's impartiality might reasonably be questioned, including but not limited to instances in which ... the judge has a personal bias or prejudice concerning a party." The implications are sobering because the institutional bias that comes with judicial deference is much more systematic and far reaching than any personal bias.

DEFERENCE TO AGENCY FACT-FINDING: LOST JURY RIGHTS AND JUDICIAL BIAS. When a court reviews an agency adjudication, the judges rely on the agency's fact-finding, as preserved in its administrative record. And this deprives parties of both jury and due process rights.

When a court defers to agency fact-finding, it deprives Americans of their right to a jury trial. As it happens, juries (like other procedural rights) are a constitutional right in the first instance; not merely later when one gets to court – a point decided in some of the earliest American constitutional cases. But even after one appeals from an agency to a court, one still does not get a jury trial. The excuse is that an agency's administrative record is like the record of a lower court. But an agency record is not the record of a court, let alone the verdict of a jury. When a court relies on such a record, the court itself violates jury rights.

Even worse is the bias. Where the government is a party to a case, the judges are relying on a record that is merely one party's version of the facts. Accordingly, when thus deferring to the administrative record, the judges are favoring one of the parties. Judicial deference to the administrative record is therefore another type of systematic bias, in violation of the Fifth Amendment's due process of law.

In court cases, there are two types of questions, those of law and those of fact. The combination of the two types of deference – to an agency's interpretation and to its record – is therefore especially disturbing. It means that, where the government is a party, there is systematic judicial bias in favor of the government on both the law and the facts. What, then, is left for the unbiased judgment of a judge and jury?

JUDICIAL BIAS EVEN AFTER HOLDING AGENCY ACTS UNLAWFUL. Even after courts hold agency actions unlawful, they continue to deny due process rights. For example, they usually will hesitate to declare an unlawful agency action void – instead remanding it to the agency. Moreover, when a district or circuit court interprets an ambiguous statute administered by an agency, the Supreme Court, under the *Brand X* doctrine, allows the agency in subsequent matters to disregard the judicial precedent and follow its own interpretation – thereby denying Americans the ability to secure precedent through litigation.

* * *

The courts should condemn the extralegal adjudication conducted by agencies, not least because it guts procedural rights. Instead, the courts add their own assaults on procedural rights. The result is the double violation of such rights, both administrative and judicial.

JURISDICTIONAL BOUNDARIES

Although the US Constitution generally repudiates extralegal power, there are some interesting qualifications at the edges. What are these limits to the argument? They tend to involve jurisdictional boundaries.

The preeminent jurisdictional qualification concerns the states. The states have varying constitutions, and although most of them establish principles very similar to those of the US Constitution, some have clearly gone in other directions – as when Virginia amended its constitution in 1971 to authorize administrative power. A state that goes too far in this direction may be vulnerable under the US Constitution's guarantee of a republican form of government. Up to that point, however, the Constitution does not prevent the states from taking their own paths.

Another jurisdictional caveat is local. When the English developed constitutional ideals against extralegal power, they largely succeeded in defeating the king's centralized prerogative power, but they typically did not think their ideals were applicable to local and other non-centralized extralegal power – what nowadays would be considered localized administrative power. This localized administrative power – such as the power exercised by justices of the peace, commissioners of sewers, and bankruptcy commissioners – was in tension with English constitutional ideals, but the English generally did not pursue such ideals at the local level.

And this pattern has been repeated in America. Although many state constitutions embrace ideals that preclude extralegal power, such constitutions have often been understood to permit some local administrative power. Moreover, where Congress acts in place of the states (in the territories and the District of Columbia), it has always felt free to authorize at least some local administrative measures, such as licensing regulations and non–Article III judges.

Another jurisdictional limit is at the borders. Congress for a long time (until the early twentieth century) understood that it could not nationally authorize the executive to regulate through licensing in domestic matters. Nonetheless, the US Constitution has always been understood to allow Congress to authorize licensing regulation in cross-border matters – traditionally Indian traders and steamboats and now, for example, airplanes and pilots.

Yet another jurisdictional boundary arises from military law. As recognized by the Constitution, the military has always been subject to its own legal system, in which military law and adjudication can be delegated.

Finally, it should be recalled that the argument here against administrative power is confined to edicts that bind or unbind. The Constitution does not bar the executive from making rules and establishing adjudication for the direction of its officers, for the distribution of benefits, or for determining the status of immigrants.

These jurisdictional qualifications are not merely exceptions but valuable boundaries to the Constitution's principles. By leaving room for administrative power in the states, in localities, at the borders, and so forth, these limits allow Americans to establish strong principles against extralegal power in the US Constitution. In other words, the federal barriers against extralegal power could be so unequivocal precisely because they did not reach too far – because they did not extend beyond the national regulation of domestic matters.

THE GERMAN CONNECTION

If the Constitution bars administrative power, how did this power enter American law? And why does it look so much like the old absolute power?

The answer lies in the civil law – the academic study of Roman law – which often celebrated Roman-style imperial power. On this foundation, Continental civilians justified their notions of absolute power, and English kings and their civilian-trained advisors introduced such ideas into England.

The ensuing tension between English law and civilian

absolutist ideas has shaped the development of constitutional law. The English in the seventeenth century developed constitutional ideals in opposition to absolute power, and Americans took such ideals even further in the US Constitution. But Continental peoples were not so fortunate. Their rulers and sympathetic academics, not least in Germany, tended to celebrate absolutism, and on this basis often defeated claims for constitutions, for separation of powers, and for bills of rights.

Especially in Prussia and other German states, rulers and attendant academics developed the monarch's personal absolute power into the state's bureaucratic administrative power. The Prussians were leaders in this development in the seventeenth and eighteenth centuries, and were echoed by the Russians in the 1760s and the French beginning in the 1790s. By the nineteenth century, the Prussians were considered the preeminent theorists and practitioners of administrative power.

This survival of absolute power in administrative form had consequences beyond the Continent. From there, notably Germany, absolute power in administrative form circled back to the common-law countries. The English turned to Continental administrative ideas already in the mid-nineteenth century, and Americans did so shortly afterward. Thousands of nineteenth-century Americans traveled to study in German universities, and when they returned home, they brought back ideas of administrative power. Some of them even spread their Germanic notions in Asia – as when Frank Goodnow drafted the 1914 Chinese Constitution.

The American adoption of European administrative ideas reveals that it is an understatement to say that federal administrative power revives absolute power. In fact, federal administrative power is a direct continuation of the absolutism that persisted in administrative form on the Continent.

This derivation of administrative power from Continental and especially German ideas is not only explanatory but also worrisome. In Europe, such ideas justified absolute power even within largely elected governments and, more broadly, undermined the expectation of free peoples that they could govern themselves, whether politically or even personally. Commenting on how Germans were coming to feel dependent on order imposed from above, Max Weber called them "Ordnungsmenschen."

Similarly, in this country, Americans are becoming accustomed to being ruled. This was Tocqueville's fear, and increasingly it is a reality. The danger is not merely a loss of civil liberties but a loss of the independent and self-governing spirit upon which all civil liberties depend.

ADMINISTRATIVE POWER
AND EQUAL VOTING RIGHTS

To understand how profoundly administrative governance threatens civil liberties, consider the growth of equal suffrage and the expansion of administrative power. Voting rights and the administrative state have probably been the two most remarkable developments in the federal government since the Civil War. It therefore is worth pausing to ask whether there is a connection.

Federal law was slow to protect equal suffrage. In 1870, the Fifteenth Amendment gave blacks the right to vote. In 1920, women acquired this right. And in 1965, the equality for blacks began to become a widespread reality.

Administrative power tended to expand in the wake of these changes in suffrage (a curiosity first noted by Thomas West). In 1887, Congress established the first major federal administrative agency, the Interstate Commerce Commission. In the 1930s, the New Deal created a host of powerful new agencies. And since the 1960s, federal administrative power has expanded even further. Of course, it would be a mistake to link administrative power too narrowly to the key dates in the expansion of suffrage. But growing popular participation in representative politics has evidently been accompanied by a shift of legislative power out of Congress and into administrative agencies.

The explanation is not hard to find. Although equality in voting rights has been widely accepted, the resulting democratization of American politics has prompted misgivings. Worried about the rough-and-tumble character of representative politics, and about the tendency of newly enfranchised groups to reject progressive reforms, many Americans have sought what they consider a more elevated mode of governance.

Some early progressives were quite candid about this. Woodrow Wilson complained that "the reformer is bewildered" by the need to persuade "a voting majority of several million heads." He was particularly worried about the diversity of the nation, which meant that the reformer needed to influence "the mind, not of Americans of the older stocks only, but also of Irishmen, of Germans, of Negroes." Elaborating this point, he observed: "The bulk of mankind is rigidly unphilosophical, and nowadays the bulk of mankind votes." And "where is this unphilosophical bulk of mankind more multifarious in its composition than in the United States?" Accordingly, "in order to get a footing for new doctrine, one must influence minds cast in every mold of race, minds inheriting every bias of environment, warped by the histories of a score of different nations, warmed or chilled, closed or expanded by almost every climate of the globe." Rather than try to persuade such persons, Wilson welcomed administrative governance. The people could still have their republic, but much legislative power would be shifted out of an elected body and into the hands of the right sort of people.

Rather than narrowly a matter of racism, this has been a transfer of legislative power to the knowledge class – meaning not a class defined in Marxist or other economic terms but those persons whose identity or sense of self-worth centers on their knowledge. More than merely the intelligentsia, this class includes all who are more attached to the authority of knowledge than to the authority of local political communities. Which is not to say that they have been particularly knowledgeable, but that their sense of affinity with cosmopolitan knowledge, rather than local connectedness, has been the foundation of their influence and identity. And in appreciating the authority they have attributed to their knowledge, and distrusting the tumultuous politics of a diverse people, they have gradually moved legislative power out of Congress and into administrative agencies – to be exercised, in more genteel ways, by persons like ... themselves.

The enfranchised masses, in short, have disappointed those who think they know better. Walter Lippmann worried that "what thwarts the growth of our civilization is ... the faltering method, the distracted soul, and the murky vision of what we grandiloquently call the will of the people." More recently, Peter Orszag urges that "bold measures are needed to circumvent polarization" – in particular that America needs to overcome the resulting "gridlock of our political institutions by making them a bit less democratic."

Of course, the removal of legislative power from the representatives of a diverse people has implications for minorities. Leaving aside Wilson's overt racism, the problem is the relocation of lawmaking power a further step away from the people and into the hands of a relatively homogenized class. Even when exercised with solicitude for minorities, it is a sort of power exercised from above, and those who dominate the administrative state have always been if not white men, then at least members of the knowledge class.

It therefore should be no surprise that administrative power comes with costs for the classes and attachments that are more apt to find expression through representative government. In contrast to the power exercised by elected members of Congress, administrative power comes with little accountability to – or even sympathy for – local, regional, religious, and other distinctive communities. Individually, administrators may be concerned about all Americans, but their power is structured in a way designed to cut off the political demands with which, in a representative system of government, local and other distinctive communities can protect themselves.

Administrative power thus cannot be understood apart from equal voting rights. The gain in popular suffrage has been accompanied by disdain for the choices made through a representative system and a corresponding shift of legislative power out of Congress. Although the redistribution of legislative power has gratified the knowledge class, it makes a mockery of the struggle for equal voting rights and confirms how severely administrative power threatens civil liberties.

Is It Practicable to Abandon Administrative Power?

Although administrative power is the nation's preeminent threat to civil liberties, many commentators worry that the nation cannot get along without it. In fact, the resulting economic problems suggest that the nation cannot afford to retain administrative power. But even so, it remains to be considered whether government is practicable without it.

For example, is administrative power the only means of rapid legislative change? Actually, when Congress wishes, it can act faster than most agencies, while relying on their expertise. Popular complaints about congressional "gridlock" therefore do not usually reflect the realities of institutional impediments, but instead typically serve to justify circumventing the political obstacles inherent in representative government.

Let's pretend, however, that gridlock is an institutional rather than a political impediment. How much administrative power actually involves genuine emergencies – matters that simply cannot wait for Congress to act? In fact, most administrative power effectuates long-term policies, and most claims of emergencies are merely excuses to shift power out of Congress.

Does complexity require administrative power? Federal statutes obviously can be just as complex as agency rules. The only difference is that statutes are adopted by Congress rather than by agencies. Of course, the underlying question (asked by Richard Epstein) is whether our complex society really needs complex rules, and there is reason to fear that the administrative answer to this is deeply mistaken.

Even if rules were adopted by Congress rather than agencies, how would the courts be able to handle the vast amount of adjudication currently handled by agencies? Apologists for administrative power protest that there are over ten thousand administrative adjudicators whose work could not be handled by the courts. But the vast bulk of such adjudication does not impose legal obligation. Thus, rather than administrative power, most such adjudication is merely the ordinary and lawful exercise of executive power – for example, in determining the distribution of benefits or the status of immigrants.

Accordingly, the question as to whether courts could handle what is now administrative adjudication must focus on the agency adjudication that imposes legal obligation. For example, the SEC employs only 5 administrative law judges, the Occupational Safety and Health Review Commission has 12, and the National Labor Relations Board has 34. In fact, outside the Social Security Administration, which distributes benefits, there are only 257 administrative law judges. This is not an overwhelming number, and it suggests that the scale of administrative adjudication is grossly overstated. The work of at least these 257 administrative law judges could easily be handled with the addition of an equivalent number of real judges.

What about the value of impartial administrative expertise? It is not clear that agencies have greater expertise than the private sector. Indeed, industry has much influence over agency regulation in part because of industry's greater knowledge. Some agencies are so short of expertise that they rely on regulated industries to write the regulations – as happened, for example, with the 2010 net neutrality rules.

More generally, expert knowledge must be distinguished from expert decision making. A decision to adopt a regulation in one area of expertise will almost inevitably have consequences in other fields of knowledge, and expertise in the one area is therefore not enough to resolve whether the regulation should be adopted. Indeed, a person with specialized expertise will tend to overestimate the importance of that area and underestimate the significance of others. As a result, although experts can be valuable for their specialized knowledge, they usually cannot be relied upon for decisions that take a balanced view of the consequences. This is why administrative power so frequently seems harsh or disproportionate: the administrative experts focus so closely on what they care about that they fail adequately to see other aspects of the question. It therefore makes sense to get the views of experts, but not to rely on them for decisions about regulation.

Ultimately, the question as to whether the government can get along without administrative power should be answered by its proponents. The arguments about the need for administrative power are empirical, and those who assert the need to depart from the Constitution must bear the burden of proof. Nonetheless, the advocates of administrative power rarely, if ever, back up their claims with serious empirical evidence.

Meanwhile, the empirical evidence of the danger from administrative power is mounting. Not being directly accountable to the people – or even to judges who act without bias – administrative power crushes the life and livelihood out of entire classes of Americans, depriving them of work and even of lifesaving medicines. It therefore is difficult to avoid the conclusion that, overall, the administrative assault on basic freedoms is unnecessary and even dangerous.

What Is To Be Done?

Lenin asked his fellow Russians, "What is to be done?" Fortunately for Americans, the answer is not revolution but a traditional American defense of civil liberties.

To this end, Americans will have to work through all three branches of government. Of course, none of the branches has thus far revealed much capacity to limit administrative power. But this is all the more reason to consider what they can do before it is too late.

First, although Congress has repeatedly authorized and acquiesced in administrative power, it still perhaps can redeem itself. Most basically, Congress should reclaim its legislative power. And, of course, it need not do this all at once; instead, it can convert rules to statutes at a measured pace, agency by agency. By leaving so much lawmaking to the executive, our legislators have allowed not only power but also leadership and even fundraising to shift to the president. Ambitious legislators might therefore realize the advantages of reclaiming their constitutional role.

Congress also should bar judicial deference to agencies on questions of law or fact, as this violates due process and other constitutional limitations. Congress additionally should abolish administrative law judges and replace them with real judges (a reform it can partly fund by shifting money from the unconstitutional adjudicators to the courts). More generally, Congress should remove immunity for administrators – beginning with those who have desk jobs in agencies with a track record of violating constitutional rights.

The executive offers a second mechanism against administrative power. Presidents come and go, and a president worried about administrative power should not be content merely to put bad administrative policies on hold until the next election; more seriously, he should end administrative paths of governance. For example, he could require agencies, one by one, to send their rules to Congress for it to adopt. He also could require federal lawyers to refrain from seeking judicial deference, lest they participate in the courts' due process violations. For any president, such steps would be a remarkable constitutional legacy.

A third and more predictable approach will be through the courts. The judges have repeatedly acquiesced in administrative power. Between 1906 and 1912 and again in 1937, the judges who stood up against it were threatened, and each time they gave way. Subsequently, even without threats, the judges have bent over backward to accommodate such power.

They thereby have corrupted their own proceedings – for example, by refusing jury rights even in court, by abandoning their office of independent judgment, and by engaging in systematic bias in violation of the due process of law. Overall, administrative power is one of the most shameful episodes in the history of the federal judiciary.

Nonetheless, Americans can persuade the judges to do their duty. The judges have high ideals of their office of independent judgment. And they are dedicated to their role in upholding the law, especially the Constitution. Accordingly, once they understand how administrative power corrupts the processes of the courts and violates constitutional liberties, at least some of them will repudiate it.

Ultimately, the defeat of administrative power will have to come from the people. Only their spirit of liberty can move Congress, inspire the president, and brace the judges to do their duty.

Americans therefore need to recognize that administrative power revives absolute power and profoundly threatens civil liberties. Once Americans understand this, they can begin to push back, and the fate of administrative power will then be only a matter of time.

MOLLIE ZIEGLER HEMINGWAY

TRUMP VS. THE MEDIA

THE DAY AFTER he was inaugurated, President Donald Trump visited the CIA and announced that his attacks on the media would continue. "I have a running war with the media. They are among the most dishonest human beings on earth, right?" he said.

The next week, his advisor, Steve Bannon, told the *New York Times* that the media had been "humiliated" by the paper's biased 2016 election coverage. "I want you to quote this," he said. "The media here is the opposition party. They don't understand this country. They still do not understand why Donald Trump is the president of the United States."

On February 17, Trump tweeted to his twenty-five million followers that the "fake news media" is "not my enemy, it is the enemy of the American People!" He reiterated this in a public speech a week later, making sure to clarify he was singling out "fake news."

NBC News political director Chuck Todd responded on social media: "This not a laughing matter. I'm sorry, delegitimizing the press is unAmerican." Journalists wrote tributes to themselves about the importance of journalism, and shared the most indignant reactions to Trump on social media. Many media outlets and editors said the president's insults were renewing their sense of mission.

The *Washington Post* changed its motto to "Democracy dies in darkness." The *New York Times* ran an ad campaign claiming, "The truth is more important than ever," a statement indicating that for the paper the importance of truth was conditional on whether its management agreed with the politician in charge.

The media shouldn't have been surprised by what Trump was doing. In speeches and on social media throughout the campaign, Trump played the part of a busy media critic, calling various news outlets fake, disgusting, and dishonest. His frequent attacks on the media were lapped up by voters, frustrated by years of uneven coverage of conservative politicians and issues. Media outlets spent much of 2016 absolutely trashing Trump and assuring viewers and readers that Hillary Clinton would easily be elected. Trump pulled off a surprise victory that demonstrated the chasm between half of the electorate and the national political media.

The media should have made short-term systematic changes to its news-gathering process to make sure that it would never again be so out of touch with the Americans it covers. Instead, it reacted even more hysterically, pushing conspiracy theories that Trump had won because of a scourge of fake news or Russian meddling. Believing its anti-Trump coverage had been too limited during the campaign, the media began on all-out assault of negative news against him, pushing dozens of what turned out to be false stories, such as those suggesting that transgender teen suicide rates had spiked in the immediate aftermath of Trump's election, that three states had had their elections hacked, that Trump's treasury secretary nominee had foreclosed on a ninety-year-old woman for a twenty-seven-cent payment error, that federal agencies were purging scientific data from websites, that Trump had removed a bust of Martin Luther King, Jr., from the White House, and that top management at the State Department had resigned in protest.

The response to Trump's election from the media has been an admixture of anger and confusion. For decades, the press in America has been accorded a variety of perks and privileges based on the assumptions that it was integral to the success of civil society and that it would exercise its power responsibly. However, Trump's victory has advanced the developing realization among many Americans that the media has completely abdicated its responsibility and shown itself hostile to the values and ideas many Americans hold. Much of the population no longer believes the media should be treated deferentially and given the power to shape, much less control, public opinion.

How'd We Get Here?

Complaining vociferously about the press is a Republican tradition dating back at least to Dwight Eisenhower's 1964 convention speech. Ike received a prolonged standing ovation when he said, "Let us particularly scorn the divisive efforts of those outside our family, including sensation-seeking columnists and commentators, because I assure you that these are people who couldn't care less about the good of our party."

At nearly every appearance President George H. W. Bush made during his unsuccessful reelection campaign in 1992, he would display his favorite bumper sticker: "Annoy the media: Re-elect Bush." The crowd would hoot and holler as Bush complained about a media that clearly signaled its preference for Bill Clinton.

Political candidates as different as Richard Nixon and John McCain made similar complaints. Conservative radio talk-show hosts spent decades dissecting the framing and spin of stories in the major media. Conservatives complained so much about media bias that it almost became trite. Liberal media critics such as Eric Alterman – who authored the 2003 book *What Liberal Media?*, which attempted to rebut GOP charges of media bias – said complaints about the media were little more than conservatives "playing the referees." Whatever the case, journalists accepted the complaints as a part of doing business and made little to no apparent effort to improve.

In fact, they got worse.

At some point, something broke. The regular complaints about media bias were harder to ignore as the problems became more obvious. The episodes of major media malpractice are simply too numerous to list, but a few stand out for having a profound impact on undermining Americans' institutional trust in the news media.

In 2005, Hurricane Katrina hit the Gulf and led to what Dan Rather – yes, the former *CBS News* anchor who pushed fraudulent documents to discredit George W. Bush – called "one of the quintessential great moments in television news." Yet, media critic W. Joseph Campbell wrote in *Getting It Wrong: Debunking the Greatest Myths in American Journalism* that the erroneous and over-the-top reporting on Katrina "had the cumulative the effect of painting for America and the rest of the world a scene of surreal violence and terror, something straight out of *Mad Max* or *Lord of the Flies*." This reporting pushed racist stereotypes, scaremongering, and a political focus that emphasized national control over local solutions.

Typical of the media's antipathy to Republicans, the national news coverage laid seemingly all the problems with the hurricane response at the foot of President George W. Bush. While the Bush administration was not above criticism, comparatively little blame for the dysfunctional disaster response was placed on Louisiana's notoriously corrupt and incompetent state and local governments, which at the time were predominantly Democratic. The mayor of New Orleans during Hurricane Katrina would go to prison in 2014 for taking hundreds of thousands of dollars in bribes from city contractors, and this corruption began well before Katrina. At the time of his sentencing, Nagin was the seventeenth elected official from the New Orleans area to be convicted on federal corruption or fraud charges since the hurricane.

In 2006, an exotic dancer hired by members of the Duke University lacrosse team alleged she'd been violently gang-raped. A year later, the three men she'd accused were not just found not guilty but actually declared innocent as the case completely fell apart. In the interim, many major media outlets reported on the story in a biased and hysterical fashion, convicting the three men of rape, racism, and a host of other sins in the court of public opinion. The media used the episode to force a national conversation about the need to accept all manner of politically correct liberal pieties.

New York Times public editor Dan Okrent criticized his paper's Duke coverage in 2007. Speaking about it years later, he stated: "It was white over black, it was male over female, it was rich over poor, educated over uneducated. All the things that we know happen in the world coming together in one place and journalists, they start to quiver with a thrill when something like this happens." Okrent's comments weren't terribly representative of widespread media concern, however. Since the Duke case fell apart, there's been comparatively little reflection about the dangers of self-righteous Democratic prosecutors run amok or the need for the media to focus on facts and evidence when it is tempted to indulge narratives that comport with its biased perceptions.

In 2009, a Tea Party movement began to push back against what its participants perceived as radical policies in the Obama administration pointed toward the growth and centralization of the federal government. The backlash was almost entirely predictable. Obama campaigned as a centrist and pragmatist, but once elected he governed like a socialist ideologue. His first two major legislative moves involved creating a trillion-dollar spending bill that was supposed to rescue the economy from the depths of recession but disproportionately rewarded Democratic special interests. Not only was the economy not rescued, it never recovered – after eight years Obama was the first president in modern American history who never had a year of GDP growth over 3 percent. Obama's second major legislative move was the sprawling two-thousand-page bill to nationalize health care known as Obamacare, which has been a rolling disaster ever since it was implemented and has triggered a number of alarming regulatory restrictions and court decisions enhancing federal power. Additionally, Obama brazenly lied about the fact that the proposed law would kick millions of Americans off their existing health insurance plans.

In retrospect, Tea Party concerns about Obama's nascent presidency were entirely grounded in legitimate objections that his expensive schemes would fail and do great harm to the notion of limited government. Nonetheless, the media treated these legitimate concerns as the contemptuous and irrational yawps of the racist Republican grassroots.

The Tea Party movement was launched by the impassioned plea of CNBC journalist Rick Santelli, yet fell into major mainstream media opposition. An early CNN report featured reporter Susan Roesgen fighting with participants about their views on the president's policies. She described the event as "anti-government, anti-CNN since this is highly promoted by the right-wing conservative network Fox." Roesgen was let go by CNN, but negative and dismissive coverage continued as the protest movement grew. In one case, completely unsubstantiated claims of racial slurs and spitting on Congressmen were given wide play by the media. Protesters who showed up at town halls were disparaged as mentally unhinged and possibly violent.

And though voter concerns about the media were treated as pure paranoia, there was mounting evidence that the media was engaged in conspiratorial behavior designed to target those resistant to advancing a liberal policy agenda. In 2010, a secret e-mail list called "Journolist" was revealed. During the 2008 campaign, hundreds of journalists used it to shape narratives to help then–Democratic candidate Barack Obama. Participants, who included mainstream reporters as well as overtly liberal journalists, discussed how to suppress negative information about Obama's longtime pastor Jeremiah Wright. Ideas included attacking conservatives as racist. One contributor said, "If the right forces us all to either defend Wright or tear him down, no matter what we choose, we lose the game they've put upon us. Instead, take one of them – Fred Barnes, Karl Rove who cares – and call them racists." Another discussion compared members of the Tea Party movement to Nazis.

The relationship between the media and conservatives continued to sour after that. On July 31, 2012, Republican candidate for president Mitt Romney paid his respects at Poland's Tomb of the Unknown Soldier in Warsaw. He was making an international trip as part of his presidential campaign. Campaign reporters had all agreed, for some reason, that Romney had made horrific campaign-ending mistakes by saying security problems at the London Olympics were "disconcerting," referring formally instead of casually to Labour leader Ed Miliband, and revealing he had taken a meeting with the secretive MI-6 agency. At the time, Romney shook hands with military veterans and chatted with Warsaw's mayor. As he made his way to his vehicle, a group of reporters from top media outlets began screaming.

"Governor Romney are you concerned about some of the mishaps of your trip?" a CNN reporter shouted. A *Washington Post* reporter famously shrieked, "What about your gaffes?" And a *New York Times* reporter yelled the follow-up question: "Governor Romney, do you feel that your gaffes have overshadowed your foreign trip?"

A few months later, when Romney was critical of the Obama administration's handling of the Benghazi attack that killed four Americans, including an ambassador, the media immediately pushed back, suggesting that the real problem was Romney's critique. The Obama administration falsely placed blame for the attack on anger at an American filmmaker's work critical of Islam, and the media by and large accepted these outlandish claims. Obama officials put out videos in other countries claiming that Americans were not to disparage other religions, despite the First Amendment protecting the right of Americans to do just that. Moderating a presidential debate, political reporter Candy Crowley helped President Obama when Mitt Romney had him on the ropes regarding his handling of the aftermath of the terror attack, taking Obama's side in suggesting that the presidential administration always clearly regarded it as a coordinated terrorist attack instead of a riot in response to a video. The Obama administration's position on what caused Benghazi would have been clarified by a *60 Minutes* interview the day after the incident that had Obama refusing to rule out the possibility Benghazi was a terrorist attack, but *60 Minutes*, likely well aware it would hurt his reelection chances, didn't broadcast the interview – and instead quietly released a transcript of Obama's remarks a few days before the election. In trying to explain the extraordinary deference on Benghazi of *CBS News*, it helps to know that Obama's deputy national security adviser, Ben Rhodes – the same man who would later brag in the pages of the *New York Times* about dishonestly manipulating reporters to pass the Iran nuclear deal – is the brother of *CBS News* president David Rhodes.

In another debate, Mitt Romney talked about his efforts to bring more women into public service while he was governor. He said that he combed through binders full of resumes of qualified women to accomplish his goal of increasing the number of women in the workforce.

Somehow this became another media obsession, where "binders full of women" became shorthand for Mitt Romney's alleged misogyny. On October 12, 2016, in the midst of an uproar over Donald Trump's sexually offensive commentary caught on an old tape, Matt Viser, the deputy Washington bureau chief for the *Boston Globe*, would write that "'Binders full of women' – a comment about resumes of female applicants for state government jobs – seems, at this point, quite quaint." Yet, like so many of his peers, Viser spent much of the 2012 campaign pushing the Obama campaign's messaging that "binders full of women" meant Mitt Romney had problems with women.

Naturally, the accusations of misogyny were nothing compared to the charges of racism. Romney ran ads correctly pointing out that the Obama administration had issued rules gutting the wildly popular welfare reform legislation that was broadly agreed to have dramatically reduced the size of America's welfare rolls. It didn't matter that Robert Rector, the policy wonk who wrote the welfare reform legislation, said Romney was correct. Instead, media "fact-checkers" badly mangled the details of the legislation and the media seized on the misinformation to make ridiculous claims that Romney was making coded appeals to racism. This devolved to the point of a television shouting match between MSNBC's Chris Matthews and then–Republican National Committee head Reince Priebus, where Matthews accused Priebus of playing the "race card" for saying that "work requirements" should be a part of receiving welfare benefits.

What happened to Mitt Romney was sadly typical of what has happened to all Republican candidates for high office. Even someone as previously beloved by the media as John McCain was slowly transformed by biased characterizations into a Hitler-like representation during his campaign against Barack Obama in 2008. But when it happened to Mitt Romney – a squeaky clean, unfailingly nice, completely moderate Mormon from Massachusetts – Republicans realized that the media would do it to anyone.

The problems continued in the second Obama term, as additional scandals came out but were barely covered, much less given the regular breathless attention political scandals are normally given. When Internal Revenue Service officials revealed that actors in the agency, some of whom were in frequent contact with the White House, had targeted conservative opponents of Obama and limited their ability to gain tax-exempt status, it was treated as if it were not a huge deal. This largely passed under the radar, even though for many Americans it was a scandal that eclipsed Watergate many times over.

Not Just Politics

The media problems weren't just about politics, either. Media bias reached a critical mass where it was seen as a fundamental threat to the cherished traditions, values, and religion of millions of Americans. Media figures couldn't hide their contempt for Americans who did not share the same progressive values as them. Shortly after he retired as editor of the *New York Times* in 2011, Bill Keller gave a speech in Austin, Texas, about the paper's bias. He said it was crucial for coverage of politics to be balanced and fair at the paper, but revealed that when it came to moral and social issues, that was a different matter altogether.

Asked directly if the *Times* slanted its coverage to favor "Democrats and liberals," he added: "Aside from the liberal values, sort of social values thing that I talked about, no, I don't think that it does." He was admitting the paper didn't care about biased coverage when it came to little things like whether marriage, the bedrock institution of society, should be redefined or whether ending human life in the womb should be allowed throughout all nine months of pregnancy.

At the time, the paper was in the midst of a decades-long major media campaign to redefine marriage to include same-sex couples. It was also in the middle of decades of struggles to cover religion well, particularly traditional religion. That struggle was still going on in December 2016 when executive editor Dean Baquet admitted, "We don't get religion." (He got that right; a *New York Times* report from eight months before the time of this writing claiming that the New Testament "calls for the execution of gays" remains on the paper's website uncorrected, despite being called out for being wildly wrong by numerous prominent outlets and religious voices.) And the paper has never been known for covering the abortion topic well, either.

When David Shaw wrote his landmark exposé in the *Los Angeles Times* in 1990 about the level of bias of major media in favor of abortion, "Abortion Bias Seeps into News," the *New York Times* was one of the publications whose slant on abortion was already legendary.

Shaw's well-researched look at the topic mentions that the media uses language that frames the abortion debate in terms favorable to those who support the practice, quotes abortion-rights advocates more frequently and favorably than opponents, and ignores or gives minimal attention to events and issues favorable to abortion opponents.

That's exactly what happened in 2013 when Philadelphia abortionist Kermit Gosnell was on trial for the murders of a woman and some of the children whose lives he ended in his filthy clinic. He kept trophies of baby feet in jars. His employees testified that he snipped the spinal cords of children he'd just delivered. He performed abortions without sufficient painkillers for poor immigrant women. His clinic was soaked in cat urine and so messy that medical teams couldn't evacuate patients safely. He kept fetal parts in the refrigerator next to employee lunches.

It had all the makings of a major media maelstrom: a prolific serial murderer, a sensational trial, innocent victims. It even had angles for noncrime reporters, with troubling issues surrounding drugs, clinic regulations, immigration status, and racism.

Yet the media had to be shamed into giving the story more than a cursory mention. And even when major outlets devoted a bit of coverage to it here and there, the coverage was reluctant and paltry. One *Washington Post* reporter who had written dozens upon dozens of stories favorable to abortion-rights groups said that she hadn't covered the Gosnell incident because it was a "local crime story." The idea that national media doesn't cover local crime would be news to people who have read about the Newtown, Connecticut, shootings; the Trayvon Martin killing; the police shooting of Michael Brown in Ferguson, Missouri; or the riots in Baltimore.

On other social issues the bias was also clear. When the Supreme Court redefined marriage to include same-sex couples in a tight ruling condemned by the dissenters as a dangerous threat to rule of law and religious liberty, many media outlets responded by cheering the ruling, downplaying its threats, and even changing their logos to include pro–gay marriage imagery. *Washington Post* ombudsman Patrick Pexton wrote a 2013 column in response to a reader's plea that the paper publish journalism instead of advocacy and propaganda on the issue. In the article, Pexton characterized those who uphold marriage as the institution built around sexual complementarity as the equivalent of racists, admitted he didn't even know or understand the arguments in favor of defining marriage as the union of man and woman, and defended the paper's one-sided coverage as a matter of justice.

Whether the topic has been religion, the family, human life, guns, conservative governance, or even sports, the media bias has become more pronounced and the trouble with accuracy, an epidemic. Once conservatives saw the problems, they couldn't unsee them, even in the case of more nuanced issues, such as the media downplaying massive annual pro-life marches while hyping Leftist marches, reacting hysterically to disasters that occur during Republican presidencies while giving the benefit of the doubt to the handling of oil spills or natural disasters that occur during Democratic tenures, spinning comments made by Republicans as sexist and bigoted while downplaying or trying to provide exculpatory context for charged comments by Democrats, using anonymous sources to tear down political opponents, hiding balancing viewpoints at the end of stories instead of featuring them more prominently in the text, using terms with negative connotations for causes that it dislikes and terms with positive connotations for those it favors, and finding other ways of shading the truth.

Enough's Enough

Looked at from the perspective of conservative voters who feel that they have been repeatedly lied to and abused by media elites for decades, it's not hard to understand how we ended up with President Trump. The media, however, is so unrepentant and lacking in self-awareness that it is having real trouble admitting it's done anything wrong, and instead is indulging its worst impulses of hyperbole and hysteria. The fact remains that the current political situation is the logical result of the hostile and distrustful environment it cultivated, rather than some black-swan event unleashed by the sudden onset of irrationality of voters in flyover states.

It was the media's decades-long approach of putting its thumb on the scale by covering conservatives and conservative causes poorly that created a lose-lose situation for conservatives. There was no way for them to operate successfully in a system where the media allowed them to be respected as the principled opposition only as long as they were shackled and limited by biased news coverage. And conservative voters were beyond sick of it. The media would say things that weren't true and cover issues dishonestly, and then accuse others of being liars or gaffe-makers for disagreeing. No candidate – not even squeaky-clean moderates like Mitt Romney – would keep the media from painting Republicans and their beliefs as dangerous. It was enough to make half the country give up on the enterprise of working with the media altogether.

Most Americans had no way to combat media crimes and their power to shape the culture and electoral outcomes, particularly if they were focused on their work and home life. And even most politicians weren't quite capable of combating this media power.

Along came Trump, the brilliant master of exploiting public opinion. A New York real estate developer and reality TV celebrity, he had spent decades studying the media and how to make it work to his advantage. Understanding that conservatives had lost trust in the credibility of the media to cover politics accurately, the media became one of his primary targets, and he played it like a fiddle. Trump voters loved that he was beating up the bully they had been impotent to vanquish. They loved that he destroyed the media's power to declare things gaffes, much less campaign-destroying gaffes. Figures such as Chuck Todd can lament Trump's ability to put the media in its place as being "un-American" all he wants. The fact is that Trump wouldn't have this power had the media not set things up through decades of shoddy coverage targeting its political opponents. The media did this to itself.

Trump's unique power to bring attention to the problems of the media also meant that his 2016 campaign proved a case study in identifying and examining pernicious media trends. Among the trends he identified that are worth exploring are the media's overwhelming desire to push narratives in spite of its inability to see the future; its undeniable coordination with the Democratic party; its attempts to present opinions as facts, and vice versa; and the blatant double standards in its coverage motivated by partisanship.

OBJECTIVITY AND OVERCONFIDENCE

While a few reporters here and there resisted the tide, there's no point in pretending that the media covered Donald Trump in a fair or nonhistrionic fashion. *New York*

Times media writer Jim Rutenberg said what most journalists were thinking in his front-page August 8, 2016, article "Trump Is Testing the Norms of Objectivity in Journalism."

"If you're a working journalist and you believe that Donald J. Trump is a demagogue playing to the nation's worst racist and nationalistic tendencies, that he cozies up to anti-American dictators and that he would be dangerous with control of the United States nuclear codes, how the heck are you supposed to cover him?" Rutenberg asked. The premise was that most journalists would inevitably agree that Trump was a dangerous demagogue, and that they should continue to stay on the Trump beat even though they were unable or unwilling to change their opinion. If a reporter viewed Trump's presidency as "potentially dangerous," his reporting should reflect that, Rutenberg said.

He advised reporters to "throw out the textbook American journalism has been using," move away from a model of balanced coverage, and become openly oppositional. He acknowledged that such a change would "throw the advantage" to Hillary Clinton and he acknowledged that supporters of Trump would take an even-worse view of the media. Journalism shouldn't try so hard to be fair but instead "stand up to history's judgment" and "ferret out what the candidates will be like in the most powerful office in the world," he said.

What does that even mean? How could reporters speculate on the future? And why would they try? In his 2002 "Why Speculate?" speech, novelist Michael Crichton stated, "Because we are confronted by speculation at every turn, in print, on video, on the net, in conversation, we may eventually conclude that it must have value. But it doesn't. Because no matter how many people are speculating, no matter how familiar their faces, how good their makeup and how well they are lit, no matter how many weeks they appear before us in person or in columns, it remains true that none of them knows what the future holds."

New York Times executive editor Dean Baquet didn't condemn the approach Rutenberg advocated but praised it. "I thought Jim Rutenberg's column nailed it," he said in an interview with Harvard's NiemanLab.

The general media consensus was to speculate that Trump would be a bad president. Therefore, it justified increasingly negative coverage of Trump, and kinder coverage of Clinton. To talk honestly about both candidates' negative traits was derided by journalists as "false equivalence," since one candidate was, in its mind, worse than the other.

But not only was Crichton right about speculation being largely worthless, the self-righteousness and misplaced confidence that accompanies so much media speculation is definitively discrediting. Never has this been more obvious than in the 2016 presidential campaign. The media felt empowered to take sides, because, to paraphrase the last president, it thought it had the power to determine who is on the right side of history. Voters had other ideas.

It was decided early on in newsrooms that Hillary Clinton would easily trounce Donald Trump. From the moment Trump announced his candidacy in June 2015, it was treated as a joke. Even after he won the Republican primary, besting many strong competitors, the general narrative was that he would not beat Clinton. The *New York Times* gave Clinton an 85 percent shot of winning. Statistician Nate Silver was lambasted by other liberals for giving Clinton only a 71.4 percent chance of winning. In turn, several prominent left-leaning media outlets went so far as to criticize Silver for not rating Clinton's chances of winning the election high enough. Surely, the prediction of the *Huffington Post* polls that Clinton had a 98 percent chance of winning has earned a prominent place in the annals of worthless speculation. The *New York Times* had a probability gauge that fluctuated throughout election night as results came in. It was in the 9:00 P.M. hour in the East that it began to look like Trump had a real chance of winning. The liberal hosts and talking heads on the news couldn't conceal their sadness and anger that night as the reality sunk in.

And yet, they had dropped their journalistic standards as they tried to elect Clinton, justifying the departure from even a pretense of objectivity on the grounds that Trump was dangerous, and they had lost. Their team had lost. And it was increasingly clear that Democrats were their team.

TEAM DEMOCRAT

The 2016 campaign featured the unauthorized release of e-mails from Democratic officials and Hillary Clinton campaign operatives via WikiLeaks, a group that publishes private or classified information from anonymous sources. The leak revealed details about how these officials interacted with the media, including journalists at CNN, POLITICO, the *Wall Street Journal*, and the *Washington Post*. This included information about a Democratic operative and former CNN contributor, Donna Brazile, repeatedly leaking debate questions that would be featured in a debate hosted by CNN to Hillary Clinton; a POLITICO reporter running the text of stories by Clinton operatives before publishing them; and a *New York Times* reporter allowing the Clinton campaign to nix an unflattering quote from an interview, contravening the newspaper's official policy forbidding quote approval.

The information once again confirmed the view of many Republicans that the media was at times behaving as the communications arm of the Democratic Party.

There can be little doubt that the media worked hand in glove with the Clinton campaign. A good example of how close the relationship worked took place with the media coverage of efforts to highlight Clinton's support from beauty pageant winner Alicia Machado.

At the end of the first presidential debate of 2016, Hillary Clinton shoehorned in a reference to the former beauty contestant who had won a contest run by Trump in 1997.

Trying to show Trump's misogyny, which was another major campaign theme of hers, she said, "And one of the worst things he said was about a woman in a beauty contest. He loves beauty contests, supporting them and hanging around them. And he called this woman 'Miss Piggy.' Then he called her 'Miss Housekeeping,' because she was Latina. Donald, she has a name ... Her name is Alicia Machado ... And she has become a U.S. citizen, and you can bet she's going to vote this November."

All is fair in politics, and if Hillary Clinton wanted to run a "war on women" campaign attack against Donald Trump, it would just mean she was following in the footsteps of previous Democratic candidates. Almost immediately, media outlets ran detailed, if thinly sourced and one-sided, front-page and top-of-the-newscast stories, some including previously taken photo shoots of Machado with an American flag. That meant these stories and photos were ready to go and waiting for Clinton to sound the alarm by mentioning her name. There was no daylight between actual Hillary Clinton campaign talking points and the stories that ran on front pages across the land.

Note how differently media outlets covered the story when it first broke in 1997. CNN began its report on Machado by saying, "When Alicia Machado of Venezuela was named Miss Universe nine months ago, no one could accuse her of being the size of the universe. But as her universe expanded, so did she, putting on nearly 60 pounds." CNN added, "Since winning the crown, the former Miss Venezuela went from 118 pounds to – well – a number that kept growing like the size of the fish that got away."

Trump told reporters, "Some people when they have pressure eat too much. Like me. Like Alicia." Critics wanted the pageant to drop her and take away her crown, but the pageant officials, including Trump, just encouraged her to get her weight down. CNN's report ended with Trump telling a "rowdy pool of reporters" that "a lot of you folks have weight problems. I hate to tell you."

But when Clinton brought up Machado's attack in the first debate, the *New York Times* put two of its top reporters on the case, and they wrote an article entitled, "Shamed and Angry: Alicia Machado, a Miss Universe Mocked by Donald Trump." NBC's *TODAY* bought the Clinton spin hook, line, and sinker, conducting an interview with Machado titled "Donald Trump Hasn't Changed since Fat-Shaming Me in 1996, Alicia Machado Says."

Within seventy-two hours of the debate, the Lexis-Nexis database showed that major media outlets had run hundreds of stories using Clinton's framing of the story. It wasn't just that they ran the story – the Clinton campaign even set up conference calls with reporters – but that they covered it without skepticism.

A less compliant media might have noted that the Mexican attorney general's office said Machado was romantically involved and had a daughter with notorious drug lord

José Gerardo Álvarez-Vázquez, also known as "El Indio." A less compliant media might have noted that a Venezuelan judge claimed Machado threatened to ruin his career and kill him in response to his indictment of her then boyfriend for murder. A less compliant media might have noted that Machado was accused – albeit never prosecuted – of driving the getaway car in that murder.

Clinton wanted to push the idea that Machado had become a US citizen recently and would be voting for her. This was a natural contrast to the Trump campaign, which expressed skepticism about current US immigration policy and whether it served American interests. Such obvious problems with Machado's story and the fact that Machado was walking proof of Trump's contention that America's immigration policy is broken were barely noted by the media.

LIES, DAMNED LIES, AND FACT-CHECKING

Beginning in the second term of the Bush administration, various media enterprises got the idea to do something called "fact-checking." Not just the type of fact-checking they should have been doing in Journalism 101, mind you. No, the reelection of Bush had disappointed many journalists, and there was a sense from them that the Bush administration was getting away with not telling the truth.

The "fact-checking trend" meant that journalists would gain more power. They wouldn't just get to determine which stories saw the light of day and which were killed or downplayed; they would pick the angle and framing for the stories and determine who was quoted and how. And through fact-checking, they would tell people what to think about claims made in these stories.

It shouldn't surprise anyone that the fact-checking

enterprises issued their findings in a biased fashion, with the benefit of the doubt and contextual loopholes provided for Democratic politicians in a way that was closed off for Republicans. One typical example is that the Pulitzer-winning PolitiFact rated Barack Obama's (false) claim in support of his health care legislation, "If you like your health care plan, you can keep your health care plan," as some variation of true six times before Obama's reelection in 2012. After he was re-elected, when they had to actually implement Obamacare, millions of Americans immediately lost their health insurance plans. A claim PolitiFact had called true half a dozen times became PolitiFact's 2013 "lie of the year."

Instead of killing off the fact-checking trend, the media incorporated it into its coverage of the 2016 general election campaign. For example, Donald Trump repeatedly said throughout his primary campaign that President Obama and Hillary Clinton were founders, cofounders, or MVPs of ISIS. He said it three times in January of 2016 alone. He said that Clinton and Obama "created" ISIS, that Clinton "invented" ISIS and was responsible for ISIS, and that Clinton should "take an award" as the "founder" of ISIS.

These claims went mostly unnoticed by the media while Donald Trump was defeating Republican opponents, even if they were made in nationally televised speeches and interviews. But when he made a similar claim again in August after the candidates had been nominated, all hell broke loose.

To be fair, Trump's speaking style couldn't be more removed from the anodyne and cautious political rhetoric journalists have grown accustomed to and demanded from Republicans in particular. This was a challenge for political journalists. Trump's sentences ran on into paragraphs. He avoided specificity or contradicted himself when he was specific. His sentences trailed into other sentences. It was frustrating.

But it's not as if his point was that difficult to understand. He opposed the Obama administration's handling of the Middle East region and how it led to the rise of ISIS. That's a downright normal political attack. But the media for some reason decided Trump was arguing that Obama and Clinton had literally filed articles of incorporation for the group. And they treated this literal claim as a fact that needed to be debunked.

This led to some funny contradictory fact-checks, such as when Bloomberg fact-checked this claim as false on account of Abu Musab al-Zarqawi founding the group while CNN fact-checked the claim as false on account of Abu Bakr al-Baghdadi founding the group.

Politifact gave Trump a "Pants on Fire" rating, even after admitting that President Barack Obama's leadership in Iraq and Hillary Clinton's push to change regimes in Libya led to the explosion of ISIS. The group's ruling was based on its belief that Trump was being hyperliteral.

Radio host Hugh Hewitt practically begged Donald Trump to phrase his ISIS arguments differently. "I'd just use different language to communicate it," Hewitt told him. Trump responded, "But they wouldn't talk about your language, and they do talk about my language, right?" Again, Trump was exploiting the media's double standards for how politicians are allowed to talk.

People accuse their political opponents of being responsible for bad things all the time. Clinton accused Trump of being ISIS's top recruiter. Bush's CIA and NSA chief said Trump was a "recruiting sergeant" for ISIS. Former New York City mayor Rudy Giuliani said Hillary Clinton could be considered a "founding member of ISIS." Senators Elizabeth Warren of Massachusetts and Chris Murphy of Connecticut declared that Senate Republicans were arming ISIS. Carly Fiorina and Rick Santorum blamed ISIS on Obama and Clinton. Senator John McCain said Obama was directly responsible for the Orlando ISIS attack due to his failure to deal with the group. President Obama said that Republicans trying to prioritize Christian victims of ISIS were ISIS's most potent recruiting tool. Heck, President Obama and *Vanity Fair* even blamed George W. Bush for ISIS.

There was no good reason to adopt a hyperliteral posture when checking Trump, and it added to the belief that the media was behaving unfairly to Trump.

Meanwhile, fact-checking organizations gave Hillary Clinton a very wide amount of latitude on statements that quite obviously were not literally true. On her claim that she "never received nor sent any material that was marked classified," PolitiFact rated the statement "half true" over a month after it was reported that Clinton had herself sent a classified e-mail on her insecure e-mail server. PolitiFact later stealth-edited the fact-check to claim the statement was false after FBI director Jim Comey's press conference acknowledging as much, but how PolitiFact ever defended such a brazen lie says a lot about the organization's partisan double standards.

It's Only Crazy When Trump Says It

Perhaps nothing better illustrates the media's double standards during the 2016 campaign as well as the coverage of Hillary Clinton's health. Throughout August and early September, the Trump campaign and its supporters were focused on the belief that Hillary Clinton didn't have the mental or physical stamina to handle the presidency. They hyped a serious coughing attack at a rally and questioned why the media wouldn't cover it.

The media responded not by covering her health but rather by arguing that it was sexist to question her health. CNN ran a story headlined, "Clinton's Health Is Fine, but What about Trump?" It didn't explain how anyone was to know her health was fine. Sanjay Gupta, a former Clinton advisor who became a CNN medical reporter, agreed that her health was fine. A panel convened to discuss the issue wondered if Trump's health wasn't the problem.

Neither Trump nor Clinton was forthcoming about personal health, but there were signs that Clinton might have legitimate issues to explore. Clinton's e-mails revealed that she told the FBI she couldn't recall something more than three dozen times. It was unclear if this was related to the concussion and blood clot she suffered at the end of 2012 limiting her productivity.

The *Washington Post*'s Chris Cillizza, who had written extensively about his belief that John McCain had serious health problems in 2008, wrote a piece defending Clinton against questions about her health. It was headlined, "Can We Just Stop Talking about Hillary Clinton's Health Now?" and was published on September 6. (John McCain was reelected to the Senate in 2016 by the way.)

Less than a week after Cillizza begged people to stop talking about Hillary Clinton's health, she had to leave a 9/11 commemoration due to health problems. She struggled to make her way to a van and passed out before she could climb in. Aides threw her in the vehicle and drove off. The campaign's story changed throughout the day. At first, she had merely tripped. Then she had become overcome by heat, despite it being a relatively cool day. Later she did a photo opportunity that featured her hugging a little girl. Later came the news she had been diagnosed with pneumonia. At each point of the story changing, the media largely reacted uncritically to what people had seen.

Another double standard was in how the media covered Donald Trump's answer in the final debate to a question about whether he'd certify the results of the election if he didn't win. He said he'd wait and see how things went. For a solid seventy-two hours, the media reaction was nothing but outrage. Yet when Hillary Clinton failed to win the election and joined legal recount efforts, and her supporters reacted with everything from riots to a months-long campaign of delegitimization, the media wasn't concerned at all.

THE END OF OUR COLLECTIVE AMNESIA

In November of 2014, *Rolling Stone* published a cover story built around the claim that a woman had been raped by fraternity members at the University of Virginia. Sabrina Erdely's story was the latest piece of journalism to push the idea of a rape epidemic on campuses. While the story was initially met with widespread acclaim and resulted in the University of Virginia suspending the fraternity in question, it was later revealed to have been based on a false account that had been irresponsibly hyped by the reporter.

The magazine retracted the piece a few months later after the Columbia Graduate School of Journalism lambasted *Rolling Stone* for failing to uphold basic journalistic standards. The magazine's publisher and the reporter are fighting defamation lawsuits.

What the *Rolling Stone* debacle showed was the fraudulence of the media's claims about adherence to checking details and upholding standards. This was also on display in the aftermath of Trump's election when reporters reacted by running stories that turned out to be false or grossly mischaracterized.

Following Trump's surprising win, the *Washington Post* had a great idea. They asked his supporters why they voted for him. Among the many interesting answers were several that specifically mentioned the media: Nicole Citro said, "As Trump cleared each hurdle during the campaign, and I saw how the media, the establishment and celebrities tried to derail him, my hope began to grow that I would be able to witness their collective heads explode when he was successful." Diane Maus's answer was, "The media did the United States a huge disservice in covering this campaign." As Lori Myers explained, "I voted for Donald Trump because the media was so incredibly biased. They were unhinged in their obvious role as the Clinton campaign propaganda machine. The collusion was just too much." And Samantha Styler said, "I am a gay millennial woman and I voted for Donald Trump because I oppose the political correctness movement, which has become a fascist ideology of silence and ignorance. After months of going back and forth, I decided to listen to him directly and not through minced and filtered quotes from the mainstream media."

Perhaps these examples show that we've entered the final stages of the longstanding social compact between voters and the media. It's not just that much of the country no longer trusts the media – the fact that Donald J. Trump is president is proof enough of that. It's also that, in a rather ironic twist of fate, the actual facts make it impossible to trust the media. After the University of Virginia story, can anyone still view *Rolling Stone* as reliable? And there's the gnawing suspicion that *Rolling Stone* is just the one that happened to get caught. Who knows what other publications have gotten away with that we don't know about?

Put another way, what we might be seeing is the end of the Murray Gell-Mann Amnesia effect. That was Michael Crichton's explanation, in his "Why Speculate?" speech, for why media carried a totally undeserved credibility. As Crichton explained:

> *Briefly stated, the Gell-Mann Amnesia effect is as follows. You open the newspaper to an article on some subject you know well. In Murray's case, physics. In mine, show business. You read the article and see the journalist has absolutely no understanding of either the facts or the issues. Often, the Article is so wrong it actually presents the story backward – reversing cause and effect. I call these the "wet streets cause rain" stories. Paper's full of them. In any case, you read with exasperation or amusement the multiple errors in a story, and then turn the page to national or international affairs, and read as if the rest of the newspaper was somehow more accurate about Palestine than the baloney you just read. You turn the page, and forget what you know.*

Crichton went on to note that people tend to exercise discretion in discounting serial liars or exaggerators in other areas of life. And in courts of law, there is a doctrine of *Falsus in uno, falsus in omnibus.* "But when it comes to the media," he said, "we believe against evidence that it is probably worth our time to read other parts of the paper. When, in fact, it almost certainly isn't."

But what if the errors are now so routine, the narrative persuasion so blatant, the defensive defiance and elitism of journalists so extreme, and the partisan bias so pronounced that people are no longer slipping into amnesia?

What if they're just done – sick and tired of the entire media industry and distrustful of many of the stories they encounter on TV and in newspapers? What does it mean going forward?

Members of the media once enjoyed an elevated position – celebrity status, even – on the theory that they would behave responsibly with the power they had to police public conversations. They were to aim for objectivity, civility, and the provision of important and helpful information rather than just advance partisan narratives at the expense of facts.

By 2016, the reality was that while the Democrats supported the media more than the Republicans did, the credibility afforded the media by both groups was off a cliff.

Two weeks before the 2016 election, a Suffolk University/*USA Today* poll asked one thousand Americans what they thought was the primary threat to election integrity. The poll was conducted months after President Obama had started talking about Russian meddling in the election and weeks after the Office of the Director of National Intelligence officially blamed Russia for ties to the hacking of the Democratic National Committee's e-mail and the successful spearfishing operation of John Podesta.

Still, 45.5 percent of those polled chose "the media" as the primary threat to election integrity. Only 10 percent chose "foreign interests such as Russian hackers."

That same poll showed that voters believed members of the media were aiding Hillary Clinton as the Democratic candidate for president. In fact, they were ten times more likely to say the media, including major newspapers and television stations, wanted Hillary Clinton to win.

Even earlier in 2016, trust in the media had hit historic lows.

Gallup reported in September 2016 that Americans' trust and confidence in the mass media "to report the news fully, accurately and fairly" dropped to its lowest level in polling history, with only 32 percent saying they have a great deal or fair amount of trust in the media. That was down eight points since the previous year. Among Republicans, the situation was much worse. Only 14 percent of them had confidence in the media.

Polls since the media began its claims of having a Trump-inspired renaissance have shown a slight uptick in Democratic support, but that only supports the idea that the media is composed of partisan actors whose interests align with Democrats and are hostile to Republicans.

As partisan actors, they lose their power to mediate public debates and discussions. Their claim to have anonymous sources who should be trusted is lost. The public now sees the major mass media as tabloids and scandal sheets that act as propaganda organs for a political party. The media's credibility is gone. And they did it to themselves.

While some might see the fact that Trump portends the end of the hated liberal-media consensus as cause for celebration, this is also cause for concern. The media has long been an important check on the exercise of power of elected leaders. If the media does believe that it has an important role to play in holding elected leaders accountable, it only has one choice: Renounce partisanship, report the facts, stop pushing narratives, diversify newsrooms culturally and intellectually, and slowly but surely recover its credibility one honest report at a time. If the nascent coverage of the Trump administration is anything to go by, the media is uninterested in doing self-examination and the hard work this requires. Even Trump's fiercest critics are fed up with the media's impotence resulting from its bias and incompetence. "Much of the reporting on the Trump administration thus far seems to be so poorly sourced, riddled with caricature and negative wishful thinking as to be actively misleading, for all intents and purposes 'fake news,'" wrote Trump-critic James Kirchick in *Tablet*. "The beneficiary of the resulting confusion and hysteria is not *The New York Times* or its readers. It's Donald Trump." Kirchick is right, but after decades of systematic media bias, the biggest loser of all has been ordinary Americans. Until the media at least acts like it respects the concerns of all Americans, regardless of whether they share its narrow progressive views, it is doomed to irrelevance in Donald Trump's America.

DAVID B. KOPEL

THE TRUTH ABOUT
GUN CONTROL

When The Truth About Gun Control *was published in early 2013, Second Amendment rights were under the worst assault yet in the twenty-first century. Thereafter, the national campaign for gun control foundered on its proponents' greed. Republican senator Tom Coburn and Democratic senator Charles Schumer almost worked out a deal for background checks on private gun sales – but Schumer would not budge from his insistence that the deal also include gun registration, which Coburn would not accept. As* The Truth *notes, gun registration has historically been a tool for subsequent confiscation. This persisted in New York City under Mayor Michael Bloomberg.*

In 2016 – as in 2000 and 2004 – the national Democratic party lost because it nominated a long-time enemy of lawful gun ownership. If not for the Second Amendment issue, Hillary Clinton would have won Pennsylvania, Michigan, Wisconsin, and the presidency.

At the national level, the Second Amendment is currently safer than if the 2016 elections had turned out differently. Yet, in states such as California, antirights extremists are already moving toward confiscation, from standard magazines over ten rounds to lawfully registered semiautomatic firearms.

The arms prohibition movement has never enjoyed strong grassroots support, but it is now backed by some of the richest men in the world. Michael Bloomberg literally has more money than every pro–Second Amendment group combined. So does George Soros. There are also many more billionaires who are making long-term investments for registration, prohibition, and confiscation. They have used their wealth adroitly to radicalize the Democratic party on the gun issue. The Second Amendment will survive in the long term only if the spending by the malefactors of great wealth is exceeded by the volunteerism of the defenders of the American way of life.

THE SECOND AMENDMENT is under siege, and not for the first time. Today's war on Second Amendment rights, led by President Obama and New York City Mayor Michael Bloomberg, continues an American culture war that has been going on for half a century. The roots of the gun-control movement can be traced back even further, to Reconstruction and attempts to disarm the freedmen, and before that to the British gun-confiscation program that sparked the American Revolution.

President Obama, having finished his last election, is wielding his newfound flexibility and using the murders at Sandy Hook Elementary School in Newtown, Conn., to promote massive bans on firearms and magazines. Yet the president's prohibitions would have made no difference at Sandy Hook. The killer fired 156 rounds during the 5 minutes it took the police to arrive – a rate of fire that could be duplicated by many firearms produced since the 1860s. He changed magazines repeatedly, dumping half-full magazines on the floor.

The gun-control debate always has its micro-issues du jour – plastic guns, "cop-killer bullets," so-called assault weapons, waiting periods, gun registration, and so on. The first three things on the list do not really exist. All the issues are simply the battles of the day in a much larger struggle. What is ultimately at stake is the same question that precipitated the American Revolution: whether the American people are the sovereigns in their own country or whether they should be ruled from above, for their own good, according to the supposedly benevolent commands of the elitist rulers of a top-down, European-style society.

THE HISTORY OF THE RIGHT TO KEEP AND BEAR ARMS

Self-defense is the most fundamental of all natural rights. So agreed the founders of international law, including Francisco de Vitoria, Francisco Suárez, Hugo Grotius, Samuel Pufendorf, and Emmerich de Vattel. They built the classical system of international law through moral and logical reasoning, starting with self-evident truths about individual human rights. Foremost among these rights was self-defense.

A necessary corollary to the natural right of self-defense is the right to defensive arms. For most people, some sort of arm is the only practical way in which they can vindicate their inherent right of self-defense. A woman who is attacked by a gang of three rapists usually needs a weapon to defend herself.

Thus, as the U.S. Supreme Court correctly stated in the 1876 case *U.S. v. Cruikshank*, the Second Amendment right to bear arms, like the First Amendment right to assemble, is an inherent human right that predates the Constitution. The First and Second Amendments protect these rights but do not create them. Rather, each right "is found wherever civilization exists."

Or, as John Locke wrote in *The Second Treatise of Civil*

Government, because God has created every person, every person therefore has the right and the duty to protect his or her God-given life from criminals, including criminal governments.

John Adams and Thomas Jefferson disagreed on much. But they agreed on the fundamental right to self-defense. Adams supported "arms in the hands of citizens, to be used at individual discretion" for "private self-defence." Like Adams, Jefferson was a great admirer of the Italian scholar Cesare Beccaria, who founded the modern science of criminology, with his international best seller *On Crimes and Punishments* (*Dei Delitti e Delle Pene*). An oft-quoted passage from Beccaria observes:

> *The laws which forbid men to bear arms ... only disarm those who are neither inclined nor determined to commit crimes. Can it be supposed that those who have the courage to violate the most sacred laws of humanity and the most important in the civil code will respect the lesser and more arbitrary laws...? These laws make the victims of attack worse off and improve the position of the assailant. They do not reduce the murder rate but increase it, because an unarmed man can be attacked with more confidence than an armed man.*

The Colonies, the Revolution, and the Constitution

To the Americans of the 13 colonies, self-defense was both a right and a duty. Americans had been used to having firearms from the first days of European settlement. Unlike in Europe – where the aristocracy maintained a monopoly on hunting – hunting in America was wide open from the beginning of white settlement (indeed, from the days when the first Indians crossed the Bering Strait).

All colonies except Pennsylvania required gun ownership by militiamen (most adult males). Many colonies also mandated gun ownership by the head of a household – including a woman, if she was the head – and sometimes required the carrying of guns when traveling or when going to public meetings, such as church services.

The right and duty of self-defense applied to a householder protecting her children and to militiamen protecting their communities from foreign enemies or from tyranny. Self-defense was a seamless web; the difference between self-defense against a criminal invader in the home, against a gang of highway robbers, or against a criminal tyrant with his standing army was only one of scale. The tyrant's gang was just bigger than the other ones.

The American Revolution began because of gun control. For years the Americans and the British intensely disputed whether the king and Parliament had the authority to govern the domestic affairs of the Americans and tax their internal trade. The dispute turned into a war when King George and his ministers attempted to disarm the Americans.

In the fall of 1774, the king embargoed the delivery of firearms and gunpowder to America. At the same time, royal governors began sending out the Redcoats to seize the "public arms" – the firearms and ammunition that some colonies stored in central armories to supply arms to militiamen who could not afford their own. The reason these seizures did not start an immediate war was that they were carried out in predawn raids, before any resistance could assemble.

But in the early hours of April 19, 1775, Paul Revere and William Dawes rode to warn the people that the British were coming. The spark struck out by their steeds in their flight kindled the land into flame.

Church bells rang and guns fired, spreading alarm. The Americans turned back the British at Concord Bridge. Although the British accomplished their objective to seize guns during house-to-house searches at Lexington and Concord, the Americans swarmed into action, harrying the British on their retreat back to Boston. "Every man was his own commander," one American later recalled. The British suffered far more casualties than the Americans that day and might have been wiped out, had not the Americans begun to run out of gunpowder.

The British gun-confiscation campaign continued, with the British navy burning down Falmouth (today known as Portland, Maine) when the citizens refused to surrender their arms.

During the war, the American militia usually needed support from the Continental Army to prevail in open-field battles against British regulars. But everywhere, the militia, on their own, denied the British access to the countryside. Although the British, with control of the sea, could move quickly from one seaport to another, wherever they went there would be instant armed resistance, for the militia would rise wherever the British deployed. As historian Daniel Boorstin later put it, "The American center was everywhere and nowhere – in each man himself."

Recognizing that an armed people could not be governed without consent, the British proposed (as detailed in British Under Secretary of State William Knox's "What Is Fit to Be Done with America?") that once the Americans had been defeated, "the Arms of all the People should be taken away." American manufacture of firearms would be outlawed and the militias prohibited. Firearms were not only a tool that the Americans used to fight for self-government, but firearms possession in itself also fostered the spirit of self-government.

The original public meaning of the Second Amendment, and its analogues in state constitutions, was safeguarding the natural right to own and carry arms for all legitimate purposes. This included the inherent natural right of self-defense (which was not controversial at the time), and it also ensured that there would be an armed body of people from whom the militia could be drawn. As Michigan Supreme Court Justice Thomas Cooley, the most eminent constitutional scholar of the latter 19th century, wrote, "The meaning of the provision undoubtedly is, that the people, from whom the militia must be taken, shall have the right to keep and bear arms; and they need no permission or regulation of law for the purpose."

The Racist Origins of Gun Control

Before the Civil War, the great antislavery writer Lysander Spooner used the Second Amendment to argue that slavery was unconstitutional. Since a slave is a person who cannot possess arms, and the Second Amendment guarantees that all persons can possess arms, no person in the United States, therefore, can be a slave. "The right of a man 'to keep and bear arms,' is a right palpably inconsistent with the idea of his being a slave," Spooner wrote.

On the other hand, in the infamous *Dred Scott* decision, U.S. Supreme Court Chief Justice Roger B. Taney announced that free blacks were not U.S. citizens; if they were, he warned, free blacks would have the right "to keep and carry arms wherever they went."

Immediately after the Civil War, Southern states enacted Black Codes that were designed to keep the ex-slaves in de facto slavery and submission. Mississippi's provision was typical: no freedman "shall keep or carry fire-arms of any kind, or any ammunition" without police permission. In

areas where the Ku Klux Klan took control, "almost universally the first thing done was to disarm the negroes and leave
them defenseless," recounted the civil-rights attorney Albion
Tourgée, who represented Homer Plessy in *Plessy v. Ferguson.*
The Ku Klux Klan was America's first gun-control group, as
well as America's first domestic terrorist organization.

Congress responded with the Freedmen's Bureau Act,
insisting that "the constitutional right to bear arms, shall
be secured to and enjoyed by all the citizens." Congress
followed up with the Civil Rights Act and the 14th
Amendment to ensure that no state could ever again violate the civil rights of Americans.

Repeatedly, the congressional proponents of the 14th
Amendment announced that one of its key purposes was to
guarantee that the freedmen could exercise their Second
Amendment right to own guns for self-defense, especially
against Klansmen. Senator Samuel Pomeroy (R-Kan.) extolled
the three "indispensable" "safeguards of liberty under our
form of government": the sanctity of the home, the right to
vote, and "the right to bear arms ... [so] if the cabin door of
the freedman is broken open and the intruder enters ... then
should a well-loaded musket be in the hand of the occupant
to send the polluted wretch to another world."

Reconstruction and the 14th Amendment forced Southern
states to repeal laws explicitly forbidding blacks to have guns.
So the white-supremacist legislature in Tennessee enacted
the 1871 "Army and Navy" law, barring the sale of any handguns except the "Army and Navy model." The ex-Confeder-
ate soldiers already had their high-quality Army and Navy
guns. But cash-poor freedmen could barely afford lower-cost,
simpler firearms not of the Army and Navy quality.

Many Southern states followed Tennessee's lead, with
facially neutral laws banning inexpensive guns or requiring permits to own or carry a gun. As one Florida judge

explained, the laws were "passed for the purpose of disarming the negro laborers ... [and] never intended to be applied to the white population." (*Watson v. Stone*, Florida, 1941.)

Jim Crow laws became the foundation of gun control in America. These laws spread north in the early decades of the 20th century, aimed primarily at immigrants (Italians and Jews in New York City) or labor agitators (California).

In the 1950s and 1960s, a new civil-rights movement arose in the South. White-supremacist tactics were just as violent as they had been during Reconstruction. Blacks and civil-rights workers armed for self-defense.

John Salter, a professor at Tougaloo College and chief organizer of the NAACP's Jackson Movement during the early 1960s, wrote, "No one knows what kind of massive racist retaliation would have been directed against grass-roots black people had the black community not had a healthy measure of firearms within it."

Civil-rights professionals and the black community generally viewed nonviolence as a useful tactic for certain situations, not as a moral injunction to let oneself be murdered on a deserted road in the middle of the night. As the 1959 NAACP national convention resolved, "We do not deny but reaffirm the right of individual and collective self-defense against unlawful assaults." Dr. Martin Luther King, Jr., agreed, supporting violence "exercised in self-defense," which he described "as moral and legal" in all societies; he noted that not even Gandhi condemned it.

The NRA Enters the Fray

National alcohol prohibition, enacted in 1920, spurred national violence, which resulted in the conservative Eastern business establishment – along with some religious pacifists – demanding handgun prohibition. In their view, the solution to the failure of alcohol prohibition was more prohibition.

The handgun-prohibition campaign of the 1920s drew the National Rifle Association, which had been a political force since the turn of the century, even more deeply into the political arena. The NRA had been founded by Union Army officers in 1871 to promote citizen marksmanship and civic virtue. Among its early presidents were Ulysses S. Grant (former president of the United States) and Winfield Scott Hancock("the hero of Gettysburg" and the 1880 Democratic presidential nominee).

In the early twentieth century, as today, the NRA's main political strength was its ability to mobilize its ever growing membership to contact government officials and express opposition to constricting the rights of law-abiding citizens.

After the NRA defeated the first handgun-prohibition campaigns, Franklin Roosevelt's first attorney general, Homer Cummings, attempted to push a bill to require the national registration of all handguns, coupled with a per-handgun tax that was more than a week's wages for a working man. Cummings hoped that his bill would set the stage for a handgun ban.

The handgun restrictions were part of the National Firearms Act (NFA), which also imposed stringent controls on machine guns and short-barreled shotguns. Once Congress heard from NRA members and removed handguns from the bill, the NRA dropped its opposition, and the NFA, including its severe controls on machine guns, became law.

Eighty-nine years later, the phony issue of "assault weapons" is based on a hoax invented by the gun-prohibition lobbies and spread by willfully ignorant media. There are some ordinary guns that *look* like machine guns. The Colt AR-15 rifle and the Ruger Mini-14 rifle are two examples. These guns do not function like machine guns.

They fire only one round each time the trigger is pressed, just like any other ordinary gun. They are not more powerful than other guns; as rifles go, they are intermediate in power. That is why, in their most common caliber, .223, they are often used for hunting small game, such as rabbits or coyotes, or midsize game, such as deer. In their most common calibers, they are not powerful enough for big game, such as elk or moose.

Yet many underinformed people think these guns are machine guns. They do not know that machine guns have been severely regulated since 1934. To acquire a machine gun requires a $200 transfer tax, fingerprinting, federal registration, and notification of local law enforcement. Since 1986, the manufacture of new machine guns for sale to anyone outside the government has been prohibited.

Gun-prohibition groups have fooled some people into believing that guns like the AR-15 are machine guns. As gun-prohibition strategist Josh Sugarmann explained in a 1988 memo, the guns' "menacing looks, coupled with the public's confusion over fully automatic machine guns versus semi-automatic assault weapons – anything that looks like a machine gun is assumed to be a machine gun – can only increase the chance of public support for restrictions on these weapons."

Today, semiautomatic handguns comprise 82 % of new handguns manufactured in the U.S. Citizens buying such guns often choose guns with *standard* magazines holding 11 to 20 rounds. For rifles today, magazines of up to 30 rounds are factory standard.

Ordinary citizens choose these handguns, rifles, and magazines for the same reason that ordinary police officers usually do: because they are often the best choice for lawful defense of self and others.

Police officers who have a Springfield Armory semi-auto pistol with a 16-round magazine on their hip and an AR-15 rifle with a 30-round magazine in their patrol car are not carrying those guns to go hunting or because they are intent on mass murder. These guns are standard police guns today because police, like ordinary citizens, know that criminals do not always attack one at a time and that violent attackers do not always fall down after a single hit – especially if the attackers are energized by methamphetamine or other drugs.

In such circumstances, the police officer, like the law-abiding citizen, may not have two seconds to spare to change magazines.

Tyranny and Genocide

Attorney General Cummings' repeated efforts for national gun registration were thwarted by the NRA. Then in 1941, Congress enacted the NRA's idea to ban gun registration.

Congress was looking in horror at mass shootings, and at mass murders by many other methods, taking place in Nazi-occupied Europe and in the Soviet Union. Congress could see how gun-registration lists compiled by democratic governments – such as the Weimar Republic in Germany or the Third Republic in France – were being used for gun confiscation once the totalitarians took over.

So when Congress passed the Property Requisition Act to allow the federal government to take property needed for national defense against tyranny, Congress made sure that the American people would retain their ability to resist tyranny. The 1941 act forbade the federal government to seize guns, to require the registration of guns (except for the guns already covered by the 1934 NFA), or "to impair or infringe in any manner the right of any individual to keep and bear arms...."

Where Hitler or Stalin ruled, gun control was an essential step toward genocide. Gun-registration lists were used to confiscate guns from the prospective victims. After the victims were helpless, the extermination began.

Gun confiscation for genocide was not practiced solely by Hitler and Stalin. *Every* episode of genocide in the past century has been preceded by assiduous efforts to first disarm the victims: Turkish Armenia, the Holocaust, the USSR, Soviet-occupied Poland, Guatemala under the military dictatorship in the 1950s, Mao's China, Chiang Kai-shek's White Terror, Uganda under Idi Amin, Cambodia under Pol Pot, Srebrenica, Zimbabwe, Darfur. And many more.

Consider three steps: 1) registration; 2) confiscation; 3) extermination. Steps 1 and 2 do not always result in step 3. But step 3 is almost always preceded by steps 1 and 2.

Gun prohibitionists scoff at the idea that armed victims could fight genocide. History shows that they can. Especially in Eastern Poland, Belarus, and Lithuania during the Holocaust, some Jews were able to obtain arms and carry out guerilla warfare against the Nazis, saving many lives.

Of course not every government that uses registration lists for mass confiscation is intent on genocide. There is no genocide in Australia or Great Britain. But it is indisputable that the *genocidaires* seem to consider gun confiscation to be a crucial precondition for genocide.

The Modern Gun-Control Debate

During World War II and the early Cold War, gun control in America was not exactly a popular idea. As Americans were seeing, Nazis and Communists could inflict tyranny and murder because guns had previously been registered and confiscated.

Things changed in the mid-1960s. Violent crime was

rising sharply. Race riots scorched nearly every big American city. The assassination of Martin Luther King, Jr., in April 1968 and two months later of Senator Robert Kennedy (by a Palestinian angry at Kennedy's strong support for Israel) broke the dam.

In September, Congress enacted the Gun Control Act of 1968 (GCA). As amended, the GCA is the main federal law for ordinary firearms. Many state and local governments also enacted far-reaching new gun laws.

This was hardly enough to satisfy the prohibitionists. They aimed to do to the American people what the Ku Klux Klan had tried to do to the freedmen: disarmament, although this time, disarming people was said to be for their own good.

Their first major breakthrough was the District of Columbia in 1975. Acquisition of new handguns was outlawed. Use of any firearm for self-defense in the home was prohibited.

The most left-leaning state in America — Massachusetts — was supposed to be next, with a handgun-confiscation initiative on the ballot in November 1976. The gun-confiscation lobby called themselves People vs. Handguns. The people thought otherwise. Confiscation was rejected in a 69 percent landslide, partly because of widespread police opposition.

So prohibitionists decided that if they could not confiscate handguns, perhaps they could get the public to just ban new handguns. California's 1982 "handgun freeze" initiative was crushed, with 63 percent voting no.

The prohibitionists tried and failed again in 1993–94 in three left-leaning Wisconsin towns: Milwaukee, Kenosha, and Madison. The long-term result of the Wisconsin confiscation votes was that the people of Wisconsin voted overwhelmingly in 1998 (1,205,873 to 425,052) to add a right to arms to their state constitution.

Beginning with the first state constitution right-to-arms guarantee (Pennsylvania, 1776), 44 states now have a constitutional right to arms. In every state in which the people have had the opportunity to vote directly, they have endorsed the right to arms by landslide margins. Since 1968, the people of 25 states have chosen, either through their legislature or through a direct vote, to add a right to arms to their state constitution, to readopt the right to arms, or to strengthen an existing right. In addition, 37 state constitutions specifically protect the right of self-defense – sometimes as part of the arms right and sometimes stated separately.

Right to Carry

By the early 1970s, the legal carrying of handguns for protection in public places had been suppressed in most states. The typical system was that carrying required a permit; the permit required "good cause" in the view of a government administrator; and ordinary citizens who merely wanted to protect themselves were almost never considered to have good cause. About a half-dozen states were exceptions to this general rule.

Starting in Florida in 1987, state after state enacted licensing-reform laws. The laws prevented abuse of discretion by using objective standards. If an adult passes a fingerprint-based background check and a safety class, then she "shall" be issued a concealed-handgun carry permit. Today in 42 states, a law-abiding, competent adult has a clear path to a lawful concealed carry.

So in those 42 states, when Americans go to a shopping mall, a restaurant, a park, or most other public places, they are in a place where some people are lawfully carrying firearms.

Whether licensed carry causes a statistically significant decline in violent crime is a subject of scholarly debate. The evidence is overwhelming that there is no statistically significant *increase* in crime. In every state where "shall issue" has become the law, it has disappeared from the gun-control debate within a few years. Most Americans have acclimated to an environment in which public carrying of defensive handguns is common, safe, and unremarkable.

Forty-five years ago, it was common to assert that hunting was declining, so as a once-rural nation was now urban, gun ownership would soon be a discarded relic of America's past. However, the Second Amendment isn't just about hunting.

Rural, urban, and suburban, Americans have continued their 400-year-old practice of arming themselves more heavily than the people of any other nation in the world. As of 1948, Americans owned guns at a per capita rate about equal to what the French and Norwegians do now. (One gun per three persons.) Per capita gun ownership has tripled since then, so there are now slightly more American guns than there are Americans.

The right to keep and bear arms is not a 1791 anachronism. It is alive in the hearts and minds of the American people.

The Supreme Court

For a long time, the U.S. Supreme Court paid little attention to the Second Amendment, Likewise, the court was timid about the First Amendment for most of America's history; it was not until 1965 that it dared to hold that a congressional statute violated the First Amendment (*Lamont v. Postmaster General*, striking a statute requiring registration for exercising First Amendment rights).

Although the Second Amendment appeared in several

dozen Supreme Court cases before 2008, it was almost always as a minor character – a typical individual right among a litany of other individual rights.

The court upheld the National Firearms Act (stringent laws about short shotguns and machine guns) in the 1939 case *U.S. v. Miller.* Unfortunately, the opinion written by the notoriously indolent Justice James Clark McReynolds was so terse and opaque that scholars spent decades arguing about what it meant.

The Supreme Court spoke up decisively in 2008. *District of Columbia v. Heller* ruled that the government could not ban the acquisition of handguns, nor could it ban armed self-defense in the home. *McDonald v. Chicago* (2010) ruled that state and local governments must obey the Second Amendment – just as they must obey the First Amendment and almost all the rest of the Bill of Rights.

THE PHILOSOPHY OF GUN BANS

Gun rights are not liberal vs. conservative, urban vs. rural, Democrat vs. Republican, or any other stereotype. The great Democratic Vice President Hubert H. Humphrey embodied liberalism's optimistic faith in the federal government and the federal Constitution. He believed that "one of the chief guarantees of freedom under any government, no matter how popular and respected, is the right of citizens to keep and bear arms.... The right of citizens to bear arms is just one more guarantee against arbitrary government, one more safeguard against the tyranny which now appears remote in America, but which historically has proved to be always possible."

In the culture war, the gun-prohibition movement has explicitly sought to make gun owners into social pariahs, like cigarette smokers: instead of being considered a personal right, gun ownership would be viewed as a repulsive personal habit. Dr. Mark Rosenberg, who in 1994 was director of the Centers for Disease Control's National Center for Injury Prevention and Control, stated that the CDC hoped to make the public perceive firearms as "dirty, deadly – and banned."

President Obama in January 2013 announced that he would be seeking more funds for CDC gun-control research. Much of this "research" has been junk science designed to create factoids about why ordinary people should not own guns. Even before 2013, the Obama administration was funneling grants to prohibitionists in order to produce antigun factoids as, supposedly, medical science. Guns are to be stigmatized as "disease vectors" and gun owners claimed to be disease carriers.

State-Imposed Pacifism

Gun prohibition has many bases, among them the pacifist-aggressives – people who want to use the force and violence of criminal law to make everyone else live by their personal philosophy of not using defensive force against violent attackers.

For example, the Presbyterian Church (USA) has declared that it disapproves of "the killing of anyone, anywhere, for any reason." Because the church believes defensive gun ownership is immoral, it supports the confiscation of all handguns. The United Methodist Church, which helped found the National Coalition to Ban Handguns (now named the Coalition to Stop Gun Violence), declared that people should submit to rape and robbery rather than endanger the criminal's life by shooting him.

The Brady Center runs a "God Not Guns" coalition, which proclaims that the exercise of Second Amendment rights is inherently sinful, demonstrating a refusal to trust in God. Their work is promoted by Jim Wallis, an evangelical Christian who is the founder of the pacifist, hard-left *Sojourners* magazine and who is the leading figure of the Christian Religious Left in modern America.

Not all pacifist-aggressives are religious. Marxist and radical feminist Betty Friedan insisted that battered women must not use violence against their attackers because "lethal violence even in self-defense only engenders more violence." David Clarke, the father of the D.C. handgun and self-defense ban, claimed that his antigun laws "are designed to move this government toward civilization.... I don't intend to run the government around the moment of survival." In other words, it is more "civilized" for you to be murdered by a criminal than to defend yourself with a gun. A perverse definition of *civilization*.

For religious reasons or others, the gun-prohibition movement aims to outlaw self-defense with a firearm. As Sarah Brady announced to the *Tampa Tribune* in 1993, "To me, the only reason for guns in civilian hands is for sporting purposes." Her husband, Jim Brady, identified the circumstances in which he believes people should be allowed to possess handguns: "[F]or target shooting, that's okay. Get a license and go to the range. For defense of the home, that's why we have police departments." Sarah Brady's long-term goal, she told *The New York Times*, is a "needs-based licensing" system. Under the Brady system, all guns would be registered. The local police chief would decide if a person who wanted to buy a gun had a legitimate "need." Sarah Brady listed hunters and security guards as people who have a legitimate need, but not regular people who wanted guns for self-protection.

Gun prohibitionists denounce self-defense as a person's "taking the law into her own hands." This is false. Using deadly force or the threat thereof to defend against a violent felony is legal in all 50 states. There are many circumstances when exercising the choice to use force for self-defense or defense of another is entirely lawful. Using such force, therefore, cannot be "taking the law into one's hands" any more than exercising other lawful choices, such as signing a contract.

When criminals use force, though, they are violating the law and thereby taking the law into their own hands. When citizens use or threaten force to stop the lawbreaking, they are taking the law back from the criminals and restoring the law to its rightful owners: themselves.

The gun-prohibition movement is ultimately based on an authoritarian wish that the American people were not the people for whom the word *individualism* was coined by Alexis de Tocqueville. They yearn for America to be like Europe, where gun ownership is a sporting privilege for a few and not a right of the people.

They want a top-down society in which (supposedly) sophisticated and intelligent elites make wise and rational decisions about how ordinary people should live their lives. To these authoritarians, the self-sufficiency that gun ownership represents is an insult.

The authoritarians agree with the German sociologist Max Weber's 1919 lecture "Politics as a Vocation," in which he announced that the very definition of a state is "the monopoly of the legitimate use of physical force." Few Americans have read Weber, but his principle has been the core of the gun-control movement and is anathema to the gun-rights movement.

David B. Kopel

Barack Obama

For whatever ideological reason, Barack Obama has a long record of embracing the antigun agenda. He is currently campaigning for a national gun-registration system. Instead of using the politically toxic word *registration*, he calls for a "national database" of guns. He endorses laws that he says will expand background checks. What he does not say is that every major congressional bill that has been introduced in the past several years under the title of "background checks" was written by Michael Bloomberg's staff and contained provisions for national gun registration.

Could prohibition then follow registration? Consider the record of Barack Obama before he became president. He endorsed handgun prohibition in general, and the D.C. and Chicago handgun-prohibition laws in particular. He endorsed the prohibition of all semiautomatic firearms (which are the overwhelming majority of new handguns and a large fraction of long guns).

He called for banning all gun stores within 5 miles of a school or park. This is the same as calling for a ban on gun sales, since every inhabited portion of the United States is within 5 miles of a school or park.

Ever since 1968, federal law has required that the only way a customer can purchase a firearm from a licensed retailer is through a transaction at the gun store, where the buyer picks up the gun. The only other place where the retailer may sell guns is at a gun show, and there the retailer must comply with all the same rules – such as background checks – as for sales for his storefront. (Hysterical claims about "Internet gun sales" ignore the fact that an interstate Internet seller must ship the gun to a licensed firearms dealer in the customer's home state; the customer can only pick up the gun after the in-state dealer completes the standard background check.)

President Obama has endorsed legislation to give the Bureau of Alcohol, Tobacco, Firearms, and Explosives nearly limitless discretion to outlaw rifle ammunition.

He proposed a 500 percent tax increase on guns and ammunition.

He has voted for legislation to ban every so-called assault weapon (very broadly defined) and even old-fashioned bird-hunting guns – such as every double-barrel and break-open shotguns in 28 gauge and larger.

Barack Obama has endorsed federal legislation that would eliminate the laws of the 42 states that allow ordinary citizens, after passing a fingerprint-based background check and a safety-training class, to obtain a permit to carry a concealed handgun for lawful self-defense.

WHO ARE THE SOVEREIGNS?

While some nations consider law to be the vehicle of the state, the American tradition views the law as the servant of the people. As the Supreme Court put it, "the people, not the government, possess the sovereignty" (*New York Times v. Sullivan*, 1964).

In the years leading up to the American Revolution, Patriots and Tories alike began to use the term "Body of the People" to mean "a majority of the people" and eventually "the united will of the people." Legitimate sovereignty, Patriots said, flowed not from "the Crown" but from the "Body of the People." Locating sovereignty in the people, and not in the Crown, meant locating the power to enforce the law in the people as well.

During the debate over ratification of the Constitution, federalist Noah Webster assured America:

*Before a standing army can rule, the people must be dis-
armed, as they are in almost every kingdom in Europe. The
supreme power in America cannot enforce unjust laws by
the sword, because the whole body of the people are armed,
and constitute a force superior to any band of regular troops
that can be, on any pretense, raised in the United States.*

It is true that the United States protects the right to
bear arms more vigorously than other nations do. The
U.S. protects most other rights better as well.

By reserving more power for themselves, Americans
grant less power to the government. The American system of adversary courtroom procedure; jury trials; checks
and balances among the three limited branches of government; the dual, limited sovereignty of local and national
governments; and the widespread ownership of firearms
all reflect the assumption that any government is not to be
blindly trusted to control itself. Only if the people retain
for themselves the direct right to enforce the law can the
people's liberty be secure.

America chose to be different, a shining city on the hill,
a beacon of freedom. From the very first days of colonial
settlement, America rejected British and European precedent. That American laws recognize the right of individuals to use force for protection is consistent with the
American principle of retaining extensive power in the
hands of the people.

Simply put, Americans do not trust authority, as do the
subjects of the British Commonwealth or Japan. Unlike
the British, who so meekly acceded to their government's
Firearms Act of 1920, they do not trust the police and
government to protect them from crime. They do not
trust the discretion and judgment of police officers to
search whatever they please.

America places more faith in its citizens than do other nations. The first words of America's national existence, the Declaration of Independence, assert a natural right to overthrow a tyrant by force. In much of the world, the armed masses symbolize lawlessness; in America, the armed masses are the law.

George Orwell observed:

And though I have no doubt exceptions can be brought forward, I think the following rule would be found generally true: that ages in which the dominant weapon is expensive or difficult to make will tend to be ages of despotism, whereas when the dominant weapon is cheap and simple, the common people have a chance. Thus, for example, tanks, battleships and bombing planes are inherently tyrannical weapons, while rifles, muskets, long-bows and hand-grenades are inherently democratic weapons. A complex weapon makes the strong stronger, while a simple weapon — so long as there is no answer to it — gives claws to the weak.

Certainly the political ideology of the Founders of the American Republic and the authors of the Second Amendment was consistent with Orwell's viewpoint that dispersion of physical power in society is both a cause and an affirmation of dispersion of political power. Hubert Humphrey agreed.

One aspect of the American ideals of classlessness, individualism, and self-reliance is the archetypal hero. The armed Canadian hero is a government employee (the mounted policeman); the armed Japanese hero is an aristocrat (the samurai). Unlike the British knight (with expensive armor), the Japanese samurai (with a handcrafted, exquisite sword), or the Canadian mounted policeman (carrying a government-issued handgun that ordinary persons were not allowed to carry), the classic armed American hero – the cowboy – sported a mass-produced Colt .45 that could be bought at a hardware store.

The cowboy's Colt revolver was known as the great equalizer. The name is right because firearms make a smaller, less-powerful person functionally equal to a larger person. A firearm allows the smaller person to defend herself at a distance from the larger person. As an inscription on a Winchester rifle put it:

> *Be not afraid of any man,*
> *No matter what his size;*
> *When danger threatens, call on me*
> *And I will equalize.*

First Lady Eleanor Roosevelt lived this philosophy. As first lady and then as a civil-rights activist giving speeches in the segregated South, she spoke out for equality for all citizens. Because of death threats from the KKK and similar types, she carried a revolver for protection.

She was not a redneck, nor an angry white man, nor an insurrectionist, nor an enemy of the federal government, nor a conspiracy nut, nor any of the other things that anti-gun bigots claim about gun owners. She was a patriotic American and one of the world's greatest champions of human rights.

She led the U.S. delegation to the United Nations and helped create the Universal Declaration of Human Rights. Like the U.S. Declaration of Independence, the U.N. Declaration recognizes the necessity "as a last resort, to rebellion against tyranny and oppression."

The fundamental human right to keep and bear arms is the inherent right of all persons, not just Americans, to use firearms to protect themselves from large-scale criminals such as tyrants and *genocidaires* – and from lone criminals invading a home or attacking a school.

GREG LUKIANOFF

FREEDOM *FROM* SPEECH

When I wrote Freedom from Speech *in the summer of 2014, things on campus had already taken a troubling turn. When I began writing in 2001, the university groups most responsible for censorship on campus were administrators, followed by faculty (who were largely responsible for the first "politically correct" speech codes in the 1980s). Students were a distant third; indeed, students were the most reliably pro-free speech constituency on campus. But that all changed in the academic year of 2013–14, as described in this piece.*

Since Freedom from Speech *was first published, the situation has become much worse. In the fall of 2015, campuses blew up with student protests. But unlike the student protesters of the '60s and '70s, these students demanded more administrative oversight, more restrictions on free speech and academic freedom, and that administrators and even professors be fired for violations of their clearly protected speech. Things would get even worse in 2017 with the rise of violent antispeech protests and protesters shutting down speakers and even classes. In response, Jonathan Haidt and I have a new book coming out in July 2018:* The Coddling of the American Mind: How Good Intentions and Bad Ideas Are Setting Up a Generation for Failure. *In it, we explore how harmful the situation on campus has become – not only for free speech but also for reasoned debate, critical thinking, and even students' mental health.*

THE ACADEMIC YEAR of 2013-14 was a strange time for freedom of speech in the United States. Despite the continued strength of the First Amendment's legal protections for unpopular speech, stories about individuals (famous or otherwise) caught saying something offensive to someone or some group have become a media obsession. It seems as if every day brings a new controversy regarding the purportedly offensive remarks of a celebrity, an official, or an ordinary citizen, followed by irate calls for the speaker to suffer some sort of retribution.

In the spring of 2014, recordings of racist remarks by Los Angeles Clippers owner Donald Sterling dominated CNN coverage for months, inspiring public outrage that likely will result in Sterling losing his basketball franchise. Not long before that, the controversy of the day involved Phil Robertson, the patriarch of A&E's popular television show *Duck Dynasty*, for making insulting remarks about homosexuals and African Americans. That incident was preceded by the fall of Paula Deen, whose career collapsed (perhaps temporarily) after she admitted to having used a racial epithet at some undefined time decades in the past. The list of celebrities who have made headlines for allegedly offensive statements seems to be ever expanding; high-profile offenders include Gary Oldman, Don Imus, Mel Gibson, Jerry Seinfeld, Isaiah Washington, and Alec Baldwin.

Oftentimes, the speakers are not merely vilified but even lose their jobs over their comments. Juan Williams at NPR, Rick Sanchez and Roland Martin at CNN, and Martin Bashir and (again) Alec Baldwin at MSNBC all lost their media positions because of controversial remarks. Admittedly, many of the offending comments were not particularly sympathetic, but the public's appetite for punishing attempts at candor gone wrong, drunken rants, or even private statements made in anger or frustration seems to be growing at an alarming rate.

Even satirical comedian Stephen Colbert ran afoul of the speech police when he made a joke on his show that used racial insensitivity to mock racial insensitivity. The #CancelColbert movement quickly picked up steam but ultimately did more to produce Twitter chatter than to threaten the career of the popular comedian. It did, however, shine a light on the thought pattern of the modern American censor: there must be zero tolerance for anything that anyone might consider offensive, regardless of the context.

And then there was the case of the Mozilla Corporation's Brendan Eich, who was pressured to resign from his brief stint as the company's CEO after it re-emerged that he had donated $1,000 to the campaign for California's Proposition 8, a ballot initiative opposing same-sex marriage, back in 2008. The Eich incident was troubling on many levels. Not only did it demonstrate a surprisingly short national memory – until fairly recently, the majority of Americans opposed gay marriage, including both President Obama and Hillary Clinton – but it also seemed to indicate that some religious or social conservatives would have to choose between their beliefs and their professions. Eich's coerced resignation sent such a disquieting message that a coalition of 58 gay-rights activists, scholars, columnists, and pundits across the ideological spectrum signed a statement titled "Freedom to Marry, Freedom to Dissent: Why We Must Have Both." The statement warned that the Eich case "signal[ed] an eagerness by some supporters of same-sex marriage to punish rather than to criticize or to persuade those who disagree."

Some argued that the Eich incident was not about "free speech," because free speech binds only governments and does not prevent private employers from firing employees (or encouraging them to step down) based on their beliefs. This argument is incorrect. It's true that what happened to Eich was not an actual First Amendment violation, but that does not mean it had nothing to do with free speech.

Though often used interchangeably, the concept of freedom of speech and the First Amendment are not the same thing. While the First Amendment protects freedom of speech and freedom of the press as they relate to duties of the state and state power, freedom of speech is a far broader idea that includes additional cultural values. These values incorporate healthy intellectual habits, such as giving the other side a fair hearing, reserving judgment, tolerating opinions that offend or anger us, believing that everyone is entitled to his or her own opinion, and recognizing that even people whose points of view we find repugnant might be (at least partially) right. At the heart of these values is epistemic humility – a fancy way of saying that we must always keep in mind that we could be wrong or, at least, that we can always learn something from listening to the other side. Free speech as a cultural value will be my primary concern in this Broadside, not the state of First Amendment jurisprudence. And the national obsession with punishing jokes, rants, drunken tirades, and even deeply held beliefs shows a growing hostility toward free speech as a cultural value.

Given this climate, it is unsurprising that American higher education, where unpopular speech has been restricted for decades, has earned media attention for being especially intolerant in the past year. My organization, the Foundation for Individual Rights in Education (FIRE), which exists to combat violations of student and faculty free speech and other constitutional rights, has been busier than ever in 2013–14. In this Broadside, I will be discussing at length recent campus incidents and trends, including "disinvitation season" (the increased push by faculty and students to disinvite guest speakers on campus) and the emergence of demands for "trigger warnings" (written and/or spoken warnings to students that books, films, or other course material might be emotionally upsetting) on campus.

But those examples are just two symptoms of an academic environment that has long been souring on robust free speech and expression. Alan Charles Kors and Harvey Silverglate extensively exposed the rise of speech codes and political correctness on campus in their 1998 book *The Shadow University: The Betrayal of Liberty on America's Campuses*, and I updated and built upon their work in my 2012 book *Unlearning Liberty: Campus Censorship and the End of American Debate*. In *Unlearning Liberty*, I argued:

> *Administrators [on campus] have been able to convince well-meaning students to accept outright censorship by creating the impression that freedom of speech is somehow the enemy of social progress. When students began leaving college with that lesson under their belts, it was only a matter of time before the cultivation of bad intellectual habits on campus started harming the dialogue of our entire country. The tactics and attitudes that shut down speech on campus are bleeding into the larger society and wreaking havoc on the way we talk among ourselves.*

I continue to believe that the increased national focus on punishing offensive speech stems, in large part, from the "bleeding out" of the bad intellectual habits of American higher education. However, I do not think – nor have I ever thought – that blame for the erosion of support for the cultural value of freedom of speech can be laid entirely on the ivory tower. The "it's all academia's fault" argument does not adequately explain why freedom of speech seems to be on the decline across the globe, even in countries that claim to value civil and political rights.

The suppression of "offensive" speech is very common outside the U.S., and it often occurs in countries that seemingly share the classical-liberal tradition. In April 2014, a British politician was arrested for "religious/racial harassment" after delivering a speech in which he approvingly quoted a passage from a book by Winston Churchill that disparaged the Islamic faith and its adherents. Censorship in general is on the rise in the U.K., from the jailing of people caught making "grossly offensive" comments on social media to the banning of R&B singer Robin Thicke's hit song "Blurred Lines" by student unions at more than 20 British universities. In February 2013, the interior minister of Iceland – a country that views itself as very socially progressive – crafted legislation to ban online pornography.

Furthermore, Europe has recently seen the spread of the doctrine of the "right to be forgotten." The European Court of Justice ruled in May 2014 that search engines like Google are required to remove links from their search results at the request of private parties to whom the information pertains unless the companies can present a public-interest justification for leaving the links active. Both this vague standard and the odd incentive structure it creates (relying on Yahoo and Google to spend money to defend individual articles and links) threaten the freedom of the press and the public's freedom to access information. In July 2014, for example, Google deleted from its search results three articles from the *Guardian* about a retired Scottish soccer referee who once "lied about his reasons for granting a penalty kick." Complying with the European Court's ruling, Google decided that because the referee had since retired, he was no longer a public figure and thus his right to privacy now trumped the public's right to know about his involvement in the incident. It is hard to understand why the public's right to access information about a scandal should expire once the responsible party retires from public life.

Elsewhere, India – the world's largest democracy – has asked Google and Facebook to screen user content for "disparaging" or "inflammatory" postings, thereby taking yet another step in a national movement to suppress speech that author Salman Rushdie has called a "cultural emergency." Meanwhile, Turkey has overachieved in the censorship realm, with its law forbidding criticism of Mustafa Kemal Ataturk (the founder of modern Turkey), its law forbidding insults to the Turkish nation, its temporary implementation of a nationwide block on access to Twitter and YouTube, and its prime minister's practice of warning the news media not to publish "insults" against him.

The "It's all academia's fault" argument cannot explain these developments, nor can it explain why higher education, which is an institution that relies on being a "marketplace of ideas," would turn against free speech in the first place. I believe we are facing a long-term threat to freedom of speech that is much more substantial than the expansion of "liberal groupthink" or "political correctness" from campus.

The increased calls for sensitivity-based censorship represent the dark side of what are otherwise several positive developments for human civilization. As I will explain in the next section, I believe that we are not passing through some temporary phase in which an out-of-touch and hypersensitive elite attempts – and often fails – to impose its speech-restrictive norms on society. It's worse than that: people all over the globe are coming to expect emotional and intellectual comfort as though it were a right. This is precisely what you would expect when you train a generation to believe that they have a right not to be offended. Eventually, they stop demanding freedom *of* speech and start demanding freedom *from* speech.

To be crystal clear, I am in no way absolving higher education of its culpability in exacerbating the movement against free speech. Higher education deserves profound criticism for maintaining and promoting illiberal and unconstitutional speech codes and punishing students and faculty for what they say. However, I believe the even greater failure of higher education is neglecting to teach the intellectual habits that promote debate and discussion, tolerance for views we hate, epistemic humility, and genuine pluralism. I will spend most of the following pages discussing how the rise of "disinvitation season" on campus and the mounting calls for "trigger warnings" represent an increasingly suffocating environment for speech on campus.

If, as I suspect, this push for freedom *from* speech is something like a predictable and natural (if pernicious) force, the single institution that could be doing the most to combat it is higher education, both within and outside the United States. Unfortunately, far from teaching the intellectual discipline that welcomes a free and robust exchange of ideas, campuses are actively accelerating the push for freedom from speech.

"Problems of Comfort":
Why We Can Expect the Threats
to Free Speech to Get Worse

We live in what is likely the most peaceful and nonviolent period in human history. Psychologist Steven Pinker made this argument thoroughly and eloquently in his 2011 book *The Better Angels of Our Nature: Why Violence Has Declined,* which compares not only the rates of violence but also the harshness (e.g., public celebrations of torture, animal cruelty, and execution) of previous eras with those of today. The evidence keeps stacking up that the average person's likelihood of dying violently has never been lower.

Meanwhile, more medications than ever are available for the treatment of physical pain, illness, and psychological ailments. The daily presence of disease, discomfort, backbreaking labor, and violence that existed long before the advent of aspirin or antibiotics is hard for us to imagine, but that reality shaped the way previous generations of individuals, religious leaders, and philosophers thought about life.

We also have a greater ability to move from neighborhood to neighborhood, from state to state, or even from country to country than any previous generation. One might imagine that this freedom would lead to the widespread dissemination of different viewpoints. However, as books like Bill Bishop's *The Big Sort: Why the Clustering of Like-Minded America Is Tearing Us Apart* (2008) and Charles Murray's *Coming Apart: The State of White America, 1960–2010* (2012) have demonstrated, we are increasingly using our mobility to congregate within counties, towns, and even neighborhoods populated by politically like-minded people.

Wanting to live in communities that reflect our values is an understandable and very human impulse. However, since it decreases the likelihood – and the accompanying discomfort – of communicating across deep philosophical, religious, or political divides, such self-sorting comes with serious downsides. The social science of what happens when like-minded people talk only among themselves is quite striking: those who are broken up into groups with similar beliefs tend to become more extreme in their opinions and less able to understand the views of those who disagree with them. And psychologists and social scientists such as Jonathan Haidt have found that this polarization is a growing part of the American culture. Many of the resources available to us in the Internet age are further exacerbating the problem. We can now obtain the majority of our information from niche media sources that are specifically tailored to reinforce our existing worldviews, and we can easily converse with those who share our opinions while avoiding or even ganging up on those who do not.

There's no doubt that having an abundance of options and greater physical comfort than we have ever enjoyed as a species is a good thing, but it comes with consequences. These are what I call problems of comfort: the kinds of challenges that get more severe not only *while* other things are getting better but in large part *because* other things are getting better. Obesity is the paradigmatic example of a problem of comfort. This epidemic, with its many negative health effects, is a predictable result of an overabundance of fatty and sugar-rich food. Today's technology, pharmaceuticals, advanced medical care, and limitless sources of cheap calories would be considered unimaginably wonderful by, say, Stone Age human beings. Yet I sincerely doubt that our ancestors would envy our self-obsession, our fearfulness, or our lack of preparedness for adversity.

This lack of readiness is quite understandable. A society in which people can avoid physical pain comparatively easily will produce people who are less prepared to deal with it. Similarly, an environment in which people can easily avoid emotional and intellectual pain will produce people who are less prepared to deal with and are more intolerant toward harsh disagreement, objectionable words, and differing perspectives.

We are instinctively drawn to increased comfort and decreased pain. The same instinct is driving our rising desire for intellectual comfort, by which I mean a yearning to live in a relatively harmonious environment that does not present thorny intellectual challenges, and in which disagreement is downplayed or avoided altogether.

But intellectual comfort is as dangerous as it is seductive.

First of all, placing a premium on intellectual comfort is at odds with the three great pillars of the modern world that Jonathan Rauch discussed in his 1993 masterpiece *Kindly Inquisitors: The New Attacks on Free Thought.* These pillars are democracy (how we determine who gets to wield legitimate state power), capitalism (how we determine the allocation of wealth), and the intellectual system that Rauch dubbed liberal science (how we determine what is true). As Rauch put it, liberal science is the idea that the "checking of each by each through public criticism is the only legitimate way to decide who is right." Such checking and criticism cannot occur without creating intellectual discomfort. In fact, all three pillars rely on competition – often fierce competition – which, by nature, is not particularly comfortable. For liberal science to thrive, it must take place in an environment where the right to dissent is protected – an environment of free speech and inquiry.

Settling conflicts with discourse and reason rather than wars or duels has been one of the greatest sources of peace and prosperity in human history. But make no mistake about it: we are still in combat with one another. We simply use words instead of weapons to determine who gets to wield power and decide what is considered to be true. In such high-stakes matters, it should come as no surprise that our dialogue can (and perhaps *should*) be heated, passionate, and often disquieting. But the idea that we can truly tackle hard issues while remaining universally inoffensive – an impossible pipe dream even if it were desirable – seems to be growing increasingly popular.

Safeguarding intellectual comfort is also at odds with scientific and cultural advancement. Science teaches us to be wary of "confirmation bias," our tendency to be receptive to only the evidence that confirms our point of view. Humans excel at believing that we are right without verifying our beliefs. There is a very good reason that it took so long for the scientific method to catch on; the idea of testing our assumptions and following what experimentation tells us, even if the results contradict our most basic beliefs, is counterintuitive, in the most literal sense. Applying this method to important personal or societal issues can be particularly upsetting. If we refuse to accept this intellectual discomfort and instead embrace complacency and certainty, we fall victim to confirmation bias, and progress inevitably stalls.

As people come to expect intellectual comfort, some will increasingly demand that the world conform to their expectations. Others will simply avoid political and intellectual discussions or even comedy and satire that they find disquieting. Such reactions dull the exchange of ideas and cement polarization. Worse still are those who come to see themselves as defenders of the feelings of others, even when such help is not requested or desired. As I discuss in *Unlearning Liberty*, these self-righteous censors often construct a "hero narrative" about themselves in which they are morally pure crusaders who must protect society from the objectionable opinions of the unenlightened masses.

The quest for intellectual comfort is almost as inevitable as the quest for physical comfort. We cannot expect people to want less of either in the future. However, the pursuit of increased intellectual comfort, with its accompanying expectation that others should confirm our views, is deeply harmful to intellectual, political, and scientific progress. (I also believe it's harmful to individual happiness and personal growth, but that's a topic for another book.)

As readers can already tell, I am approaching this topic from a more fundamental standpoint than the liberal-vs-conservative or progressive-vs-conservative perspective that is common in culture-war discussions. Among the many problems of the left-vs-right approach is the fact that it necessarily oversimplifies highly complex issues. I have made no bones about the fact that campus censorship is largely motivated by people from the political left. At the same time, I know that there are conservatives who oppose freedom of speech and the right to engage in offensive, blasphemous, or sexually explicit expression. And many on the left side of the spectrum, such as Nadine Strossen, Wendy Kaminer, Nat Hentoff, Floyd Abrams, and Glenn Greenwald, are true free-speech purists. If we characterize the push toward censorship as a phenomenon that comes from only the left, we automatically let half the population off the hook and demonize the other half, many of whom may potentially be allies in the fight for free speech.

I will, however, acknowledge one aspect of the standard American political divide that has great relevance to the rest of this Broadside. In his excellent 2012 book *The Righteous Mind: Why Good People Are Divided by Politics and Religion*, Jonathan Haidt explored the foundations of human morality and tried to determine how they cohere and from where they originate. He concluded that political conservatives have multiple sources for their moral norms that include the values of traditional societies around the world, such as sacredness, loyalty, and respect for authority. In contrast, Haidt wrote, American liberals and progressives primarily emphasize the "care ethic," whereby one's analysis of the morality of an issue begins and ends with whether or not the proposed action demonstrates care for the well-being or feelings of others, with particular focus on the needs of a relatively large category of people defined as "victims." As progressive author and professor George Lakoff put it in *The Political Mind*, "Behind every progressive policy lies a single moral value: empathy." Lakoff's assertion lends support to Haidt's argument that progressive morality is largely one-dimensional, driven primarily by the care ethic. If true, this theory does an excellent job of explaining why the push for sensitivity-based censorship increasingly comes from the left wing of the political spectrum. Whichever portion of the spectrum emphasizes care above all other values will be more sympathetic to attempts to prevent offensive or challenging speech and to provide those they view as vulnerable with as much freedom *from* speech as possible.

Campus Speech, Disinvitation Season, and the Movement from the "Right Not to Be Offended" to the "Expectation of Confirmation"

While I believe the threat to free speech is global and extends far beyond American higher education, we can nonetheless learn a great deal from what is happening on American campuses. American higher education is immensely influential and, perversely, has been on the cutting edge of censorship and other illiberal trends for decades. Therefore, examining campus attitudes about both free speech and freedom from speech may offer a preview of what the world will look like in 10 to 20 years. Also, since higher education may offer our best hope of fighting the calls for freedom from speech, it is important to see how uninterested most campuses are in helping solve the problem. In fact, they are often making it worse.

In *Unlearning Liberty* and in my other writings, I have examined how higher education pioneered the idea that some students, professors, and administrators have the "right not to be offended." This mythical right manifests itself in campus speech codes that ban "hurtful," "inconsiderate," or "offensive" speech, as well as in the kind of absurd overreactions to and punishments of speech that we see on a daily basis at FIRE. I am sad to report that since *Unlearning Liberty* was published, the bar for what can get you in trouble in college appears to have sunk even lower.

Constitution Day (which is honored yearly on Sept. 17) in 2013 was a particularly bad day for free speech on campus. At Modesto Junior College in California, student and decorated military veteran Robert Van Tuinen was told that he could not hand out copies of the U.S. Constitution to his fellow students. On the same day, at California's Citrus College, student Vincenzo Sinapi-Riddle was informed that he could not freely protest the National Security Agency (NSA) and its surveillance program on campus. Both students were required to restrict their protests to tiny "free speech zones," and had to get advance administrative permission before conducting them. Four months later, another group of students at the University of Hawaii at Hilo were told that they could not distribute copies of the Constitution to their schoolmates. (FIRE, with the help of attorneys from the national law firm Davis Wright Tremaine, filed suit against all three colleges.)

In June 2014, students at the University of Chicago got together to sign a petition against well-known gay-rights advocate and sex columnist Dan Savage for uttering the word *tranny* – an abbreviation for *transsexual* that is often used as an epithet – during a panel discussion at the school. Although Savage was arguing for the reclamation of this word as a tool of empowerment, his use of it did not sit well with some. One student argued that Savage should not be allowed to say the "T-slur" (the student refused to use the actual word) no matter what the context, and like-minded students petitioned the University of Chicago's Institute of Politics to implement a ban on "hate speech" at future lectures (an effort that the institute fortunately rejected).

But the campus-speech story that received the most media attention was doubtlessly "disinvitation season 2014," when college speaker after college speaker faced disinvitation efforts from students and faculty alike. While many were rightly outraged when such efforts were successfully directed at famous conservatives and libertarians like Condoleezza Rice, Charles Murray, and Ayaan Hirsi Ali, the public has become sadly accustomed to intolerance for conservative voices on campus. The public took greater notice, however, when the disinvitation efforts were successfully directed at former University of California, Berkeley, Chancellor Robert Birgeneau and International Monetary Fund head Christine Lagarde, both of whom are high-profile figures and neither of whom is conservative.

The term *disinvitation season* has been something of a dark joke within FIRE for years – one that has grown less funny with each passing year. FIRE had been loosely tracking some of these incidents for about a decade, but we decided in May 2014 that we needed to engage in more systematic research. While we are under no illusion that we have identified every disinvitation effort that has taken place since the turn of the century (please contact us at disinvitation@thefire.org if you know of additional examples), we have compiled an extensive database of examples of disinvitation efforts over the past 15 years.

So far, FIRE has uncovered 257 incidents since 2000 in which students or faculty have pushed for speakers who were invited to campus (for both commencement and other speaking engagements) to be disinvited. Of those incidents, 111 were "successful," in that the speaker ultimately did not give a speech. Those 111 successful disinvitations took three main forms: 75 occurred via the revocation of the speaker's invitation to campus; 20 were from speakers withdrawing in the face of protest; and 16 were "heckler's vetoes," in which speakers were shouted down, chased off stage, or otherwise prevented from delivering their remarks by student hecklers.

Although these 257 disinvitation efforts span 15 years, more than half (137) have happened since 2009, when we first noticed an uptick in the frequency of such incidents. And of the 111 "successful" disinvitation attempts, 59 occurred during or after 2009. The available data strongly indicates that the problem is only getting worse; the past 5½ years have already seen more attempts at disinvitations, and more successful disinvitations, than the nine years preceding them.

There is, unsurprisingly, a clear political trend in the likelihood that a speaker will face a disinvitation attempt. Speakers are far more likely to encounter such efforts from opponents to their political left than from those to their right. Since 2000, those pushing for disinvitation targeted speakers with views more conservative than their own nearly twice as frequently (118 attempts) as they targeted speakers with views more liberal than their own (61 attempts).

The fact that conservatives are the focus of so many disinvitation efforts is made far more striking by the fact that – especially when it comes to commencement addresses – conservatives are *far* less likely to be invited to deliver speeches in the first place. According to research from Harry Enten at the polling aggregation website and blog FiveThirtyEight, in the 2013 and 2014 commencement seasons, *not a single* Republican political figure was invited to speak at the commencements of any of the top 30 universities or top 30 liberal-arts universities. In contrast, 25 Democratic political figures spoke at those same schools' commencements, 11 of whom gave the main address.

Enten noted, "In an increasingly polarized political atmosphere, the current lack of Republican commencement speakers at top universities and colleges makes a lot of sense; a decent number of people, including Democrats, don't like to hear differing views." The underlying assumption here is quite disheartening. In an academic environment in which students were properly trained, one would hope the community would not only tolerate opinions with which they disagree but would also actively seek them out, as curious, creative, and disciplined minds should be taught to do. Instead, we have come to accept the reality of an academic environment in which students crave freedom from speech and from speakers with whom they disagree. We can and should expect better.

I am not alone in thinking this. The disinvitation problem has become severe enough that both William Bowen, the former president of Princeton University, and Michael Bloomberg, the Independent former mayor of New York City, scolded students for their arrogance and closed-mindedness in their 2014 commencement addresses. Bowen, who replaced the disinvited Chancellor Birgeneau as Haverford College's graduation speaker, decried the agitators' approach as "immature" and "arrogant" and called Birgeneau's disinvitation a "defeat" for the school.

Bloomberg, for his part, used his commencement address to warn Harvard graduates that "tolerance for other people's ideas and the freedom to express your own are ... perpetually vulnerable to the tyrannical tendencies of monarchs, mobs, and majorities, and lately we've seen those tendencies manifest themselves too often, both on college campuses and in our society."

As an attorney who focuses on free speech and the First Amendment, I fully support the rights of faculty and students to make their opinions known about a university's decision to invite any speaker. That being said, freedom of speech and academic freedom depend on our ability to handle hearing opinions we dislike and to engage those opinions constructively and creatively. Free inquiry and academic freedom, in particular, require some amount of epistemic humility and a willingness to acknowledge that even the opinion or person we find the most abhorrent might reveal some portion of the truth of which we are unaware. It is also important to recognize that even if a speaker *does* happen to be entirely wrong, we might learn more about our own beliefs or about the complex relationships among beliefs by allowing that person to speak.

Rather than teaching students to be skeptical of confirmation bias, we appear to be teaching them to have an expectation of confirmation: a sense of entitlement to an environment in which their beliefs are not contradicted (at least not too harshly). Expectation of confirmation is yet another manifestation of the desire for intellectual comfort, and it is also likely to increase over time. If we don't fight the growth of this expectation among students, we can be confident that disinvitation season will get worse and worse every year, until universities decide that the only people they can safely invite to speak will be those who have nothing to say. Still worse, catering to this expectation plays into an unhealthy narrative – that hearing from only those with whom you agree is somehow a laudable goal, rather than poison to intellectual growth.

Disinvitation season, thanks in part to its intersection with celebrities and public figures, may be the most high-profile symptom of campus illiberalism, but it isn't the only campus trend to catch the public's notice in recent months. The push for "trigger warnings" has also received considerable attention, and it may have even darker implications for the future of free and open discourse and debate.

Impossible Expectations: Trigger Warnings

In May 2014, the *New York Times* called attention to a new arrival on the college campus: trigger warnings. Seemingly overnight, colleges and universities across America have begun fielding student demands that their professors issue content warnings before covering any material that might evoke a negative emotional response. By way of illustration, the *Times* article (titled "Warning: The Literary Canon Could Make Students Squirm") pointed to a Rutgers student's op-ed requesting trigger warnings for *The Great Gatsby*, which apparently "possesses a variety of scenes that reference gory, abusive and misogynistic violence," and *Mrs. Dalloway*, which the student called "a disturbing narrative" that discusses "suicidal inclinations" and "post-traumatic experiences." The article generated significant discussion, with readers questioning why college students would need trigger warnings – which are generally billed as a way to help those who suffer from post-traumatic stress disorder (PTSD), a serious mental-health condition – before reading the type of material that any college student should expect to encounter on any college campus.

The *New Republic*'s Jenny Jarvie has traced the genesis

of trigger warnings to online chat rooms and message boards frequented by survivors of highly traumatizing experiences like rape. In her March 2014 article "Trigger Happy," Jarvie noted that the warnings, which "began as a way of moderating Internet forums for the vulnerable and mentally ill," spread through feminist forums like wildfire, prompting writer Susannah Breslin to proclaim in April 2010 that feminists were using the term "like a Southern cook applies Pam cooking spray to an overused nonstick frying pan." From there, the phenomenon mushroomed into a staggeringly broad advisory system that, as Jarvie explained, now covers "topics as diverse as sex, pregnancy, addiction, bullying, suicide, sizeism, ableism, homophobia, transphobia, slut shaming, victim-blaming, alcohol, blood, insects, small holes, and animals in wigs." In May 2012, the *Awl*'s Choire Sicha penned an article titled "When 'Trigger Warning' Lost All Its Meaning." In it, Sicha discussed "how far afield 'trigger warnings' have gone," calling the trend "insulting" and "infantilizing."

Despite such criticism, trigger warnings are gaining traction – and are no longer confined to Internet forums. The leap from online communities to college campuses is not surprising, as campuses have long been at the vanguard of accommodating student, faculty, and administrator demands for emotionally and intellectually comfortable environments. Some believe that campuses have a duty to shield students from difficult material, while others espouse the older view, popularized by colleges like Yale in the 1970s, that colleges should be places where students are encouraged to "think the unthinkable, discuss the unmentionable, and challenge the unchallengeable." This contrast is stark and has certainly unsettled many professors.

In early 2014, Oberlin University took a dramatic step toward heightening students' intellectual comfort by posting a trigger-warning policy on its website. Although the policy did not mandate the use of trigger warnings, it heavily encouraged the faculty to employ them as a means of "making classrooms safer."

It is crucial, at this point, to note how thoroughly the definition of *safety* has been watered down on campus. The term is no longer limited to physical security – far from it. In my career, I have repeatedly seen *safety* be conflated with *comfort* or even *reassurance*. It is hard for me to overemphasize how dangerous this shift is. Our society appears to have forgotten the moral of the fable "The Boy Who Cried Wolf." When there is confusion as to whether *safety* refers to physical harm or to mere discomfort, how can professors and administrators quickly assess the danger of a situation and make appropriate decisions to safeguard the physical security of their students? Making sure that such important words do not lose their meaning through inappropriately distorted usage is an essential part of fighting the movement toward freedom from speech.

Oberlin's policy – which was quickly tabled when panicked professors found out about it – shows how expansive and invasive trigger warnings can be. Its stated purpose was to protect students suffering from PTSD due to sexual assault, but its list of potentially triggering topics extended far beyond sexual or physical abuse. Professors were asked to "understand that sexual misconduct is inextricably tied to issues of privilege and oppression" and to therefore consider how topics like "racism, classism, sexism, heterosexism, cissexism, ableism, and other issues of privilege and oppression" could affect their students.

The breadth of this list reveals that trigger-warning policies often have little to do with the needs of actual PTSD sufferers. Bear in mind that PTSD is the current evolution of the term "shell shock," which was developed after

World War I to describe long-term psychological harm due to sustained exposure to horrific experiences during wartime. In the 1970s, PTSD became the preferred term for referring to traumatized veterans of the Vietnam War. The term has tremendous emotional force, but its use in the trigger-warning debate is yet another troubling employment of an important word. What colleges like Oberlin describe as PTSD bears little resemblance to its original meaning, which focused on the results of exposure to severe and often prolonged physical violence, atrocities, or other life-threatening or terrifying events. Survivors of sexual assault have experienced the type of trauma that fits this definition, but it is hard to see how people who have merely been exposed to "classism" – something that virtually anyone can claim to have encountered in some way at some point – can be put in the same category.

Oberlin is not alone. Around the time that Oberlin was instituting its trigger-warning policy, the student government at the University of California, Santa Barbara, (UCSB) passed a "Resolution to Mandate Warnings for Triggering Content in Academic Settings," which the UCSB administration is currently in the process of implementing. The resolution provides a "suggested list of Trigger Warnings [that] includes Rape, Sexual Assault, Abuse, Self-Injurious Behavior, Suicide, Graphic Violence, Pornography, Kidnapping, and Graphic Depictions of Gore."

Bailey Loverin, the student who co-authored the UCSB resolution, was inspired to do so after watching a film depicting rape in class. Although she identifies as a survivor of sexual abuse, she has specifically stated that she "was not triggered by [her] classroom experience." Rather, she found it "disturbing and sickening." In other words, she felt highly uncomfortable while watching the film.

Her discomfort – and her worries about the emotional comfort of her classmates – culminated in the passage of a policy that will likely force all UCSB professors to scour their course materials for anything that might be upsetting to students. The rules of political correctness seem to counsel against responding with the real answer: that college is where you are supposed to learn about the world as it truly is, which includes covering some horrific and dreadful topics. This endeavor should make anyone with a conscience uncomfortable at times, but that discomfort is a necessary part of real, adult-level education.

A quick look at recent campus dustups gives a more complete understanding of what the results of trigger-warning policies will be. In February 2014, students at Wellesley College were outraged when an artist placed a statue of a man sleepwalking in his underwear on campus. There is nothing overtly sexual or threatening about the statue, which was erected as part of a sculpture exhibit. If anything, the sleepwalker seems vulnerable: his eyes are closed, he is unaware of his surroundings, and he is barely dressed. Despite this, students called it "a source of apprehension, fear, and triggering thoughts regarding sexual assault for many members of our campus community" in a Change.org petition seeking its removal.

One of the most powerful aspects of art is its capacity to provoke thought and debate, often by raising some hackles. Yet Zoe Magid, who started the petition, asserted that artwork that makes people uncomfortable has no place at Wellesley: "We really feel that if a piece of art makes students feel unsafe, that steps over a line." Make sure to note how *unsafe* is used in this context.

At UCSB (again), a professor used the idea of triggers to defend getting into a physical altercation with campus protesters. In March 2014, Mireille Miller-Young, a UCSB feminist-studies professor, spotted a young woman carrying a pro-life sign that displayed images of aborted fetuses. She tore the sign from the activist's hands and went so far as to shove another protester who tried to retrieve it. When questioned by the UCSB Police Department, Miller-Young – who was pregnant at the time – declared that she "felt 'triggered' by the images on the poster." She also portrayed herself as a defender of student comfort, claiming that "other students in the area were 'triggered' in a negative way by their imagery." In other words, she placed greater value on the emotional comfort of those with whom she identified than on the physical security of the women she assaulted. In the video of the incident, Miller-Young seems positively gleeful to have taken the protesters' signs, and her actions make her argument that she was personally triggered, as opposed to simply angry, difficult to believe. That defense appears to be little more than a post hoc way of making her seem more sympathetic.

It is easy to dismiss events like that as rare acts of lunacy. One can argue that Miller-Young was just a lone professor making a transparent attempt to garner sympathy for – or otherwise excuse – illegal behavior. It is also easy to dismiss the rising popularity of trigger warnings as a flash in the pan that will fade in the face of public ridicule. Yet the policies and confrontations that stem from the concept of trigger warnings are just further symptoms of the increasing expectations of intellectual comfort and freedom from speech on campus. While it is possible that the particular problem of demands for trigger warnings will be short-lived (though I doubt it), there will persist a larger problem of a limitless "care ethic" in which outsiders are responsible for safeguarding the emotional state of all, even at the risk of impeding discourse on dead-serious topics that must be explored.

The UCSB case also highlights how such policies will inevitably be abused. An unfortunate truth of human nature is that if we are given a cudgel that may be wielded against people and views we oppose, some of us will gladly swing it. I can say with near 100 percent confidence that students and even other faculty members will use trigger rationales to silence voices on campus that they merely dislike.

And professors know it is already shockingly easy to get in trouble for what you say at today's colleges. Take the 2014 example of art instructor Francis Schmidt of Bergen Community College in New Jersey, who was suspended without pay and ordered to undergo psychological counseling for posting on Google Plus a picture of his daughter wearing a T-shirt featuring a quote from the warrior queen Daenerys Targaryen, a character on HBO's mega-hit *Game of Thrones*: "I will take what is mine with fire and blood." Depressingly, the quote was interpreted by administrators as a serious threat of violence. A security official even claimed that the "fire" reference could be a proxy for the gunfire of an AK-47. A strikingly similar case, this time involving a quote from the sci-fi cult television classic *Firefly*, took place at the University of Wisconsin-Stout in 2011.

Broaching sex-related topics in the classroom can be particularly risky, with professors at Appalachian State University; the University of Colorado, Boulder; and the University of Denver all facing harassment charges and removal from teaching for the inclusion of sexual content in their class materials and discussions, even though the content was demonstrably relevant to each course.

In an environment like this, imposing on professors the duty to anticipate and be responsible for their students' emotional reactions to material will simply create new rationales for students or administrators seeking to punish provocative instructors. Such an expectation would be disastrous for teaching and would place professors in an impossible position.

Oberlin Professor Marc Blecher has pointed out that instructors without tenure would be particularly vulnerable to this effect, telling the *New York Times*, "If I were a junior faculty member looking at this [the Oberlin policy] while putting my syllabus together, I'd be terrified." In May 2014, seven humanities professors from seven colleges penned an *Inside Higher Ed* article stating that "this movement is already having a chilling effect on [their] teaching and pedagogy." They reported receiving "phone calls from deans and other administrators investigating student complaints that they have included 'triggering' material in their courses, with or without warnings." Sometime in the not-so-distant future – if it has not happened already – professors *will* be punished for not providing a trigger warning before discussing material that a student finds objectionable.

The seven professors also raised an important point about how trigger-warning policies may well harm, rather than help, the very students they claim to protect: "Trigger warnings may encourage students to file claims against faculty rather than seek support and resources for debilitating reactions to stressors." Students with PTSD are suffering from a serious mental-health condition and should seek professional assistance for it. In her article "Treatment, Not Trigger Warnings," Sarah Roff, a psychiatrist who specializes in the mental effects of trauma (including flashbacks and panic attacks), explained that training students to avoid certain topics can be quite detrimental:

> *One of the cardinal symptoms of PTSD is avoidance, which can become the most impairing symptom of all. If someone has been so affected by an event in her life that*

reading a description of a rape in Ovid's Metamorpho- ses *can trigger nightmares, flashbacks, and panic attacks, she is likely to be functionally impaired in areas of her life well beyond the classroom. The solution is not to help these students dig themselves further into a life of fear and avoidance.*

Proponents of trigger warnings argue that safeguarding the comfort of traumatized students is well worth the potential costs. Their position holds great emotional appeal. In the words of Shakesville's Melissa McEwan, a leading trigger-warning advocate, "We provide trigger warnings because it's polite, because we don't want to be the asshole who triggered a survivor of sexual assault because of carelessness or laziness or ignorance." The vast majority of us don't want to hurt others, particularly those who have already been badly hurt.

This emotional appeal can serve as a formidable weapon, especially as Haidt's care ethic becomes unbound from other moral or practical considerations. Those who oppose trigger warnings are accused of being insensitive to the needs of vulnerable groups. It is also considered illegitimate to question the sincerity of emotional responses, which makes it easy for students who dislike certain ideas (or individuals) to try to silence them by claiming to have been triggered by them. Casting doubt on such an asser- tion would constitute "victim blaming," which only a coldhearted monster would do. Alleging that someone is insensitive to the emotional state of victims is a powerful and effective shortcut to taking the moral high ground in contemporary debate.

The fear of being demonized in this manner is justified, given the power of the modern "Twitter mob" and other manifestations of popular outrage. In fact, such concerns are particularly valid on campus, where professors right-fully fear for their jobs if they manage to spark the moral indignation of some subset of students, administrators, or faculty members. It is for this reason that groups that fight for professors' rights, such as FIRE and the American Association of University Professors, must do their best to bolster professorial resistance to new and impossible expectations like trigger warnings. Otherwise, we risk squandering the opportunity to work with our natural allies (in this case at least) – university professors – to oppose the push toward elevating intellectual comfort over intellectual growth.

In rereading the commentary and reactions to the *Times* article that I mentioned at the beginning of this section, I noticed that defenders of trigger warnings often struck a common note. Essentially, they argued, "What's the big deal? So you have to include two little words before you cover emotionally difficult material. Is it really that much to ask?" I have offered various answers to that question throughout this Broadside, but in conclusion, I want to stress two of them. First, the trouble with trigger warn-ings lies less in the individual practice (although it will present a huge problem for teaching) than in what that practice represents. Trigger warnings starkly reinforce the mentality that demands freedom *from* speech. Second, the trigger-warning issue is a genuinely slippery slope, as Oberlin's staggeringly broad policy demonstrates.

Supporters of trigger warnings are sometimes shocked by the negative response that the idea, as applied to col-lege content, has received in the press and blogosphere. For those who believe that Haidt's care ethic is paramount and that offering such warnings is simply a means of show-ing empathy, conscientiousness, and care, the widespread criticism of the practice is probably fairly mystifying. To those who value intellectual freedom, however, trigger warnings are yet another manifestation of the attitude that society must protect every individual from emotionally difficult speech. It is impossible to live up to this expectation, and in the course of trying to do so, we risk devastating freedom of speech and the open exchange of ideas.

Critics might dismiss my and others' concerns about what trigger warnings represent as a slippery-slope fallacy. But if there is one thing that I have discovered in fighting for free speech on campus, it is that when it comes to limitations on speech and the uniquely sensitive environment of college campuses, the slope is genuinely perilously slick.

In my career, I have seen harassment rationales – meant to prevent misogynists from forcing women out of jobs through constant abuse – being invoked to justify censoring everything from quoting popular television shows to faintly implying criticism of a university's hockey coach to publicly reading a book. The slippery slope of censorship is demonstrably not a fallacy on campus. When students take advantage of a psychological term developed to help those traumatized in the ghastly trenches of World War I to justify being protected from *The Great Gatsby*, sleepwalker statues, and, as the Oberlin policy specified, Chinua Achebe, it becomes clear that there is virtually no limit to the demands that will be made if we universalize an expectation of intellectual comfort.

Other critics see where this is headed, as well. As Professor Roff wrote in the article mentioned above, "since triggers are a contagious phenomenon, there will never be enough trigger warnings to keep up with them." And as Conor Friedersdorf wrote in the *Atlantic*:

The future before us if the most sweeping plans for "trigger warnings" become reality, is a kind of arms race, where different groups of students demand that their highly particular, politicized sensitivities are as deserving of a trigger warning as any other. Everyone from anarchists to college Republicans will join in. Kids will feel trauma when their trauma isn't recognized as trauma. "Trigger warnings" will be as common and useless as "adult content" warnings on HBO.

Everyone will be worse off.

Friedersdorf is right. The "offendedness sweepstakes" (to borrow a phrase from Rauch) pushes the bar ever lower for what is deemed unacceptably offensive, while the realm of unacceptable speech grows ever larger. This is a global race to the bottom, and it is being run most fiercely in higher education. In the process, candor, discussion, humor, honest dialogue, and freedom of speech are imperiled.

Conclusion: Fighting the Problems of Comfort

My primary goal in this short work has been to explain that threats to free speech, while rampant on college campuses, are not unique to higher education or even to the United States, and why we can expect them to intensify over time. I have also offered a preview of where I fear we are headed. While this view may strike some as unduly pessimistic, I think it is necessary to correctly diagnose the problem if we are sincere about tackling it.

If I am right, and the move toward greater physical, emotional, and intellectual comfort is a predictable historical force, understanding what is coming may help us prepare for it. My fear is that future generations will not see much point in delving into emotionally difficult topics and that those of us who argue that doing so is intellectually "good for you" will sound a lot like parents telling stubborn children that they should eat their Brussels sprouts.

I am constantly on the lookout for potential cures for this problem. Litigation plays an important role in the fight, as does having students engage in proper Oxford-style debates (like we see today in the Intelligence Squared series). Comedians and satirists may also join the pushback against the infinite care ethic; after all, it is blazingly clear that politically correct censorship and comedy are natural enemies. And, of course, nothing can replace teaching students at every level of education the old-fashioned intellectual habits of epistemic humility, giving others the benefit of the doubt, and actually listening to opposing opinions. Such practices need to make a comeback if we are to have a society in which it is at all productive (let alone pleasurable) to talk about anything serious.

I hope to write extensively in the coming years about the potential solutions to problems of comfort, the expectation of confirmation, and the desire for freedom from speech. But unless higher education stops encouraging these inclinations and starts combating them, it will be a hard battle indeed.

Then again, the fight for freedom of speech has never been easy.

ANDREW C. MCCARTHY

ISLAM AND FREE SPEECH

Free speech, a bedrock protection of our constitutional republic, is increasingly an endangered species in modern America. When we retrace the self-destructive steps away from our founding principles, we find a good deal of the trail blazed by the Western "progressive" determination to meld the antithetical cultures of liberty and sharia — Islam's totalitarian societal framework cum legal code, petrified a millennium ago. Islamic law takes lethal aim at free speech. Yet, in the Obama era, the United States government went so far as to embrace it in a United Nations resolution that purports to outlaw the critical examination of radical Islamic ideology under the sweet-sounding guise of banning "hostility" to religion. Framed in the aftermath of the 2015 Charlie Hebdo jihadist attack in Paris, Islam and Free Speech *examines the West's craven retreat in the face of an aggressor ideology whose jihadist adherents are just the frontlines and whose leaders are confident that victory lies in forming parallel societies that gradually suffocate liberty.*

I*ls ne sont pas Charlie!*
    That is what should have been pressed on the T-shirts, scrawled across the placards, and strung beside the trendy hashtags that festooned cyberspace. It would have been a slogan more befitting the throng that descended on the

City of Lights, particularly the Western politicos – minus U.S. President Barack Obama, the putative Leader From Behind of the Formerly Free World.

Whatever these characters might be, they most certainly are not Charlie.

It was nonetheless amid streaming "*Je Suis Charlie*" banners that 40 high-government officials led a crowd of more than 1.5 million citizens in a "unity rally" at Place de la République. Millions more partook in concurrent rallies throughout France. The ubiquitous signs were in homage to *Charlie Hebdo*, a left-wing satirical magazine featuring pungent cartoons that proclaim a doctrinaire secularism. Earlier that week, editor in chief Stéphane Charbonnier, along with several *Charlie Hebdo* cartoonists and columnists, had been brutally murdered at the start of a three-day jihadist rampage. When the smoke cleared, 17 innocents had been mowed down by gunfire in attacks reminiscent of the 2008 Mumbai massacres carried out by Pakistani jihadists aligned with al-Qaeda.

When it comes to lampoon, *Charlie Hebdo* is an equal-opportunity purveyor, with no religion immune from its japery. In one religion, however, a large plurality of adherents abide neither lampoon nor *égalité* – to say nothing of *liberté, fraternité*, the supremacy of reason, and other pillars of Western enlightenment. It was only by mocking the tenets and excesses of that religion – Islam – that the magazine became a terrorist target.

Charbonnier was presiding over the year's first editorial meeting on the morning of Jan. 7, 2015, when Chérif and Saïd Kouachi, brandishing Kalashnikov rifles, stormed *Charlie Hebdo*'s Paris offices. Besides the journalists, they killed a maintenance worker and two unarmed police officers – one assigned as Charbonnier's bodyguard, the other a Muslim just doing his duty for France.

The brothers had at least one accomplice, Ahmedy Coulibaly, who had pledged loyalty to the infamously barbaric Islamic State, also known as ISIS or ISIL – as in the Islamic State of Iraq and al-Sham (greater Syria), or the Levant. Hours after the *Charlie Hebdo* siege, Coulibaly shot and severely wounded a jogger in a southwestern suburb of Paris. The following day, consistent with ISIS's call for Muslims to assassinate Western security personnel, Coulibaly shot and killed unarmed Paris police officer Clarissa Jean-Philippe.

Finally, he homed in on another favorite jihadist target, Jews. On Jan. 9, Coulibaly took hostages at a kosher super-market in eastern Paris, warning that he would kill his captives if harm came to the Kouachis. By then, in nearby Dammartin-en-Goele, security forces surrounded the brothers, who were holding hostages in a printing factory. Ultimately, French authorities stormed both locations, shooting all three terrorists to death, but not before Cou-libaly killed four of his hostages.

The eminent historian Bernard Lewis has predicted that Europe will be Islamic by the end of the 21st century, "part of the Arabic West, the Maghreb." The story of the three jihadists who terrorized France is a story of modern, transitional Europe: its open door to Muslim immigra-tion, the antiassimilation activism of its Muslim leaders, and the jihadists who are inexorably produced.

The Kouachi brothers had been born in Paris in the early 1980s to Algerian immigrants. Orphaned, they bounced around the nearby suburbs, or *banlieues*, so many of which have become Islamic enclaves. Like an alarming number of young French Muslims, both were trained jihadists, wending their way from radical French mosques to the training camps of al-Qaeda's franchise in Yemen.

Though they roamed France freely, the brothers were

known to the authorities as would-be terrorists. Chérif, in fact, had been arrested in 2005 while trying to join the anti-American jihad in Iraq. Three years later, he was briefly imprisoned for recruiting on behalf of al-Qaeda in Iraq, the franchise that eventually evolved into ISIS. It was during a prison stay that he befriended Coulibaly, another young French Muslim born to immigrants (from Mali) who was serving a bank-robbery sentence. The two men fell in with an al-Qaeda recruiter, Djamel Beghal, then serving a 10-year sentence for conspiring to bomb the American embassy in Paris. Beghal, an eminence in Europe's growing jihadist circles, had found al-Qaeda while he was a regular at London's infamous Finsbury mosque.

When the time came for their jihad, the Kouachi brothers chose their target carefully. Al-Qaeda had placed Charbonnier on a hit list published in 2013 by *Inspire*, the terrorist network's English-language magazine. Upon bursting into the editorial conference room, the brothers called him by his nom de plume – "Charb!" – before killing him in cold blood. As they fled the scene after the shooting spree, the Kouachis treated stunned survivors and spectators to the signature jihadist cries of *"Allahu Akbar!"* ("Allah is greater!") They added a chilling coda: "We have avenged the Prophet Muhammad! We have killed *Charlie Hebdo!*"

It is little wonder he was targeted. Charbonnier was a steadfast champion of free expression. His was not a hollow, hashtag courage.

In 2006, despite radical Islam's notoriously savage approach to registering disapproval, *Charlie Hebdo* republished the unflattering cartoons of Islam's prophet that were first run by Denmark's *Jyllands-Posten* newspaper. In its way, the magazine made clear that its rebuke was aimed at Islamists, not Muslims in general. The cover of the issue republishing the cartoons featured a weeping prophet under the headline, "*Mahomet débordé par les intégristes*" ("Muhammad overwhelmed by fundamentalists").

It is a measure of the West's decline that this served only to distinguish *Charlie Hebdo* from the major-media echo chamber. According to the latter, it was *the cartoons,* not *sharia supremacist ideology,* that "ignited" the rioting in Islamic societies across the Middle East and Central Asia. It was as if, because mayhem and murder are now the *predictable* Muslim reaction to trifling slights, they are also somehow the *rational* reaction.

Another flashing indicator of Western decline: the magazine also distinguished itself by displaying the actual cartoons. Even after the deadly rioting had patently made them a news story, such pied pipers of elite opinion as the *New York Times,* the *Washington Post,* and network news divisions on both sides of the Atlantic declined to publish them. Yale University Press even banned the cartoons from a book about – yes – *the cartoons.* And *Jyllands-Posten* itself declined a request to republish the cartoons, with the telling admission, "Violence works."

In a schizophrenic France, *Charlie Hebdo*'s defiance left it in an ambivalent space. To be sure, official deference to free-expression principles made it the beneficiary of heightened – if ultimately ineffectual – police protection. But the republic is deracinating from its centuries-old foundation of vibrant political expression and secularist civil society. Consequently, the magazine was also subjected to no small amount of public scorn, its precarious state seen as self-induced. This is the fecklessness, the cultural self-loathing, and the soft bigotry of low expectations that induce Western opinion elites to forfeit such core liberties as free speech on the grounds that by dint of its incorrigibility, Muslim aggression has achieved entitlement status.

It is the mindset that whets radical Islam's appetite.

On Sept. 11, 2012, jihadists stormed an American diplomatic compound in Benghazi, Libya. The terrorists murdered the United States ambassador and three other American officials. Fraudulently, but in a manner entirely consistent with the conventional wisdom that trivial insults to Islam rationalize mass murder by Muslims, the Obama administration blamed the terrorist attack (or "protest," as officials gingerly described it) on an obscure anti-Islamic video – a trailer for a prophet-mocking film called *Innocence of Muslims* that virtually no one on earth had actually seen.

During the eight-hour Benghazi siege, President Obama, the commander in chief of the world's only superpower, failed to take any action to defend Americans fighting for their lives. He had limitless energy, though, for mounting a lugubrious defense of Muslim rage. Obama and Hillary Clinton, his then secretary of state (and now the putative Democratic candidate to replace him), filmed public-service announcements for the consumption of Islamic audiences overseas – not to condemn the killing of Americans and the rioting at U.S. facilities in several Muslim countries, but to reassure Muslims that the American government's only involvement in *Innocence of Muslims* was to deplore its anti-Islamic themes.

And to prosecute its producer. Under the guise of a parole violation for a prior, relatively minor fraud conviction, the administration shamefully trumped up a case against Nakoula Basseley Nakoula. The film producer is an Egyptian-born Coptic Christian, then residing in California – where the First Amendment still supposedly applies, obliging government officials to *secure* our liberties, including political or artistic expression, however distasteful they may find it.

Yet in the administration's calculus, *denying* Nakoula's liberty was a double bonus. Domestically, with the president campaigning for re-election, jailing the producer bolstered the fraudulent narrative that the anti-Muslim video – rather than the Islamist terrorist network that Obama claimed to have "decimated" – was responsible for the Benghazi massacre. For the consumption of overseas Islamic audiences, Nakoula's plight stood as a monitory example that this American president was willing to enforce sharia blasphemy standards.

It was hardly the only such example. Just two weeks after the Benghazi massacre, Obama also used his much anticipated annual speech before the United Nations General Assembly to declare, "The future must not belong to those who slander the prophet of Islam."

At *Charlie Hebdo*, the response to Islamic supremacist aggression was markedly different. As we've seen, after Muslims rioted over the Danish cartoons, the magazine republished them. On cue, Islamists began phase one of their tried-and-true Western strategy of "First lawfare, then warfare." A Muslim activist group sued *Charlie Hebdo* under France's elastic "hate speech" laws. The magazine's retort was to mock the Islamists' mirthless intolerance. It published more cartoons, including a cover caricature of a Muslim imam, arm in arm with an equally angry-looking bishop and rabbi, demanding that *Charlie Hebdo* "be veiled." A 2011 edition featured a smiling Muhammad on the cover, promising "100 lashes if you don't die of laughter" (and, further, inviting the prophet to become the magazine's "guest editor").

By then, a French court had decided the Islamist lawsuit in favor of *Charlie Hebdo*. In the Western rule-of-law tradition, litigants are expected to accept judicial rulings against them. In radical Islam's lawfare-then-warfare tradition, when a Western court disregards sharia blasphemy standards, dissatisfied Islamists turn to phase two, the surer methods of extortion. Thus it was that in 2011, Islamists exploded a petrol bomb that destroyed *Charlie Hebdo*'s offices. And let's again be clear that it was *radical Islam*, not the cartoons, that did the igniting.

The magazine persevered, moving to a new, ostensibly more secure location and continuing to satirize Islam's excesses, just as it satirized all things political, social, and religious. As Charbonnier once put it, "We have to carry on until Islam has been rendered as banal as Catholicism."

Later in 2011, a cover depicted the prophet as a gay man kissing a male *Charlie Hebdo* cartoonist. Islamists subsequently hacked the magazine's website, but still it persisted. In so doing, *Charlie Hebdo* made plain that Muslims were not being singled out, echoing the "progressive" moral equivalence that portrays extremism as an attribute of religion in general – as if it might just as readily be Zoroastrians and Presbyterians throwing gay men to their deaths from Syrian rooftops. The magazine dutifully limned the violent jihadists not as excessively devout Muslims but as traitors to the Islam of Muhammad. In one cartoon, for instance, an ISIS terrorist was depicted beheading the prophet after condemning him as an "infidel."

The nuances did not impress the intended audience. The week after the Sept. 11, 2012, wave of anti-American attacks, *Charlie Hebdo* lampooned the Obama administration's risible suggestion that a video, however provocative, could rationalize murder, maiming, and property destruction. It ran caricatures of a naked Muhammad in the pages of an edition whose cover cartoon displayed the prophet in a wheelchair pushed by an Orthodox Jew under the headline *"Intouchables."*

The issue was published over the objections of the

French government – the same government that would later take center stage at the postmassacre *Je Suis Charlie* rally. The Obama administration also complained. With the president taking election-season heat over his implication that civilized people could be incited to commit the Benghazi atrocities by a harmless video, White House spokesman Jay Carney grudgingly conceded that Obama was not claiming *Charlie Hebdo*'s publication "justified" violence, but the administration nonetheless faulted the magazine's "judgment" in choosing to exercise its "right" to free expression.

Obama, meanwhile, used his own judgment to rail about "slanders" against "the prophet of Islam" from his U.N. soapbox ... while al-Qaeda used its judgment to put Charbonnier on a hit list. The rest is history.

Yet how did we get to this historical anomaly in which, as the estimable scholar Daniel Pipes observes, "a majority population accepts the customs and even the criminality of a poorer and weaker immigrant community"? It is the result of a conquest ideology taking the measure of a civilization that no longer values its heritage, no longer regards itself as worthy of defense.

France's population of 66 million is now approximately 10 percent Islamic. Estimates are sketchy because, in a vestige of its vanishing secularist tradition, France does not collect census data about religious affiliation. Still, between 6 million and 7 million Muslims are reasonably believed to reside in the country. (Pew put the total at 4.7 million back in 2010; other analysts peg it higher today.) To many in France, the number seems higher, because of both the outsize influence of Islamist activists on the political class and the dense Muslim communities in and around Paris – approximating 15 percent of the local population. An online poll conducted by Ipsos MORI in 2014 found that the average French citizen *believes* Muslims make up about a third of the country's population.

As night follows day, when Muslim populations surge, so does support for jihadism and the sharia supremacist ideology that catalyzes it. The reason is plain to see, even if Western elites remain willfully blind to it. For a not-insignificant percentage of the growing Muslim millions in Europe, infiltration – by both mass immigration and the establishment of swelling Islamic enclaves – is a purposeful strategy of conquest, sometimes referred to as "voluntary apartheid."

One of its leading advocates is Sheikh Yusuf al-Qaradawi. A Qatar-based Egyptian octogenarian, al-Qaradawi is a Muslim Brotherhood icon. He is a copiously published scholar who graduated from Cairo's al-Azhar University, the seat of Sunni Islamic learning for over a millennium, and thus oversees both the International Union of Muslim Scholars and the European Council for Fatwa and Research. Thanks to his pioneering of the highly trafficked IslamOnline website and, especially, to his hugely popular al-Jazeera television program *Sharia and Life*, he has become the world's most influential sharia jurist.

Al-Qaradawi is the sharia backbone of the violent jihad to exterminate Israel – a tiny country surrounded by hundreds of millions of hostile Muslims. The sheikh also vows that Islam will "conquer" both Europe and America but acknowledges that this conquest will require a strategy more suited to a determined minority that knows it cannot win by force of arms alone. The key, he asserts, is *dawa*, the Muslim equivalent of proselytism. In radical Islam, it is hyperaggressive, pushing on every cultural cylinder, pressuring every institution, and exploiting the atmosphere of intimidation created by jihadist terrorism to blur the lines between legal advocacy and extortion.

In France, *dawa* presses against *laïcité*, the credo of secularism through the strict separation of religion and the state. Al-Qaradawi is quite clear that "secularism can never enjoy a general acceptance in an Islamic society." He is equally adamant that Muslims, who are bound to live in accordance with the strictures of sharia, must reject a secular framework because "acceptance of secularism means abandonment of sharia, a denial of the divine guidance and a rejection of Allah's injunctions." Thus, he elaborates, "the call for secularism among Muslims is atheism and a rejection of Islam. Its acceptance as a basis for rule in place of sharia is downright apostasy."

This nexus between free speech and Western democracy is worth pausing over. Notice that in focusing on the incompatibility between Islamic law and democracy's secular, pluralist underpinnings, al-Qaradawi draws the inevitable conclusion that democracy equals apostasy. The term *apostasy* is not invoked idly in Islam. As explained in *Reliance of the Traveller*, a classic sharia manual endorsed by al-Azhar scholars, the renunciation of Islam is a death-penalty offense.

Free speech does not exist in a vacuum. It is the plinth of freedom's fortress. It is the ineliminable imperative if there is to be the robust exchange of knowledge and ideas, the rule of reason, freedom of conscience, equality before the law, property rights, and equality of opportunity. That is why it must be extinguished if there is to be what al-Qaradawi calls a "place of religion" – meaning *his* religion. For all its arrogance and triumphalist claims, radical Islam must suppress speech because it cannot compete in a free market of conscience.

To sustain their movement, therefore, Islamist leaders must separate Muslims from secular society. In the West, this means forming Islamic enclaves in which sharia gradually takes root as the de facto and, eventually, the de jure law – enabling Muslims to resist the challenge of critical thinking under the guise of avoiding the near occasion of apostasy. Over time, dominion is established over swaths of not only physical territory but also legal privilege. Al-Qaradawi puts the matter succinctly:

> *Were we to convince Western leaders and decision- makers of our right to live according to our faith – ideologically, legislatively, and ethically – without imposing our views or inflicting harm upon them, we would have traversed an immense barrier in our quest for an Islamic state.*

The key to the conquest strategy is to coerce the West into accepting a Muslim right to resist assimilation, to regard sharia as superseding Western law and custom when the two conflict. For precisely this reason, the Organization of Islamic Cooperation – a bloc of 56 Muslim countries (plus the Palestinian Authority) – has decreed that "Muslims should not be marginalized or attempted to be assimilated, but should be accommodated." Recep Tayyip Erdogan, the Islamist president of Turkey who has systematically dismantled that country's secular, pro-Western system, similarly pronounces that pressuring Muslims to assimilate in the West "is a crime against humanity."

Free expression is the gateway to assimilation. Consequently, radical Islam cannot tolerate it.

As a result, France is now rife with *zones urbaines sensibles* – "sensitive urban areas." The government officially lists some 751 of them: Islamic enclaves in the *banlieues,* often referred to as no-go zones because the indigenous populations discourage the presence of non-Muslims who do not conform to Islamic standards of dress and social interaction, and of public officials – police, firefighters, emergency medical teams, and building inspectors – who are seen as symbols of the state's effort to exercise sovereignty in areas that Muslims seek to possess adversely.

Some of those zones inevitably evolve into hotbeds of jihadist activity. As the Gatestone Institute's Soeren Kern notes, citing a report by the Middle East Media Research Institute, there has been no shortage of Internet traffic suggesting, for example, "the killing of France's ambassadors, just as the 'manly' Libyan fighters killed the U.S. ambassador in Benghazi." In a low-intensity jihadist thrum stretching back several years, the torching of automobiles has become commonplace: as many as 40,000 cars are burned annually. Perhaps most alarmingly, over a thousand French Muslims, more than from any other Western country, are estimated to have traveled to Syria to fight for ISIS – meaning many will return to the country as trained, battle-hardened jihadists. Beyond the direct ISIS participants, moreover, the *Washington Post* has reported that a recent poll found 16 percent of French citizens expressing some degree of support for ISIS – an organization whose rule over the vast territory it has seized is best known for decapitations, rapine, burning prisoners alive, the execution of homosexuals, mass graves, and the enslavement of non-Muslim communities.

Once one grasps the voluntary-apartheid strategy, it becomes obvious why radical Islam's inroads in France, and elsewhere in Europe, seamlessly translate into demands for the enforcement of sharia's curbs on speech and artistic expression. What is not so obvious is just what a profound challenge to the West this constitutes.

The shocking *Charlie Hebdo* atrocity called global attention to the offensive caricatures, as well as renewed attention to the Danish cartoons, the *Innocence of Muslims* trailer, and other instances in which Islam's detractors have resorted to insult – what Obama breezily distorts as "slander" – to make their points. The focus on blatant provocation grievously minimizes the stakes of the Islamist threat.

Even free-speech enthusiasts are repulsed by obnoxious expression. One who passionately argues that it would be perilously wrong to *criminalize*, say, flag burning or the exhibition of Andres Serrano's *Piss Christ* can sympathize with calls to *discourage* their display – privately, nonthreateningly, and within the bounds of the law. After all, few sensible people would miss expression that is in poor taste and edifies neither our political discourse nor our appreciation of beauty. From that seemingly benign premise, however, it is but a short leap to the dangerous conclusion that *an outright ban* on sheer insults to Islam would be a harmless accommodation: "Yes, it would betray free-expression principles, but," we soothe ourselves, "it might serve the worthy cause of social harmony."

In fact, it would do exactly the opposite. A conquest ideology takes well-meaning accommodation as weakness and always demands more. But that is almost beside the point, because what is at risk is so much more than the right to give gratuitous offense.

As the aforementioned sharia manual *Reliance of the Traveller* instructs, classical Islamic law's suppression of artistic expression is not limited to mere sacrilege. It forbids depictions of "animate life," which are deemed offensive to Allah because they "imitate [his] creative act." "Whoever makes a picture," the manual warns, "Allah shall torture him with it on the Day of Judgment." So put aside the palpable fact that insult is frequently provocative in an enlightening, socially productive way. What is ultimately at stake in radical Islam's challenge to the West is art itself – in all its bracing genius and poignant presentation.

Perhaps even more ominous is the challenge to political speech outside the realm of art. Sharia's death penalty for apostasy is well known. What is not well known, however, is the breadth of conduct that sharia regards as apostasy. It is not limited to a Muslim's renunciation of Islam. There are various forms of what we might call "constructive apostasy" – for example, idol worship, the utterance of "words that imply unbelief," statements that appear to deny or revile Allah or the Prophet Muhammad, denial of "the obligatory character" of something scholarly consensus makes part of Islam, and even mere sarcasm regarding "any ruling of the Sacred Law." The enormity of prohibited expression far transcends *Charlie Hebdo*–style effrontery.

Hand in hand with apostasy, Islam prohibits blasphemy – by both Muslims and non-Muslims. "Wait," you're thinking, "how can a religion make rules for nonbelievers?" But remember: Islam, particularly in its extremist construction, perceives itself as not simply a religion but a full-blown societal framework, one that abides no division between private belief and public governance. It dictates terms to nonbelievers because it aims to rule them, at Allah's direction and under Allah's law.

Sharia is quite intentionally less indulgent of non-Muslims. Islamists and their apologists never tire of telling credulous Westerners that Islam permits no compulsion in matters of religion. This, however, merely means non-Muslims are not forced to *convert*. By contrast, Islam *does compel the imposition of sharia*. That is where compulsion comes in, for non-Muslims as well as Muslims. The system is designed to encourage conversion without forcing conversation, by making it starkly more attractive to be a Muslim. Sharia thus pervasively discriminates against non-Muslims (*dhimmis*): relegating them to lower-caste status, coercing their payment of a poll tax (*jizya*) for the privilege of living as infidels in an Islamic state, and exhorting Muslims to make them feel humiliated. In this, Muslim law fulfills Allah's command in the Koran's Sura 9:29:

> *Fight those who believe not in Allah nor the Last Day, nor hold forbidden which had been forbidden by Allah and his Messenger, nor acknowledge the Religion of Truth, from among the people of the book* [i.e., Christians and Jews], *until they pay the* jizya *and feel themselves subdued.*

As should be apparent, the radical Islamic interpretation of sharia is even less tolerant of perceived slights to Islam by nonbelievers than it is of irreverent displays – constructive apostasy – by Muslims. To constitute blasphemy, speech need not be insulting or slanderous. Islamists deem critical examinations of Islam to be blasphemous, especially if they reach negative conclusions or encourage unbelief. Proselytism of religions other than Islam, particularly if it involves encouraging Muslims to abandon Islam, is also strictly forbidden. In sum, if speech or expression could sow discord among Muslims or within an Islamic community, sharia would prohibit it. And truth is not a defense.

Clearly, the encroachment of sharia and its blasphemy standards in the West is not about whether a satirist should be permitted to caricature Muhammad as a gay man or salaciously discuss the aging prophet's scripturally documented connubial relations with a 9-year-old girl. It is about whether a society targeted by radical Islam can be prevented from understanding the threat and can defend itself. It is about whether a free society retains the wherewithal to engage in robust political discourse, the sine qua non of self-government.

That is the challenge. So what is the response?

France is at the forefront of the transnational progressive march toward a postnational, politically homogenous Europe that dances to the tune called by technocrats in Brussels. Classical Western liberalism is strictly déclassé.

French leaders have enmeshed the country in such multilateral treaties as the European Convention on Human Rights, the International Convention on the Elimination of All Forms of Racial Discrimination, and the International Covenant on Civil and Political Rights. As the Middle East Forum's Lawfare Project details, this burgeoning corpus of international law pays lip service to freedom of expression but sedulously restricts it with ever more elastic protections "of the reputation and rights of others." The treaties direct member states to enact nebulous laws that render illegal "the dissemination of ideas based on racial superiority or hatred," as well as "advocacy" of "religious hatred" that could be an "incitement to ... hostility."

French law, too, bans "hate speech," defined to include incitement to racial discrimination or "hatred" based on, inter alia, one's religious group. In effect, this hopelessly politicized pandering has empowered the Muslim grievance industry to criminalize aspersions against Islam. To heighten the *in terrorem* effect on the masses, legal action has been taken against prominent citizens. Legendary actress Brigitte Bardot has been convicted and fined several times – most recently for speaking against the ritual slaughter of sheep during a Muslim feast. Controversial politician Jean-Marie Le Pen (runner-up in the 2002 presidential election) was convicted for bewailing the anti-assimilationist consequences of Muslim immigration. And though ultimately acquitted (by a court that side-stepped the "incitement" issue), author Michel Houellebecq endured protracted legal proceedings after he publicly described Islam as "stupid" and "dangerous."

Of course, France has no First Amendment. Notwithstanding its enlightened tradition, it has always been easier to ban varieties of expression there than in the United States. In fact, in an overreaction to the crisis of internal strife largely self-induced by its sundry accommodations of radical Islam, France has banned Muslim women from donning the burka (the fully enveloping garment that covers even the face) in public places. The ban is probably counterproductive: its non-enforcement in Islamic enclaves only promotes the conceit that sharia has superseded French law. But unwise or not, the First Amendment would not tolerate such a ban.

Nevertheless, if President Obama has his way, the First Amendment will yield to sharia blasphemy standards. In conjunction with the aforementioned Organization of Islamic Cooperation (OIC), Obama's then Secretary of State Clinton sponsored United Nations Human Rights Council Resolution 16/18. It calls on all governments to outlaw "any advocacy of religious hatred against individuals that constitutes incitement to discrimination, hostility or violence." In arrant violation of the Constitution, the resolution would accomplish what Obama has sought since his first days in office: speech suppression predicated on mob intimidation.

In parsing the provision, bear in mind that incitement to violence is already criminalized throughout the United States, and discrimination based on race, sex, age, ethnicity, religion, and sexual preference is outlawed by numerous federal and state laws and regulations. Resolution 16/18 has only one purpose: to render illegal speech that could cause Muslims to perceive hostility toward their belief system – under circumstances in which even those who hold Islam in disfavor are not trying to ban it, and where mere hostility (a) may not be prohibited under our law, (b) is a prudent and natural response to many provocations, and (c) ironically is to be subjected to an unprecedented ban for the benefit of Islam, the scriptures and laws of which are inherently hostile to non-Muslims, women, and homosexuals.

The resolution so starkly transgresses the First Amendment that its chief proponent, Hillary Clinton, had to be armed with a plan B – something even more breathtakingly repressive. At a meeting of the "Istanbul Process" she had confederated with OIC leaders, after the customary lip-service tribute to free expression (a "universal right at the core of our democracy"), she vowed that the Obama administration would "use some old-fashioned techniques of peer pressure and shaming, so that people don't feel that they have the support to do what we abhor." Translation: government-supported extortion tactics, the Constitution be damned.

Thus does sharia suppression of speech become just one more weapon in the left's indoctrination arsenal. It is a ceaseless jihad to convert our politics, the campus, the media, and the broader culture into "progressive" enclaves. In these no-go zones, nonconforming expression, dissent, and individual liberty are suffocated by speech codes (informal or, increasingly, codified), campaigns for social and academic "justice" (where the search for excellence and truth are subordinated to left-wing mythology and piety), the push for "net neutrality" (to strangle by regulation the conservative and libertarian voices that have thrived in the Internet's free market), economic boycotts (to cripple the corporate sponsorship of competing ideas), and campaign finance reform (to suppress political speech under the guise of anticorruption). The principal target is "hatred," a strategically vague term that can be invoked to ban anything the left opposes.

Shortly after the *"Je Suis Charlie"* signs and the sunshine patriots melted away, *Le Journal du Dimanche*, a weekly newspaper, released some poll results. Less than two weeks had elapsed since the slaughter and the lionizing of gadfly cartoonists as free-speech martyrs, yet 42 percent of French citizens opposed the publication of *Charlie Hebdo*'s cartoons. Echoing the political class, they agreed that action should be taken to avoid giving offense to Muslims.

By early February, a thousand protesters who were assembled by the Muslim Action Forum demonstrated outside the British Ministry of Defence in London. Under a sign warning Britons to "Be Careful With Muhammad," the leaders distributed leaflets that condemned the use of "freedom of speech" to "sow the seeds of hatred" and "damage community relations" by "provoking Muslims." The British government, whose leaders had joined the *Je Suis Charlie* rally just a month earlier, responded by … investigating citizens who purchased issues of *Charlie Hebdo* – in the interest of "enhancing public safety" and "assessing community tensions," of course.

Like the Obama administration, they know they are not Charlie. What they may not know is that their security depends on giving offense to radical Islam, the breed of Muslim that aims to conquer them.

JARED MEYER

HOW PROGRESSIVE CITIES FIGHT INNOVATION

This last year, 2017, was a big year for local preemption. States like Texas passed a host of bills to protect residents from overbearing local governments, including one that allowed Uber and Lyft to return to Austin. There are now forty-two states that stop local governments from applying antiquated regulations to force out emerging transportation services.

But there is more work to be done. Even though advances in technology open new ways for Americans to work and reduce the need for consumer protection regulations, Wisconsin and Tennessee are the only states with preemption bills preventing local occupational licensing. Furthermore, Arizona is still the only state that stops local governments from discriminating against short-term rental platforms like Airbnb and HomeAway.

America's Founding Fathers understood that local control rests ultimately with the individual, so true localism has to be about protecting workers and their families. For this reason, states have the right and ability to overrule municipal governments. With policy debates over autonomous vehicles, unmanned aerial vehicles, and next-generation wireless networks intensifying, the need will only grow for state governments to step in when local policies stand in the way of innovation and residents' ability to earn a living.

For good reason, millions of people who have taken an Uber, shopped on Etsy, found a professional's help on Thumbtack, or booked a place to stay through Airbnb love the sharing economy. These services, and countless others like eBay, TaskRabbit, Rent the Runway, and GoFundMe have a common theme – they connect people though online platforms. Often, the sharing economy enables transactions that used to be infeasible, time consuming, or cost prohibitive.

Others see the sharing economy as an enemy to be eliminated. It is true that the work done in the sharing economy does not look much like that of 1950s-era taxi drivers, artisans, repairmen, or hotel managers, but a twenty-first century economy cannot flourish under a decades-old policy framework. As technology continues to disrupt established business models, fights between innovators and special interests will only intensify.

Opponents of the sharing economy do not want to promote innovation; they want to protect themselves from change and competition. And political opponents refuse to understand that the fundamentally different businesses of the new economy require a modern regulatory model to thrive and fulfill their potentials. Instead of embracing these advances, these groups resist any change that threatens their short-term economic interests.

To fight back, it is critical to illuminate the new economy's benefits and reveal the motives and tactics of those who desperately want to kill it. Change is central to economic growth, and Americans should not remain quiet while policy makers limit innovation to protect the politically powerful.

The Twenty-First Century Economy

Before highlighting political opposition to the sharing economy, it is important to understand the recent economic developments that are behind the business models of companies like Uber and Airbnb.

Underpinning these changes is the economic concept of "transaction costs." Nobel Prize–winning economist Ronald Coase explains that transaction costs are what it takes to bring together buyers and sellers, exchange information, negotiate prices, and enforce contracts.

As the Competitive Enterprise Institute's Iain Murray argues, the sharing economy is made possible by the substantial lowering of transaction costs resulting from recent technological advances. Peer-to-peer interaction over the Internet gives consumers and providers of goods and services the ability to quickly connect with and gather information about others.

Across all sectors of the economy, technology creates entrepreneurial opportunities for anyone with productive resources to offer. These resources can be anything from physical or intellectual services (such as handyman jobs, academic tutoring, or legal advice) to the use of property (be it a drill, car, or spare room).

On one hand, the needs served by sharing-economy companies are nothing new. There have always been people who wanted to buy a hard-to-find product, find a place to stay, access cash, eat a home-cooked meal, find assistance on a task, or figure out a way to get around. The problem was finding someone who was willing to offer the desired goods or services at a reasonable price. Imagine what it would have been like if people went from door to door asking home owners if they had an extra room to rent and for how much. Now, travelers can simply log on to Airbnb and, with a few clicks, find a room that fits their needs and budgets. Similarly, hitchhiking – a primitive version of ride sharing – was never a very efficient way to find rides.

The expansion in commercially available goods comes from the ability to put what economists refer to as "dead capital" to use. Dead capital, as the term suggests, comprises underused property. Consider a table saw, which costs about $300. For most households, this tool is probably used only a few times a year. In the past, people who did not want to spend such a sum for a one-off project could try to borrow a saw. This might have worked, but not everyone's friends or neighbors had a table saw or were willing to rent or lend it. This is no longer a problem because today, for a fraction of the cost, people can go on sites like NeighborGoods and rent saws and countless other tools from those who already own them. The sharing economy is so effective because it drastically expands a person's social network.

Beyond increased access, information is one of the hallmarks of the sharing economy. The rise of the Internet and the proliferation of smartphones exponentially increases consumers' access to information. This gives consumers a level of power that they have never had before.

Consider the following change in market dynamics. Each business transaction has three distinct parts: the buying decision, which is controlled by consumers; the selling decision, which is controlled by businesses; and information about the product or service. In the past, this information was controlled, or at least greatly influenced, by businesses. But, as author Jim Blasingame explains, all that has changed in today's economy because information is now in the hands of consumers.

Online feedback systems show how the costs of finding

information have dropped dramatically. Web 2.0 – the generation of the web that introduced user interaction, sharing, and collaboration on sites – has led to a more consumer-friendly system. The sharing economy is just the natural extension of this, with its embrace of robust feedback systems.

Buyers frequently read reviews of products to see whether other customers were happy or unhappy with their experiences. These reviews can be produced by trusted organizations and professionals, or they can come from the vast online community of past users. Peer-to-peer online interactions are like word-of-mouth reviews – only online interactions can reach exponentially more people than word of mouth ever could.

Even with all these benefits, the sharing economy is much more than a consumers' paradise. Workers also enjoy new advantages from the changing nature of work.

Americans have already absorbed many of the values of the sharing economy – particularly entrepreneurship. Indeed, millennials have been called the "start-up generation." A Bentley University survey finds that two-thirds of millennials have a desire to start their own business. And a Deloitte report shows that about seven in ten millennials envision working independently at some point in their careers.

Entrepreneurship has long been the primary escape from the tethers of traditional employment. But starting a business entails great costs and risks – such as quitting a steady job or building a business during the gaps of time between work, sleep, and other activities.

The sharing economy offers many of the benefits of entrepreneurship to a broader population, with lower cost and decreased risk. Independent contractors are the driving force behind the sharing economy's growth. Working as an independent contractor allows people to choose their own hours, and online platforms can provide work opportunities that fulfill the demand for independent work.

It is still hard to start a business and work for oneself. But, before the rise of the sharing economy, growing that business was even more difficult. This was especially true for niche products that needed to reach a customer base spread all over the world. By catering to producers of niche products, online platforms like the craft shop Etsy help to create widely successful independent companies. EBay has provided a similar type of benefit to sellers since 1995. In other words, the sharing economy enables greater levels of entrepreneurship because it makes it easier for millions of Americans to work for themselves.

For the last decade, the American economy has been generating more jobs in which workers are self-employed and contract out with other companies to offer their services. While people working for companies such as Uber and Airbnb still account for a small percentage of the US labor force, the individualized work arrangements that the sharing economy embraces make up a much larger, and growing, share of the labor force.

Research led by the American Action Forum's Will Rinehart finds that independent contractors accounted for nearly one-third of the jobs created from 2010 to 2014. Additionally, data from Christopher Koopman and Eli Dourado of George Mason University's Mercatus Center show that the number of 1099-MISC tax forms issued by the IRS to independent contractors increased by nearly 25 percent from 2000 to 2014, demonstrating that the shift toward independent work preceded the founding of Airbnb (2008) and Uber (2009). On the other hand, the number of W-2s, the tax forms used by salaried employees, slightly decreased over that same time.

Though the sharing economy is often associated with urban-dwelling millennials, older Americans also benefit from more flexibility and accessibility. Renting out homes and apartments with Airbnb and VRBO, hosting meals through EatWith, or driving for Uber or Lyft are all viable options for seniors to earn extra income. And the increased, on-demand access to goods and services also greatly helps those with limited mobility.

The key to understanding the sharing economy is the realization that the real driving force behind these changes is not flashy smartphone apps but lower transaction costs. Lower transaction costs affect every aspect of the economy.

Rather than adapting to these changes and embracing new technology, many established interests choose to fight economic advancement with politics. This tactic has been used relentlessly by hotels, taxi cartels, and labor unions against two of the most innovative parts of the sharing economy – home sharing and ride sharing.

Some Cities Can't Handle Innovation

Cities like Nashville, Tennessee, should love short-term home-rental platforms like Airbnb. For one, the city is a tourism magnet that remains short of enough hotels to meet surging demand. This is why Nashville's downtown has the highest average nightly hotel rate in the United States – ahead of cities like San Francisco, New York City, and Boston.

More importantly, some residents struggle to keep up with the increasing costs of living caused by steady economic growth. Unfortunately, rather than craft laws that embrace innovation and make it easier for both residents and tourists, Nashville's government has placed arbitrary limits on short-term rentals.

In 2015, Nashville bowed to pressure from special interests in the hotel industry and organized labor by passing an ordinance that restricted residents' ability to rent out their homes. The ordinance mandated a 3 percent cap on the number of nonowner-occupied homes in a neighborhood that could receive a short-term rental permit.

Under these new requirements, many long-time Airbnb hosts were unable to secure a permit. One of the families, P.J. and Rachel Anderson, could not get a permit because their neighborhood had already reached the 3 percent cap. The Andersons, who were longtime Nashville residents and Airbnb hosts, had the chance to relocate temporarily for a work opportunity in the music industry, something that is common in Nashville. However, they would be unable to afford to do so unless they could rent out their home while they were away. To fight back against Nashville's limits on renting nonowner-occupied homes, the family teamed up with the nonprofit Beacon Center of Tennessee and sued the city to regain their right to use their property.

In October of 2016, Circuit Court judge Kelvin Jones ruled in favor of the Andersons, striking down parts of the ordinance. While this was a positive result for all home owners, Jones's ruling did not stop restrictive laws from coming out of Nashville in the future. The ordinance limiting the Andersons from renting out their home was overruled for its unconstitutional level of vagueness, as it was unclear whether the Andersons' home qualified "as a hotel, bed-and-breakfast, or boardinghouse, which are not considered short-term rentals." However, the 3 percent cap was ruled to be constitutional and would be allowed to stay in effect if the ordinance were clarified and rewritten.

Critics allege that Nashville is being taken over by outside investors who buy houses only to rent them out through online platforms. However, an overwhelming majority of Airbnb hosts rent out the house that they live in. These types of property limits affect far more groups of people than simply wealthy outside investors. The Andersons' story is a telling example of how this ill-conceived attempt to crack down on what the city considers "illegal hotels" harms Nashville residents.

Another complaint against Airbnb in Nashville has been that it creates "party houses" and "illegally parked cars" in residential areas. While there are undoubtedly some disrespectful Airbnb guests, there are also countless rude full-time neighbors. The enforcement mechanisms that are currently used to hold residents accountable for actions such as holding late-night parties and playing loud music could easily be applied to short-term rental guests. Nuisance laws are already on the books – lawmakers do not need to solve a problem that already has a solution.

Furthermore, Airbnb's presence in Nashville helps to address a serious problem. Nashville currently hands out millions of taxpayer dollars to incentivize hotel building due to its hotel shortage. In this climate, Nashville policy makers would be wise to embrace the opportunity Airbnb and other short-term rental platforms offer for providing accommodations for visitors to the city. Yet, to satisfy the demands of special interests, they instead limit this technology's potential. And things may get worse, as the city has consistently considered placing a complete moratorium on issuing short-term rental permits.

Even if Nashville policy makers do not improve their short-term rental policy, the state of Tennessee can solve the problem. In the 2017 legislative session, a bill was introduced to create a statewide regulatory system that resembles the sensible regulations passed late last year by the Memphis City Council. This preemption bill would prohibit local government from regulating homes that offer short-term rentals differently than homes that do not. This makes sense because if a local housing regulation is deemed necessary to protect the public or minimize nuisances, then it should apply to all housing–regardless of whether the home is rented out or not.

Arizona passed a law to this effect, SB 1350, that stops local governments from standing in the way of innovation when it comes to short-term rentals. Prior to the law's passage in Arizona, the areas of Jerome, Sedona, and Scottsdale had either banned short-term rentals or severely restricted them.

Florida is considering parallel legislation that would prohibit local governments from banning or restricting short-term rentals based solely on their "classification, use, or occupancy." This would be a win for Floridians, considering that there are currently dozens of local ordinances regulating short-term rentals. These regulations include fines of $10,000 a day, government inspections with only one hour's notice, exorbitant licensing fees, special utility and water assessments, excessively restrictive time frames for the use of private pools, and requirements for privacy and noise-buffering fences. As Florida senator Greg Steube, the sponsor of the state's preemption bill, says, "Local governments' goal is often to so heavily regulate short-term rentals that they are essentially prohibited."

Given what is happening across the country, it is difficult to argue with Steube's assessment. To show how these restrictions harmed Arizonans before the passage of the bill, Christina Sandefur and Timothy Sandefur of the Goldwater Institute tell the story of Glenn Odegard, an Arizona resident who bought a hundred-year-old house in Jerome, a struggling mountain town. As they write:

Glenn tried to contribute to that restoration by resuscitating a home that had been abandoned and left vacant for 60 years after a landslide filled it with rocks and mud. Intending to offer it as a vacation rental, Glenn lovingly restored the dilapidated house to its original historic condition. His successful efforts earned the home a feature in Arizona Highways *Magazine and a spot on the Jerome Historic Home and Building Tour. Yet despite issuing the relevant permits and initially embracing Glenn's home renovation, town officials decreed he could no longer use the home as a vacation rental. Under the town's newly announced ban, Glenn and other home owners face fines of $300 and up to 90 days in jail for each day they allow paying guests to stay. His "reward" for the investment of his time, money, and labor was to be considered an outlaw.*

A bill like Arizona's is likely necessary in Tennessee since the state's problems extend far beyond Nashville – Chattanooga inexplicably bans all short-term rentals in residential areas.

Nashville's history with short-term rentals makes it clear that state lawmakers should take this decision out of the City Council's hands. There is no reason for policy makers to be afraid to rein in cities that limit the economic opportunity that comes from technological progress.

Tennessee is not the only state that needs to protect property owners' rights. Just consider the conclusion that "there is no one-size-fits-all answer for municipalities in regulating short-term rentals" in the Colorado Municipal League's November 2016 report on short-term rental regulations. While this may be true, cities across Colorado show that there are countless misguided approaches to regulating the growing home-sharing industry.

On January 1, 2017, new regulations meant to limit

short-term rentals in Denver went into effect. These restrictions, pushed by the hotel industry, represent unnecessary impediments to residents renting out their homes for some extra money.

The most problematic of Denver's rules is one that states that home owners are only allowed to rent out their primary residences. Even though most Airbnb hosts do rent out their primary residences, second homes are nonetheless an important part of the short-term rental industry. Second homes can comprise everything from vacation homes to long-time family homes that owners do not want to sell when work opportunities lead them to another city for a few years.

The second-most-active city in Colorado for Airbnb is Boulder, and Boulder County at large has certainly seen a major increase in growth as a result of Airbnb. Six of seven communities in Boulder County about doubled their number of annual Airbnb guests from 2015 to 2016. This is great news for Boulder County. Airbnb guests tend to stay more than twice as long and spend almost twice as much money in the community as other visitors. Airbnb's wide footprint in diverse neighborhoods also distributes travel income outside of traditional hotel districts.

One would expect cities to embrace this direct infusion of tourist dollars into the local economy, but Boulder has instituted similar regulations to Denver. The city requires hosts to rent out only their primary residence, and pay a hefty licensing fee and business taxes for doing so. Boulder also sets an occupancy limit of either three or four "unrelated persons."

Regulators are often at their worst when they get creative, and Durango's short-term rental restrictions are an example of this. The city's self-described "innovative policy solution" that "seek[s] to maintain neighborhood character, vitality, and vibrancy" is arguably the worst set of home-sharing regulations in the state.

Durango imposes strict restrictions on the terms by which people can participate in this sector of the sharing economy. The city only allows short-term rentals in limited areas, and then caps the number that are available per block at one. In other words, it only takes one neighbor already having a short-term rental permit for Durango to not allow another family to rent out their home. All in all, Durango offers only sixty permits for short-term rentals for a town with eight thousand housing units. This nonsensical cap effectively shuts Airbnb and short-term rentals in general out of Durango.

In a state with such a vibrant and important tourism industry, Colorado's cities are constantly thinking of new "innovative" ways to partner with special industries. Instead of competing to see which city has the worst short-term rental policy, cities should welcome an industry that provides extra income to home owners, reduces prices for consumers, and boosts the economy of the region.

Colorado and Tennessee are not alone. Across the country, policy makers in everything from small tourist towns to America's largest cities have placed severe restrictions on short-term rentals. Opponents of home sharing focus on the local level, where city council members are more likely to fall for their flawed arguments. There is no denying that opponents have had high levels of success. If the cities continue to refuse to accept innovation, then state governments have a responsibility to follow Arizona's lead by stepping in and fighting back against special interests.

"The Rent Is Too Damn High"

In October 2016, New York passed a bill that creates civil penalties of up to $7,500 for advertising a whole apartment that is for rent for less than thirty days. This means that people going on a weekend getaway or staying with their significant other across town face thousands of dollars in fines for listing their place on Airbnb.

The justification for this bill was that Airbnb and other online short-term rental platforms drive up rents in New York City. This claim would be laughable if policy makers did not take it seriously – it is now the main argument used against short-term rentals.

First, there is no way that an online platform that did not launch until 2008 can be blamed for the city's decades-long struggle with high rents. How exactly is it possible that Airbnb could have been squeezing housing options for New Yorkers before its creation? The short answer is that it was not. In a classic case of government dishonesty, politicians blame problems created by years of government overreach on the new guy in town.

In an attempt to validate their war against short-term rentals, city leaders portray home sharing as a net loss of forty-one thousand housing opportunities (the number of active Airbnb nightly listings in the city) for locals. They claim that wealthy Airbnb users set up so-called illegal hotels and turn entire apartment complexes into unregulated temporary residences. This paints a dark picture of home sharing. After all, what could possibly be a better narrative for proudly progressive mayor Bill de Blasio than the rich cutting corners at the expense of the poor?

The numbers quickly make this narrative fall apart. Airbnb's forty-one thousand active nightly listings in New

York City come out to just over 1 percent of the city's three million housing units. Additionally, in New York City, 90 percent of Airbnb posts are for residents' permanent homes. There is no way that taking a maximum of 0.1 percent of New York City's residential units off the market by using them exclusively for short-term rentals is what drives rent increases. This is especially true considering that the city has 110,000 hotel rooms. These numbers should make people question the sudden concerns over access to affordable housing from prominent leaders in the hotel industry.

The real reason for higher rents is a combination of a lot of people wanting to live in New York and an insufficient amount of housing supply to meet this demand. High levels of regulations that limit development are a major contributor to the lack of housing supply.

Land use regulations prevent denser construction and building more units in existing buildings. Construction and zoning regulations have drastically increased in scale and scope. They are now so overreaching that 40 percent of the existing buildings in Manhattan would not be able to be built today. With a high level of restrictions on how builders can meet the demand for housing, it is no wonder that New York City property is so expensive.

Simply put, living in Manhattan will always be more expensive than living in rural Oklahoma. Furthermore, there is no way to combat the housing affordability crisis without expanding the supply of housing. It is not Airbnb that causes high rents but politicians.

If anything, Airbnb is an asset to the middle class. The average Airbnb host in New York City makes about $5,500 a year from the service, money that 76 percent of users say helps them stay in their homes or apartments.

The claim that Airbnb is to blame for high rents is also

common across cities in California. Here again, housing shortages in San Francisco and Los Angeles were instead caused and perpetuated by city governments' unwillingness to increase the housing supply.

Since the 1960s, the residential construction rate in California has significantly declined and, as a result, real housing prices increased by 385 percent from 1970 to 2010. Though limits on new construction are not the sole cause for increasing housing prices, they are a major factor.

The least-affordable housing markets are those where new housing permits have not kept up with population growth. For example, in Los Angeles, there were twenty-eight thousand housing projects started in 2014. Meanwhile, Houston, a city with no housing shortage and 1.7 million fewer people than Los Angeles, started sixty-four thousand housing projects in 2014. The lack of housing in Los Angeles is not due to overcrowding – the city has . roughly eight thousand people per square mile, which is one-third of New York City's level.

In Los Angeles, home owners spend an average of 40 percent of their income on mortgage payments, while San Francisco residents spend an average of 48 percent on them. Airbnb provides an opportunity for these home owners to meet their mortgage obligations by helping them rent out spare rooms.

San Francisco, where rents for a one-bedroom apartment frequently exceed $4,000 per month, has the most serious housing shortage in America. Over the past twenty years, San Francisco has only permitted the annual construction of an average of 1,500 housing units. Over that time, San Francisco's population grew by ninety-seven thousand, and growth has been stronger in recent years.

A study by the real estate firm Trulia finds that San Francisco had the highest median rental prices per square foot and the lowest rate of new construction permits among America's ten largest tech hubs. A reason for this is that nearly 80 percent of San Francisco's housing is occupied by rent-controlled tenants or home owners. This leaves only one in five housing units available for other renters, artificially driving up rents.

Additionally, the booming, high-salary tech industry represents about 8 percent of the workforce in San Francisco, putting further upward pressure on the price of housing in an already-overburdened market. This is why some people blame tech workers for the city's housing shortage. One proposed solution is for tech companies such as Google to create more housing for employees on company property. Although this seems to be logical, the city of San Francisco explicitly forbids it.

San Francisco, unlike many other major US cities, has building permits that are discretionary rather than as-of-right. This standard makes it more difficult to gain approval for development because of the numerous legal challenges that it invites. For new housing developments in San Francisco, there is a preliminary review, which takes six months. Then there is a chance that neighbors will appeal the permit on either entitlement or environmental bases. These barriers add unpredictable costs and years of delays for developers, the financial responsibility for which is ultimately passed on to buyers and renters.

It is easy for politicians to blame corporations for problems that are ultimately their own responsibility. This is precisely what California senator Dianne Feinstein has done. In October 2015, she published an Article In the *San Francisco Chronicle* arguing in favor of the city's Proposition F, which would have limited short-term rentals in San Francisco to seventy-five days a year.

According to Feinstein, this ballot initiative would have

helped to alleviate the city's housing shortage. Predictably, Feinstein did not mention the lack of housing permits in cities across her state. It is also important to note that she and her husband have a stake in a San Francisco hotel that is worth up to $25 million. Proposition F was soundly defeated at the ballot box, but city leaders quickly moved to create other restrictions on short-term rentals.

Ironically, Airbnb might owe its existence to San Francisco's housing shortage. In 2007, the city did not have enough hotel capacity to house visitors for an industrial design conference, so Airbnb's founders Brian Chesky and Joe Gebbia decided to start a company to fix this problem.

Another tactic taken by hotel unions, such as the AFL-CIO–affiliated New York Hotel and Motel Trade Council, is to claim that Airbnb threatens "good-paying union hotel jobs in New York City and around the country." Despite the union's claim that hotels across the nation will suffer, the data indicates the overall hotel industry is managing quite fine even with the growth of home sharing. According to STR, a leading company in hotel market research, the hotel industry just had its best year on record. Hotels and home sharing can thrive together because companies like Airbnb expand the proverbial pie of lodging options. Both models offer different experiences, levels of convenience, and price points.

Airbnb helps to relieve some of the symptoms of high rents and housing shortages by giving people some help with their existing rents or mortgages. The claim that Airbnb is the reason for higher costs of housing is demonstrably false. Instead of placing blame on Airbnb for housing shortages, politicians should embrace the service and evaluate their regressive restrictions on new housing development.

Jared Meyer

A Tech Capital without Uber

Austin is home to the University of Texas at Austin, countless start-ups, and the widely popular South by Southwest festival. But even though the city is commonly referred to as the tech capital of the South and has a reputation as a millennial paradise, Uber and Lyft ceased operations there in May of 2016. Austin is the largest city in the United States without Uber or Lyft.

Local policy makers blame Uber and Lyft for leaving the city, but the Austin City Council pushed out ride sharing by regulating in search of a problem. Austin's case of regulatory overreach shows how even the country's most progressive cities are often hostile to economic progress.

In December of 2015, the Austin City Council approved an ordinance to require ride-sharing drivers to go through fingerprint background checks. Rather than altering their business models, Uber and Lyft took their protests to the voters by setting up a ballot challenge to the ordinance called Proposition 1. The proposition failed, and the companies ended their service in the city.

Complying with fingerprinting requirements would not have increased public safety. But doing so would have made it more difficult for ride-sharing companies to quickly and equitably provide work opportunities as they grew to meet ever-increasing consumer demand. Even though fingerprint background checks may sound like they increase security, they are unnecessary, ineffective, and discriminatory when used for job screening instead of for law enforcement.

Uber and Lyft both use name-based background checks instead of government fingerprinting. The companies' safety record shows that this approach works. Indeed, a comprehensive review of these name-based background checks by the Maryland Public Service Commission finds that the companies' checks are just as "comprehensive and accurate" as government fingerprint background checks. This review came after the state passed a law in 2015 that would have required fingerprinting for all ride-sharing drivers if the commission reached the opposite conclusion.

Policy makers who insist on fingerprint background checks must be watching too much *CSI*. These checks are far from the foolproof tool that they are portrayed as on TV. As the Cato Institute's Matthew Feeney argues, "Fingerprinting is not as effective as Hollywood might have you believe. The FBI fingerprint database is incomplete, in part because it relies on police departments and other local sources adding relevant data and keeping that data updated."

In other words, fingerprint background checks are only as effective as the databases of fingerprints that they pull from. In Maryland, certain traffic violations – including DUIs and reckless-driving incidents – would not show up through fingerprint background checks. Name-based background checks avoid this failure by querying thousands of courthouse and law enforcement databases to find relevant records.

Fingerprint databases also include arrests that did not lead to any convictions. If someone is arrested and fingerprinted but then found not guilty or never charged with a crime, that information would need to be updated by law enforcement for fingerprint background checks to be effective. Yet this follow-up step is often overlooked, which leads to discriminatory results.

Law enforcement personnel do not have the time to keep these records updated because fingerprint databases were designed to aid in solving crime – not vetting for-hire vehicle drivers. Since about one in three felony arrests end up with no conviction, fingerprinting leads to many qualified drivers without criminal convictions being denied work opportunities. The Urban League, NAACP, and National Black Caucus of State Legislators all oppose fingerprinting requirements for this reason.

Fixing these errors is difficult. University of Maryland professor Michael Pinard testified at a public hearing about the requirements that it would be "difficult if not impossible" for people without law degrees to challenge the faulty results from a fingerprint background check.

The most troubling result of Austin's ride-sharing regulations is not that two successful start-up companies will lose revenue by pausing their operations in the city – it is the new problems and dangers posed to Austin residents.

No background checks are perfect, but ride sharing's safety record shows that the companies' current policies are working well. The safety standards that Uber and Lyft voluntarily hold themselves to are even stricter than those required of Austin taxis. In addition to providing safer transportation than taxis do, ride sharing's business model makes it very easy to police drivers. The locations of both parties are tracked through the duration of the trips, identities are verified, and no cash changes hands because of the platform's electronic payment systems. In other words, if drivers commit crimes while working for Uber or Lyft, they must be doing so because they want to get caught.

When evaluating the potential risks of new technologies, it is important to weigh them against the real dangers posed by the status quo. For example, New York City's police commissioner, Bill Bratton, told women to use the "buddy system" when riding in the city's taxis. This is because taxi drivers are a leading perpetrator of sexual assaults by strangers, with fourteen women being raped by New York City taxi drivers in 2015. There will undoubtedly be isolated cases of bad behavior by ride-sharing drivers, but the built-in safeguards make it much easier to hold bad actors accountable, which discourages dangerous conduct.

Rather than increasing public safety by mandating fingerprint background checks, Austin policy makers are placing their constituents at greater risk. Perhaps nowhere is this unintended consequence clearer than with drunk driving. Ride sharing has been documented to lower both drunk-driving arrests and fatal accidents, partly because taxis are difficult to find late at night. In Austin – a city with the highest number of downtown bars per capita in the United States – the number of available taxis drops at midnight. This is when alcohol-related crashes and DUI arrests are at their highest levels. It should therefore come as no surprise that Mothers Against Drunk Driving is a major proponent of ride sharing as an additional reliable source of transportation.

Furthermore, as Austin resident and Texas Public Policy Foundation senior fellow John Daniel Davidson has chronicled, getting around the city has become much more challenging. During University of Texas football games, the city's many music festivals, or just regular Saturday nights, the streets are chaotic. Even though there are new ride-sharing services that require fingerprinting for their drivers, these applications are often unreliable and getting a ride is very difficult during times of high demand. And, of course, public transit options in the city remain terribly inadequate.

In addition to unfounded public safety concerns, one of Austin's main justifications for fingerprinting Uber and Lyft drivers was that the city's taxi drivers were required to go through the same process. The new regulations were nothing more than a way to harmonize regulations between all forms of for-hire vehicles, according to proponents of further regulation.

Massachusetts senator Elizabeth Warren made such a claim in a speech at the New America Foundation, asserting that Uber is "[fighting] against local rules designed to create a level playing field between themselves and their taxi competitors."

But there are two ways to level the playing field. One is to apply antiquated regulatory requirements to new technologies, as Austin did. The far-superior option is to embrace innovation by getting rid of pointless requirements that tend to protect established businesses rather than consumers, such as taxi permits that limit the supply of available cabs or ineffective and discriminatory fingerprinting requirements.

Taxis in Austin are still required to get a government permit to operate. But the city, which has a population of nearly nine hundred thousand people, only issues 915 taxi permits in total. Furthermore, these permits are owned by just a handful of companies.

Until Uber and Lyft came along, all these barriers to entry led to a lack of competitive pressures – and customer service in the taxi industry noticeably suffered. Competition allows companies to differentiate themselves through the type, price, and quality of services they offer. Rigid regulations that dictate the means transportation companies can use to meet customers' needs create a one-size-fits-all standard.

To help taxis better compete against their ride-sharing competitors, local policy makers should focus on cutting the red tape so that taxis can become more like Ubers – not the other way around. As Michael Farren of the Mercatus Center argues, if policy makers must apply regulation to new business models such as ride sharing, a better way forward would be to specify certain areas of concern (such as prescreening for quality and safety, or clarity in pricing) but then leave companies free to figure out how to meet these requirements.

Texas is not the only state where the fingerprint background check debate has left people without ride sharing. Cities in upstate New York are facing the same fight.

This is surprising given what Governor Andrew Cuomo had to say about ride sharing. Back in July 2015, the governor asserted, "Uber is one of these great inventions, startups, of this new economy and it's taking off like fire to dry grass and it's giving people jobs. I don't think the government should be in the business of trying to restrict job growth."

Two years later, New York's government still does not allow ride-sharing services to operate in upstate New York. This inability to adapt to new business models leaves millions of New Yorkers with fewer transportation options and work opportunities.

Besides Austin, Buffalo is the largest US city without Uber or Lyft. Buffalo's poverty rate of 31 percent is nearly two-and-a-half times greater than the average rate in the United States. The city's five-year labor force participation rate, which measures people who are working or looking for work, stands at 59 percent, far below the average US rate. These are all problems that could be addressed with more work opportunities, which Uber and Lyft would provide.

And Rochester, another major city in New York that does not have ride sharing, has likewise paid the price for this choice economically. The city, though it is known for its colleges and universities, has one-third of its residents living in poverty.

Just how much economic activity are these New York

cities missing out on by not having ride sharing? In November 2015, Uber estimated that the company would create an additional thirteen thousand jobs if the company expanded to all of New York. If anything, this job-creation estimate is too low; Uber has thirty thousand active drivers in Pennsylvania, a state with a similar population to that of New York when excluding New York City, the only area of the state where Uber and Lyft operate.

A February 2017 study by Land Econ Group finds that if Lyft started operating in Buffalo and Rochester in 2014, local drivers could have earned over $18 million from partnering with the company in 2017. The projection is based on the number of observed rides in cities with comparable populations, incomes, and densities. This is real income that would have helped those struggling to make ends meet in the sluggish upstate New York economy.

It is true that most new ride-sharing jobs would be part time. Half of Uber drivers work on the platform for under ten hours a week and 80 percent of Lyft drivers work on the platform for under twenty hours. Some critics of ride sharing's business model worry about part-time work, but flexible work is a feature of ride sharing – not a bug.

Because drivers set their own schedules and use their own cars, a wide array of people benefit. From single parents and full-time drivers to college students and retirees, virtually anyone can earn additional income by partnering with ride-sharing companies. This is why nearly all Uber and Lyft drivers cite flexibility as the main benefit of contracting with the companies.

New Yorkers realize these diverse benefits even if some of their elected representatives do not. A 2016 Siena College poll finds that "at least two-thirds of voters from every [New York] region and every [political] party support legislation to allow ride-sharing companies such as Uber to operate in their areas." Overall, support for legalized ride sharing was at 80 percent at the time of the poll.

In 2017, there is no excuse for major cities to leave their residents without the work opportunities and transportation options that ride sharing provides. At least thirty-seven states currently have statewide regulatory frameworks that allow ride-sharing services. While some of these frameworks are far from ideal, at least they allow ride sharing's business model to continue to operate and develop. Of course, New York and Texas are two of the states that do not have such a framework.

As the experiences of hundreds of other cities throughout the world show, ride sharing is a safe and affordable addition to a city's transportation infrastructure. Yet, some big-city mayors see the service as an affront to their progressive values. But how can companies that provide thousands of residents with jobs, increase access to transportation options (especially in underserved areas), and lower prices possibly be anything but progressive? Where the regressive policy option is to regulate ride sharing out of existence, the progressive choice is for city leaders to resist the urge to overregulate and instead embrace services that improve the lives of their residents.

Unions Can't Stand the Sharing Economy

Seattle may have allowed unions to negotiate away an entire profession when, in December 2015, the Seattle City Council voted to extend collective-bargaining rights to certain independent contractors, including those who partner with ride-sharing platforms such as Uber and Lyft. This move was the first of its kind, because federal labor law only allows employees to collectively bargain, which means having an organization negotiate pay structures and working conditions for an entire class of workers.

If successful, Seattle's collective-bargaining process will silence the opinions of drivers who may not have chosen to be in a union but will be forced to join one anyway. And once Seattle's model spreads to other cities, collective bargaining will mean many of the sharing economy's benefits will cease to exist.

The outdated union model is antithetical to the flexible, entrepreneurial workplace that many Americans – especially millennials – desire. Ride sharing is a popular work opportunity for a multitude of reasons that collective bargaining will likely limit. If the vote is successful, all drivers who want to keep working will be forced to join a union and follow the collectively bargained agreement.

Under union representation, new workers are often the first to be fired, even when they perform better than those who have more experience. Would a union defend bad drivers who had their Internet accounts deactivated because of negative reviews? Post-ride, dual-feedback systems are major factors behind ride sharing's increased levels of customer service and trust. If partnerships with unqualified drivers cannot be terminated, riders will be less safe and the incentive for drivers to offer a pleasant riding experience will be reduced.

The other union norm of maximum or minimum work hours would take away drivers' freedom to work as much or as little as they desire. For example, some drivers prefer to drive early in the morning on weekdays to avoid traffic and get lucrative airport trips. Others work during bar closing times to take advantage of the higher fares that come with the increased demand. The scheduling put in place by unions would likely favor full-time, established drivers and take away the diverse benefits that the ride-sharing model provides. Predetermined driving schedules that cannot adjust to demand would also lead to drivers idling, unable to find fares, and riders waiting on the side of the road, unable to find available cars.

There is no indication of what the costs of belonging to a union will be if collective bargaining is successful. But there is reason to worry that some part-time or seasonal drivers will lose money during the time periods that they do not drive because they still must pay the union. For example, some college students and teachers only drive during summer vacation. There is no reason that they should have to pay dues and lose money when they are not actively driving.

There is also no guarantee that the initiation fees and dues will be the same for all for-hire vehicle companies. One could imagine a situation where it costs much more to drive with Lyft than with Uber or a taxi company. This imbalance could give a lot of power to the companies with the lowest union fees, which could lead to fewer options for both riders and drivers.

Drivers are very sensitive to increases in barriers to starting work. One of the main benefits of the ride-sharing model is that there are low start-up costs. Every added cost or delay, whether fingerprint background checks or union initiation fees, makes it less likely that people will begin partnering with ride-sharing companies. The effects will be even worse for drivers who utilize multiple platforms and thus would have to pay multiple sets of dues. This practice is common, as more than 40 percent of Lyft drivers also drive with other platforms.

The National Labor Relations Act, passed in 1935, established the right to collectively bargain for all employees. This right does not apply to the independent contractors who make up the sharing economy. Independent contractors are free to join groups such as the Freelancers Union or the App-Based Drivers Association to gain access to benefits and career-development resources, but they cannot collectively bargain.

Excluding independent contractors from collective bargaining makes sense. Even people who only work with one company do not all have the same priorities regarding work arrangements. Those who use Uber for supplemental income and part-time work have vastly different concerns than those who treat the service as a full-time job. Under collective bargaining, which group's interests will the union represent? Majority rule could take away one of the cornerstones of the sharing economy: the diverse benefits that come from flexible, individualized work opportunities.

The total flexibility is what makes working in the sharing economy so desirable in the first place. The ability to quickly increase earnings to meet rent, pay down student loans, or fund a new business venture benefits people every day. This "income smoothing" is especially critical for young people and the poor, groups whose earnings often fluctuate wildly. Some 70 percent of Americans between the ages of eighteen and twenty-four, and 74 percent of those in the bottom income quintile, experience an average of 30 percent or more in income changes from month to month, according to the JPMorgan Chase Institute. Ride sharing's flexible work model empowers people with diverse priorities to help themselves and those counting on them.

Troublingly, because Seattle's rules require unions to negotiate in areas such as drivers' earnings, terminations, and hours, collective bargaining in the city could eventually lead to courts deeming drivers to be employees instead of independent contractors. The more control unions force the companies to have over drivers, the more likely this scenario becomes.

This is not what drivers want. An independent survey of 3,100 Lyft drivers finds that 82 percent of respondents agreed or strongly agreed with the statement "I like being an independent contractor." Since flexibility is one of the main benefits of the ride-sharing model, it is not surprising that 99 percent of Lyft drivers agreed that with the statement "I like to choose when I work."

Uber drivers share the same sentiment. When six hundred Uber drivers were asked the question "If both were available to you, at this point in your life, would you rather have a steady 9-to-5 job with some benefits and a set salary or a job where you choose your own schedule and be your own boss?" 73 percent said that they prefer flexibility over the traditional employment model. Opponents in organized labor fail to realize that the flexibility of being an independent contractor is vital to the sharing economy's success.

Union opposition to the sharing economy is widespread, and it extends beyond Uber and Lyft. The International Brotherhood of Teamsters explains its perception of the effects of the sharing economy in its newsletter, writing, "[Sharing-economy] companies are simply recycling old ideas and taking us backwards to a time when workers had no rights on the job." The Teamsters' complaints do not stop there, as the newsletter also warns, "Don't let the term 'sharing economy' fool you. There is no sharing. It's really just the one percent making money by stripping workers of the rights for which the labor movement has fought so hard to secure."

It is unsurprising that union advocates lament the sharing economy on the basis of reducing union membership. Naturally, union advocates seek to prevent work that

falls outside the realm of a typical union job. The 1950s
steel worker had his job protected and enhanced by a union,
so the 2017 Uber or Lyft driver must supposedly conform to
union association as well, according to their arguments.

In February 2016, the AFL-CIO, America's largest labor
union, released a statement that made clear how its leadership views sharing-economy workers – as a potential boon to
union member rolls. "Making the right policy choices begins
with ensuring people who work for on-demand companies
enjoy the rights and protections of employees," the statement reads. "The AFL-CIO is committed to ensuring new
technology – and new forms of employer manipulation – do
not erode the rights of working people. Rest assured that if
employers get away with pretending their workers aren't
employees, your job could be next."

Unions are desperate because worker preference and
demographics are working against them. Today, only 11 percent of American workers (6 percent in the private sector)
belong to unions. Unions have exerted power beyond
their small numbers due to their outsize campaign contributions, practically all to Democratic politicians. To keep
the flow of contributions and their power, and to prop up
their underfunded pension plans, unions need more dues-
paying members. Yet fewer Americans, particularly
younger workers, are joining unions.

Labor Department data show that 14 percent of workers between the ages of forty-five and sixty-four belong to
unions, compared with 10 percent of twenty-five-to-thirty-four-
year-old workers, and a historically low 4 percent of those
aged sixteen to twenty-four. Most millennials may be
prounion in theory, but when it comes to parting with a
portion of their paychecks, few are willing to support
unions in practice.

Labor unions have lost sight of the reality that to

remain viable they must meet young workers' needs. Instead, their focus is to satisfy the demands of union bosses and retirees, as evidenced by bloated union-leader salaries and unsustainable pension promises.

Of course, to unions, it does not matter whether workers even desire collective-bargaining agreements that erode their independence and flexibility. This type of opposition to independent work on the part of unions is epitomized by Robert Reich, who has called the sharing economy a "fraud" that "should be called the 'share-the-scraps economy.'" Reich, professor of public policy at University of California Berkeley and former secretary of labor under President Clinton, maintains that the sharing economy is "a reversion to the piece work of the nineteenth century – when workers had no power and no legal rights, took all the risks, and worked all hours for almost nothing."

But who is Reich to decide that the millions of Americans who have voluntarily partnered with a sharing-economy company are being ripped off? Though he is not an economist by training, he should be familiar with the economic concept of "revealed preference." People choose to partner with sharing-economy companies because, in their view, doing so is the most desirable option available to them. To make this more difficult for them to do is to essentially say, "I do not care if you enjoy driving with Uber as an independent contractor; I disapprove of your decision and will not allow it."

Instead of obsessing over trying to revive the post–World War II era of high unionization rates, politicians should embrace the emerging flexible workplace. Besides the benefits that the sharing economy offers to workers, consumers, and the economy, it is in lawmakers' political interest not to intervene in the new economy's ascent.

The Politics of the Sharing Economy

Back in 2013, at the Eighty-First United States Conference of Mayors, a bipartisan group of nine mayors from major US cities released a resolution urging "support for making cities more shareable."

Additionally, a June 2015 National League of Cities survey of 245 elected officials found that over 7 in 10 were supportive of the sharing economy, and not just because of the work opportunities it creates. The most popular response when leaders were asked to name the biggest benefit was "improved services."

Despite this past optimism and positive rhetoric, excessive regulatory barriers or outright bans still plague the sharing economy in certain cities because small, concentrated interests use the political process to receive special treatment. This problem is especially pronounced on the local level, where hotel owners, taxi cartels, and labor unions have their highest levels of influence.

In the long term, opposition to Uber, Airbnb, and the rest of the sharing economy is a losing political strategy, as Americans for Tax Reform's John Kartch argues. The Pew Research Center finds that potential young voters (ages eighteen to twenty-nine) are nearly five times more likely to use ride sharing than Americans who are at least fifty years old. Pew's research also shows that Americans of all ages and political leanings overwhelmingly reject the idea of applying the same regulations that hamper legacy industries to new services like ride sharing.

Furthermore, a Reason Foundation poll finds that only 18 percent of millennials have faith in government regulators to have the public's best interests in mind. It takes a lot to get young people to vote, but if policy makers get between millennials and their Ubers or Airbnbs, there will be major consequences at the polls in the future. As these services continue to expand, the political costs of opposing the sharing economy will only grow.

In financial and energy industries, regulations' negative consequences are far from clear to consumers. For example, most people do not know how much specific EPA regulations will increase the cost of charging a smartphone. Similarly, the effects of Dodd-Frank's financial regulations are far from clear when someone sends money on Venmo or applies for a mortgage through an app. But with Uber and Airbnb, the negative effects of government intervention are crystal clear – higher prices, fewer options, and reduced earnings opportunities.

Young Americans rightly realize that many regulations do little more than protect established interests. Furthermore, following in the footsteps of their parents and grandparents, millennials appreciate the value of entrepreneurship. The majority of young Americans hope to work for themselves in the future – a goal that the sharing economy can help realize.

Though fights over Uber and Airbnb regulations often make the news, it is important to realize that the same trends that enabled these companies' business models will transform more than vehicle transportation and short-term lodging. Technology is going to continue making the workforce and marketplace more flexible, individualized, and mobile. Americans are entrepreneurial by nature, and innovations that make it easier for people to work for themselves while providing more options to consumers should be welcomed by policy makers.

The essence of the sharing economy is consumer empowerment, and increased connectivity has transformed the relationship between consumers and service providers for the better. The world we live in today is one that prizes accessibility and convenience. It is a world that has taken power from large corporations and multinational suppliers and given it to consumers through the widespread availability of information.

Yet, in the face of these benefits, fearful regulators in cities across America continually claim that consumers are hurt by the trust they have rightly placed in the new business models that characterize the sharing economy. Rather than keeping consumers safe, local regulators now threaten the growth of the peer-to-peer system that has proven to be the most effective way to increase consumers' access to information.

As the economic trends that drive the sharing economy expand their reach into more and more industries, regulators will surely continue to find themselves in uncharted territory, and their decisions will have major effects on the level of economic growth. When these regulators encounter new business models, they need to keep in mind that the technological progress behind the sharing economy is a positive development. The sharing economy is driven by lower transaction costs, and waging a war on lower transaction costs is the definition of fighting progress.

If mayors and city councils across the United States continue to oppose the sharing economy, state policy makers have a responsibility to stand up for innovation. This may require overruling cities when local policies threaten the development of the new economy. Truly progressive thinking means not standing in the way of clear innovation and widely shared growth. If cities are going to remain a driving force for economic progress, then states need to save cities from themselves.

JAMES PIERESON

WHY REDISTRIBUTION FAILS

Whenever tax reform is a major topic of national discussion, the intertwined issues of income redistribution and inequality are usually part of the conversation. It is an article of faith among progressives that the federal tax-and-spending system is an effective means of redistributing income from the wealthy to the poor and near poor. Democratic presidential candidates from George McGovern to Hillary Clinton have hammered away at this issue for decades despite a lack of convincing evidence that the federal government is even capable of redistributing income and thereby reducing income inequality. As Congress once again tackles the perennial issue of tax reform, sensible efforts to reduce tax rates with the goal of promoting economic growth will inevitably encounter opposition from those calling for placing higher rates on corporations and the wealthy as instruments for the redistribution of wealth.

HILLARY CLINTON launched her presidential campaign in spring 2015 by venturing from New York to Iowa to rail against income inequality and to propose new spending programs and higher taxes on the wealthy as remedies for it. She re-emphasized these dual themes of inequality and redistribution in the "relaunch" of her campaign in June 2015 and in the occasional campaign speeches she delivered over the course of the summer.

Clinton's campaign strategy has been interpreted as a concession to influential progressive spokesmen like Senators Elizabeth Warren and Bernie Sanders, who have loudly pressed these redistributionist themes for several years, in response to the financial meltdown in 2008 and out of a long-standing wish to reverse the "Reagan Revolution" of the 1980s. In view of Clinton's embrace of the progressive agenda, there can be little doubt that inequality, higher taxes, and proposals for new spending programs will be central themes in the Democratic presidential campaign in 2016.

The intellectual case for redistribution has been outlined in impressive detail in recent years by a phalanx of progressive economists – including Thomas Piketty, Joseph Stiglitz, and *New York Times* opinion columnist Paul Krugman – who have called for redistributive tax and spending policies to address the challenge of the growth of inequalities in income and wealth. Piketty's best-selling book, *Capital in the Twenty-First Century* (2014), made a case for raising the top marginal tax rate in the United States from 39.6 percent (where it stands today) to 80 percent or more (where it was during the 1940s and 1950s), and then relying upon the U.S. government to redistribute those funds from the wealthy to households in greater need of them. Nobel Laureate Robert Solow of MIT put the matter bluntly in a 2014 exchange with Harvard's N. Gregory Mankiw, saying that he is in favor of dealing with inequality by "taking a dollar from a random rich person and giving it to a random poor person," presumably with the federal government acting as the middleman to implement the transaction.

Public-opinion polls over the years have consistently shown that voters overwhelmingly reject programs of redistribution in favor of policies designed to promote overall economic growth and job creation. More-recent polls suggest that while voters are increasingly concerned about inequality and question the high salaries paid to executives and bankers, they nevertheless reject redistributive remedies like higher taxes on the wealthy. According to those studies, voters do not support redistributive policies because they do not believe the government is capable of implementing them in effective ways. While voters are worried about inequality, they are far more skeptical of the capacity of the government to do anything about it without making matters worse for everyone.

Here, as is often the case, there is more wisdom in the public's outlook than in the campaign speeches of Democratic presidential candidates and in the books and opinion columns of progressive economists. Leaving aside the morality of redistribution, the progressive case is based upon a significant fallacy: it assumes that the U.S. government is actually capable of redistributing income from the wealthy to the poor. For reasons of policy, tradition, and institutional design, this is not the case. Whatever one may think of inequality, redistributive fiscal policies are unlikely to do much to reduce it, a point that the voters seem instinctively to understand.

* * *

One need only look at the effects of federal tax and spending policies over the past 3½ decades to see that this is so. The chart on page 7, based upon data compiled by the Congressional Budget Office (CBO), displays the national shares of before- and after-tax income for the top 1 percent and 10 percent of the income distribution from 1979 to 2011, along with the same figures for the bottom quintile of the distribution. For purposes of this study, the

CBO defined *income* as market income plus government transfers, including cash payments and the value of in-kind services and payments, such as health care (Medicare and Medicaid) and food stamps. The chart thus represents a comprehensive portrait of the degree to which federal tax and spending policies redistribute income from the wealthiest to the poorest groups, and to households in between.

The chart illustrates two broad points. First, the wealthiest groups gradually increased their share of national income (both in pre- and after-tax and transfer income) over this 30-plus-year period; and second, federal tax and spending policies had little effect on the overall distribution of income.

Across this period, the top 1 percent of the income distribution nearly doubled their share of (pretax) national income, from about 9 percent in 1979 to more than 18 percent in 2007 and 2008, before it fell back after the financial crisis, to 15 percent in 2010 and 2011. (Some studies suggest that by 2014, it was back up to 18 percent.) Meanwhile, the top 10 percent of the income distribution increased their share by a third, from about 30 percent in 1979 to 40 percent in 2007 and 2008, before it fell to 37 percent in 2011. This was a secular trend in the distribution of national income that persisted throughout different presidential administrations and tax regimes. The path was smoothly upward for both income groups across the period, with temporary peaks and troughs corresponding with business-cycle rallies and recessions. Economists have offered different theories to explain the trend, though most agree that the causes lie in several overlapping factors, including globalization, technological change, record stock-market gains, and increasing premiums paid to highly educated workers.

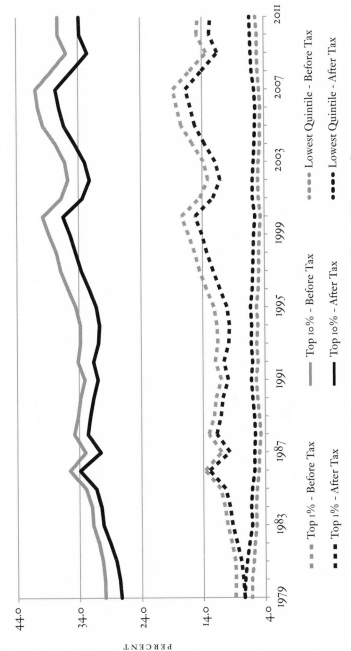

SHARE OF BEFORE- AND AFTER-TAX REVENUE
(1979 TO 2011)

PERCENT

44.0
34.0
24.0
14.0
4.0

1979   1983   1987   1991   1995   1999   2003   2007   2011

Top 1% - Before Tax   Top 10% - Before Tax   Lowest Quintile - Before Tax

Top 1% - After Tax   Top 10% - After Tax   Lowest Quintile - After Tax

Source: Congressional Budget Office, "Distribution of Household Income and Federal Taxes, 2011"
(November 12, 2014); https://www.cbo.gov/publication/49440#title1

Many will be surprised to learn that the federal fiscal system – taxes and spending – does not do more to reduce inequalities in income that arise from the free-market system. After all, the progressive income tax was designed to redistribute income by placing heavier burdens on the wealthy, and many federal spending programs were crafted specifically to assist lower-income households. Yet there are perfectly obvious reasons, on both the tax and spending sides, as to why redistribution does not succeed in the American system – and probably cannot be made to succeed.

* * *

The income tax yields revenues to the government through two main sources: progressive taxes on ordinary income (salaries and wages) and taxes on capital gains, with the latter taxed at somewhat lower rates to encourage investment. For most of this period, taxes on capital gains have yielded less than 10 percent of total income taxes and about 4 percent of total federal revenues. In terms of the income tax, most of the action is in taxes on ordinary income.

The highest marginal income tax rate oscillated up and down from 1979 to 2011. In 1979 during the Carter presidency, it was 70 percent, then it fell to 50 percent and to 28 percent in the Reagan/Bush years. It then rose to 39.6 percent in the 1990s under the Clinton presidency and fell again to 35 percent from 2003 to 2010. (It is now back up to 39.6 percent.) The highest rate on capital gains moved within a narrower band, beginning at 28 percent in 1979 and falling as low as 15 percent from 2005 to 2011. (The top rate is currently 23.5 percent.)

Over this period, regardless of the tax rates, the top 1 percent of the income distribution lost 1 percent to 2 percent of their income share due to taxes. In 1980, that group claimed 9 percent of before-tax income and 8 percent of after-tax income; in 1990 the figures were 12 percent and 11 percent; and in 2010, 15 percent and 13 percent. The top 10 percent of the income distribution generally lost 2 percent to 4 percent of their income share due to taxes, probably because those households take a greater share of their income (compared with the 1 percent) in salaries rather than in capital gains. At the other end, the poorest quintiles gained almost nothing (about 1 percent on average) in income shares due to cash and in-kind transfers from the government. In 2011, for example, the poorest 20 percent of households received 5 percent of (pretax) national income and 6 percent of after-tax income. That pattern was stable and consistent throughout the period.

Many in the redistribution camp attribute this pattern to a lack of progressivity in the U.S. income tax system, an explanation that overlooks the fact that income taxes in the U.S. are at least as progressive as those in many other developed countries. The highest marginal rate in the U.S. was 35 percent from 2003 to 2012 and today is 39.6 percent for top earners, a rate not far out of line with those of America's chief competitors, including Germany, France, the United Kingdom, and Japan, where the highest marginal rates range between 40 percent and 46 percent.

A 2008 study published by the Organisation for Economic Co-operation and Development (OECD) found that the U.S. had the most progressive income tax system among all 24 OECD countries, measured in terms of the share of the tax burden paid by the wealthiest households. According to the Congressional Budget Office, the top 1 percent of earners paid 39 percent of the personal income taxes in 2010 (while claiming 15 percent of before-tax income), compared with 17 percent in 1980 and 24 percent in 1990. According to the same study, the top

20 percent of earners paid 93 percent of federal income taxes in 2010 while claiming just 52 percent of before-tax income. Meanwhile, the bottom 40 percent of the income distribution paid zero net income taxes. For all practical purposes, those in the highest brackets already bear the overwhelming burden of federal income tax, while those below the median income have been taken out of the income tax system altogether. It would be difficult to make the U.S. income tax system more progressive than it already is in terms of the share of the tax burden carried by the wealthiest households.

*　*　*

There is a more basic reason the tax system does not do more to redistribute income: the progressive income tax is not the primary source of revenue for the U.S. government. In 2010, the federal government raised $2.144 trillion in taxes, with just 42 percent coming from the individual income tax, 40 percent from payroll taxes, 9 percent from corporate taxes, and the rest from a mix of estate and excise taxes. In 2014, due to the economic recovery, the figures had shifted to 46 percent for income taxes and 34 percent for payroll taxes. Since the early 1950s, the national government has consistently relied upon the income tax for 40 percent to 50 percent of its revenues, with precise proportions varying from year to year due to economic conditions. For several generations, progressive reformers have looked to the income tax as the instrument through which they aimed to take resources from the rich and deliver them to the poor. In reality – in the United States, at least – the income tax is not a sufficiently large revenue source for the national government to do the job that the redistributionists want it to do.

During the New Deal era, the United States chose to fund its program of old-age pensions (Social Security) through payroll taxes on employees and employers rather than from general income tax revenues. In adopting this approach, the U.S. followed a precedent established by Germany in the 1880s, when that country established a system of old-age support funded by payroll taxes. President Roosevelt insisted on the payroll tax because he felt the program would be insulated from congressional meddling if it had its own dedicated funding stream. He also feared that Congress would add unaffordable future benefits if the program received its funding from general revenues. The payroll tax also allowed FDR to cast Social Security as an insurance program that provided workers with guaranteed rights to benefits in return for their lifetime contributions. When President Johnson and Congress expanded the program in 1965 to provide medical care for seniors, they chose to fund it with an additional payroll tax. Today, Social Security and Medicare are the two most expensive domestic programs funded by the federal government – and they are paid for by payroll taxes.

As a result of the passage of Medicare and expansions in Social Security benefits, payroll taxes as a share of federal revenues doubled during the 1960s and 1970s, from 16 percent of revenues in 1960 to well over 30 percent by the late 1970s. Payroll taxes fall more heavily upon working- and middle-class incomes, which come from wages and salaries, than upon the wealthy, whose incomes come disproportionately from capital gains and whose salaries far exceed the maximum earnings subject to those taxes. In 2010, the wealthiest 1 percent paid just 4 percent of payroll taxes (compared with 39 percent of income taxes), and the top quintile of earners paid 45 percent of payroll taxes (compared with 93 percent of income taxes), while the middle quintile of earners paid 15 percent of all pay-roll taxes (and just 3 percent of income taxes). The payroll tax has progressive features, in that the wealthy still carry a heavier share than the poor, but it is far less progressive than the income tax. And in terms of the federal tax system as a whole, the more widely shared burdens of the payroll tax tend to offset or mitigate the progressive effects of the income tax.

When those two revenue streams – income and payroll taxes – are added together, the federal tax system appears substantially less progressive than when assessed solely in terms of income taxes. In 2010 (according to CBO data), the top 1 percent of the income distribution paid 24 percent of total taxes, compared with 39 percent of individual income taxes, and earned 15 percent of the (pretax) national income. The top 20 percent of the income distribution paid 69 percent of total taxes, compared with 93 percent of income taxes, and earned 52 percent of the national income. Meanwhile, the middle quintile of household incomes paid 9 percent of total taxes but just 3 percent of individual income taxes, while claiming 14 percent of the national income. The federal tax system remains modestly progressive when the two taxes are added together, because the wealthier households still pay a larger share of total taxes than they claim in total national income. Nevertheless, the federal government's reliance on payroll taxes to fund generous entitlement programs mitigates the progressivity of the income tax.

This factor makes it exceedingly difficult for the government to redistribute income in any substantial way through the federal tax system. The payroll tax as a means of funding entitlements is embedded financially and politically into the federal system. It would be difficult from a political point of view to untangle and redesign that system of funding, given the current divisions between the two political parties. It would also be unwise for a host of reasons – most of them outlined by President Roosevelt in the 1930s – to attempt a switch to general revenues to pay for those expensive and politically popular programs, because it would tempt Congress to add future benefits without regard to costs. Whatever one may think of them, payroll taxes are not going to disappear as sources of revenue for Social Security and Medicare.

That leaves redistributionists with the option of raising income tax rates on "the rich" – defined as the top 1 percent of the income distribution – but there is not enough money available by that route to make much of a difference to the other 99 percent of the population, or to those in the bottom half of the income distribution. An increase in the top marginal tax rate from 39.6 percent to, say, 50 percent might have yielded about $100 billion in additional revenue in 2010, assuming no corresponding changes in tax and income strategies on the part of wealthy households and no negative effects on investment and economic growth (all risky assumptions). That is real money, to be sure, but it represented only about 0.5 percent of GDP (using 2010 figures) and less than 3 percent of total federal spending, not enough to permit much in the way of redistribution to the roughly 60 million households in the bottom half of the income scale. This also assumes that federal expenditures actually redistribute income from the rich to the poor or to those in between, which is most definitely not the case.

* * *

Turning to the spending side of fiscal policy, we encounter a somewhat murkier situation because of the sheer number and complexity of federal spending programs.

Nevertheless, the conclusion is much the same as on the tax side: the overall flow of federal spending does little to alter shares of national income between the top and bottom of the income scale. In fact, federal expenditures, when taken as a whole, fail to redistribute income from the rich to the poor and instead allocate it upward to the top 20 percent or 30 percent of the income distribution. While we might raise taxes on the wealthy, it does not follow that those revenues would flow to those near or below the poverty line.

This generalization holds despite the fact that the federal government spends roughly half of its $3.5 trillion annual budget on a multitude of programs designed to assist the elderly, the disabled, the poor, and the near poor. The House of Representatives Budget Committee estimated in 2012 that the federal government spent nearly $800 billion on 92 antipoverty programs that provided cash assistance, medical care, housing assistance, food stamps, and tax credits for the poor and near poor. The number of people drawing benefits from antipoverty programs has more than doubled since the 1980s, from 42 million in 1983 to 108 million in 2011. The redistributive effects of these programs are limited, however, because most funds are spent on services to assist the poor, and only a small fraction of these expenditures is distributed in the form of cash or income. Most of the money, in short, goes to providers of services and not to poor or near-poor households.

This is an important feature of the American welfare state as it has evolved over the decades: it is organized to assist the poor and to alleviate the conditions of poverty, but not to redistribute income from the wealthy to the poor. The American welfare state mostly provides in-kind services and benefits to the poor as opposed to cash income, with the result that most of the actual money spent on poverty goes to households that are far from poor. Former Senator Daniel Patrick Moynihan once tartly described this as "feeding the sparrows by feeding the horses" – in other words, paying middle-class and upper-middle-class providers to deliver services to the poor. (Moynihan was in favor of delivering incomes rather than services to the poor.)

The U.S. welfare state evolved in the direction of services rather than incomes in part because the American people have long viewed poverty as a condition to be overcome rather than one to be subsidized with cash. Many also believe that the poor would squander or misspend cash payments and so are better off receiving services and in-kind benefits like food stamps, health care, and tuition assistance. For the most part, then, Americans have erected an array of "safety net" programs designed to help people who are temporarily in need move out of poverty or prevent them from falling into destitution. With regard to providing aid to the poor, then, Americans have built a social-service state but not a redistribution state.

* * *

Social Security is the only substantial federal program that transfers money from one group to another, in this case from workers and employers paying payroll taxes to retirees collecting benefits. It is by far the largest of all federal programs and claimed $850 billion, or 24 percent of the federal budget, in 2014. It is paid for by a payroll tax split equally between employees and employers. As of 2014, about 59 million Americans were collecting benefits under Social Security, with an average benefit of $1,260 per month.

Social Security has a progressive benefit formula, and it contains a feature (Supplemental Security Income) that provides cash benefits to elderly, blind, or disabled people with incomes below the poverty line. Nevertheless, in spite of those features, it was designed and still functions to provide income for retirees, not to redistribute income from the wealthy to the poor. Because retirees have paid into the system via payroll taxes, Social Security (like Medicare) is not means-tested. Everyone who has paid in is eligible to receive benefits, regardless of wealth or income. The system operates on a pay-as-you-go basis such that incomes for current retirees are funded by taxes on current workers and employers.

The National Bureau of Economic Research (NBER), in a series of studies on the redistributive aspects of Social Security, concluded that the program transfers income in various complex ways (for example, from those with short life expectancies to those with longer ones) but over the long run does not transfer it from the rich to the poor. One NBER study by Julia Lynn Coronado, Don Fullerton, and Thomas Glass bluntly concluded that "Social Security does not redistribute from people who are rich over their lifetime to those who are poor. In fact, it may even be slightly regressive." This is partly because wealthier recipients tend to live longer than others and partly because they are more likely to have nonworking spouses who are also eligible to collect benefits.

Medicare and Medicaid, two other expensive programs that together claim nearly 25 percent of the federal budget, provide important health care services to the elderly and the poor but no actual income. Medicare (like Social Security) is funded through payroll taxes and Medicaid through a roughly 60/40 mix of federal and state taxes. There are currently about 56 million elderly Americans enrolled in Medicare and about 71 million low-income Americans enrolled in Medicaid and its affiliated

program, the Children's Health Insurance Program (CHIP).
There are an additional 9 million people enrolled in Women, Infants, and Children (WIC), a separate program set up to deliver food and nutritional assistance to pregnant women and mothers of young children in families with incomes below or slightly above the poverty line. Enrollment in all these programs is growing rapidly because of the aging of the population (Medicare) and the expansion of Medicaid under the Affordable Care Act. Medicaid is now the most rapidly growing item in state budgets across the country.

The flow of money through these health care programs – more than $850 billion in federal funds in 2014 (plus another $180 billion in state funds for Medicaid) – goes mainly to hospitals, nursing homes, pharmaceutical companies, doctors, insurance companies, and health-maintenance organizations. These two programs underwrite more than 60 percent of expenditures on nursing homes in the United States and more than 30 percent of national expenditures on hospital care. Both programs have been plagued by fraud and corruption since their origins in 1965 because some doctors, nursing-home entrepreneurs, and other providers have sought to game the system for financial advantage – and in many cases have succeeded all too well. No one has ever attempted a study of the redistributive aspects of the flow of funds from Medicare and Medicaid, but one surmises from the nature of these payments (to insurance companies, nursing homes, and doctors, for example) that most of the money goes to those in the upper reaches of the income distribution.

* * *

[231]

The federal government provides cash assistance to the poor and near poor through two programs: (1) Temporary Assistance to Needy Families (TANF, popularly known as welfare), which currently provides cash benefits to about 4.5 million households at a cost of $17 billion per year to the federal government and about $14 billion (in 2014) to various state governments; and (2) Supplemental Security Income, which provides cash benefits to the disabled poor (8.5 million households) at a cost of about $50 billion per year to the federal government. These numbers work out to about $7,000 (on average) per year per household under TANF and $6,000 per year per household under SSI, in each case, about half of the average benefit under Social Security.

The cash transfers under TANF may be regarded as redistributions because they are paid for out of general income tax revenues, at least at the federal level, and the funds go exclusively to poor households. The funds paid out under SSI are collected via Social Security payroll taxes and thus, for reasons outlined above, cannot be judged as redistributions from the wealthy to the poor. SSI expenditures have increased rapidly in recent years as TANF expenditures have fallen, in part because (as the House Budget Committee Report suggests) some states have moved able-bodied welfare recipients to SSI, where they are supported exclusively by federal funds. Lower-income working families are also eligible to receive rebates on payroll taxes through the Earned Income Tax Credit (EITC). The House Budget Committee estimated that 28 million taxpayers took advantage of this program in 2011, at an estimated cost of $60 billion to the federal government in rebated taxes. (The average family with children received $2,900 in tax rebates.)

The poor are eligible to receive a bevy of in-kind benefits under Medicaid, the Supplemental Nutrition Assistance Program (SNAP, formerly known as food stamps), rental assistance, college scholarships, energy subsidies, job training, and other programs too numerous to list. Next to Medicaid, SNAP is the most expensive and far-reaching of these programs. It provided in-kind food subsidies to some 47 million people in 2014, at a cost of $74 billion to the federal government (about $16 billion of which went to administration). A qualifying individual could receive (in 2014) a maximum benefit of $194 per month, and a family of four could receive up to $650 per month. The federal government pays out these benefits on the first of each month by reloading a government-issued credit card to be used solely for purchases of food and beverages at supermarkets and convenience stores. SNAP comes close to providing a cash benefit, since recipients can use their cards to purchase a wide range of items at retail stores, and, indeed, some exchange their cards for cash in an underground market. SNAP is supported in Congress by influential lobbying groups, including agricultural interests and food manufacturers, which supply the food distributed through the program; and major retail chains, where recipients redeem their benefits.

Of the $800 billion spent on poverty programs in 2012 (as listed in the House Budget Committee Report), it appears that less than $150 billion, or about 18 percent of the total, was distributed in cash income, if we include as a cash benefit the tax rebate under the EITC. The rest of the funds were spent on services and in-kind benefits, with the money paid to providers of various kinds, most of whom have incomes well above the poverty line. It is worth noting that when President Obama sought to build out the welfare state, he did so mainly by expanding in-kind benefit programs, particularly Medicaid and SNAP.

With respect to the recipients of federal transfers, the
CBO study reveals a surprising fact: households in the
bottom quintile of the income distribution receive less in
federal payments than those in the higher-income quintiles. According to that study, households in the bottom
quintile of the income distribution (below $24,000 in
income per year) received on average $8,600 in cash and
in-kind transfers; households in the middle quintile about
$16,000 in such transfers; and households in the highest
quintile about $11,000. Even households in the top 1 per-
cent of the distribution received more in dollar transfers
than those in the bottom quintile. The wealthier households received those transfers overwhelmingly through
Social Security and Medicare; the poorer households
from a roughly equal mix of Social Security, Medicare,
Medicaid, TANF (cash welfare), and SNAP (food stamps).
The federal transfer system may move income around
and through the economy, but it does not redistribute it
from the rich to the poor or near poor.

* * *

The above programs accounted for more than 60 percent
of all federal spending in 2014. Most of the remainder of
the $3.5 trillion in federal expenditures was allocated to
budget items whose purposes are unrelated to redistribution – including defense, medical research, transportation,
agricultural subsidies, veterans' benefits, small-business
loans, and interest on the national debt. The evidence we
have suggests that the bulk of these funds flow in the direction of households well above the median national income.

American Transparency, a research organization that
posts government payments online, discovered that *Fortune* 100 companies receive more than $100 billion per

year in federal contracts and subsidies, much of it through the defense, aerospace, and transportation budgets. The same organization found that the largest farm subsidies flow into wealthy urban zip codes in New York City, Beverly Hills, Palm Beach, Miami Beach, and Sea Island, Ga. Wealthy investors are said to have purchased farmland in order to claim the agricultural subsidies attached to it.

A parallel analysis of other federal spending programs would reveal much the same pattern. Interest payments on the national debt – roughly $230 billion in 2014 – flow to foreign governments, pension funds, mutual funds, and individual investors, but very little of it goes back to households at the bottom or the lower half of the income scale. For this reason, deficit spending (now the norm in Washington, D.C.) is one of the most regressive of all federal policies.

An impressive amount of federal spending flows to charitable and not-for-profit organizations that provide their employees and executives with generous salaries and benefits. The publication *Giving USA*, which tracks charitable spending, reports that the government now supplies one-third of all funds raised by not-for-profit organizations. According to a study by the National Science Foundation, major research universities received federal grants and contracts totaling $40 billion in 2011. Johns Hopkins led the pack with $1.9 billion, followed by the University of Washington ($949 million), the University of Michigan ($820 million), and the University of Pennsylvania ($707 million). If one leaves aside the large sums allocated to these institutions, the nonprofit sector still received $215 billion in federal grants and contracts in 2010, more than 6 percent of total federal spending.

* * *

It is well known in Washington that the people and groups that lobby for federal programs are generally those who receive the salaries and income, rather than those who get the services. They – as Moynihan observed decades ago – are the direct beneficiaries of most of these programs, and they have the strongest interest in keeping them going as they are. The nation's capital is home to countless trade associations; companies seeking government contracts; hospital and medical associations lobbying for Medicare and Medicaid expenditures; agricultural groups; college and university lobbyists; and advocacy organizations for the environment, the elderly, and the poor, all of them seeking a share of federal grants and contracts or some form of subsidy or tax break.

This is the reason five of the seven wealthiest counties in the nation border on Washington, D.C., and is also why the average income for the District of Columbia's top 5 percent of households exceeds $500,000, the highest among major American cities. Washington is among the nation's most unequal cities as measured by the income gap between the wealthy and everyone else. Those wealthy individuals did not descend upon the nation's capital in order to redistribute income to the poor but rather to secure some benefit to their institutions, industries, and, incidentally, to themselves. They understand a basic principle that has so far eluded progressives and redistributionists: the federal government is an effective engine for dispensing patronage, encouraging rent seeking, and circulating money to important voting blocs and well-connected constituencies – but not for the redistribution of income.

This point also provides perspective on the "makers vs. takers" theme that one often hears in Republican criticisms of federal-transfer programs. In fact, the distinction between makers and takers is not so easy to establish. The roster of the so-called takers does not consist exclusively of poor people and deadbeats who refuse to work or pay taxes (though there is some of this). Many of the takers are elderly beneficiaries of Social Security and Medicare, middle-class professionals who provide public services of one kind or another, and financially comfortable recipients of government grants and contracts. Many of the takers, in short, are middle- and upper-middle-class voters, which is one reason efforts to scale back the government are met with so much resistance. Aaron Director, the late economist at the University of Chicago, maintained decades ago that government programs are structured and paid for primarily to satisfy middle-class voters. Despite the evolution of the American welfare state in recent decades, his proposition remains valid today.

James Madison wrote in *The Federalist* that the possession of different degrees and kinds of property is the most durable source of faction under a popularly elected government. Madison especially feared the rise of redistributive politics, under which the poor might seize the reins of government in order to plunder the wealthy by heavy taxes. He and his colleagues introduced various political mechanisms – the intricate system of checks and balances in the Constitution, federalism, and the dispersion of interests across an extended republic – to forestall a division between the rich and poor in America and to deflect political conflict into other channels. While Madison's design did not succeed in holding back the tide of big government in the 20th century, it nevertheless proved robust enough to frustrate the aims of redistributionists by promoting a national establishment that is open to a boundless variety of crisscrossing interests.

The ingrained character of the American state is

unlikely to change fundamentally anytime soon, which is why those who worry about inequality should abandon the failed cause of redistribution and turn their attention instead to broad-based economic growth as the only practical remedy for the sagging incomes of too many Americans.

JAMES PIERESON

THE INEQUALITY HOAX

LIBERALS AND PROGRESSIVES seem to thrive on crises. They are, in any case, unusually proficient in creating or calling attention to them, often as excuses to impose new taxes and regulations or to gain additional power and influence for themselves. In the 1960s they gave us the "poverty crisis" and the "urban crisis," followed in the 1970s and 1980s by the "environmental crisis," the "energy crisis," and the "homeless crisis." Later we had the "health care crisis" and, more recently, the civilization-threatening "global-warming crisis." None of these ever qualified as a genuine crisis, if by that term we mean a moment of danger that must be navigated by wise statesmanship or effective policy. Some have found it useful to turn multifaceted problems into crises in order to stampede the public into adopting policies it would otherwise (quite sensibly) reject.

Today the issue of the hour is the "inequality crisis," another overhyped issue that is being seized upon as an excuse to raise taxes, attack "the rich," and discredit policies that gave us three decades of prosperity, booming real estate and stock markets, and an expanding global economy. For several years, ever since the financial crisis of 2008, journalists and academics have been turning out books and manifestos bearing such titles as *The New Gilded Age; The Killing Fields of Inequality; The Great Divergence:*

America's Growing Inequality Crisis and What We Can Do About It; and *The Price of Inequality: How Today's Divided Society Endangers Our Future*, to list just a few of the many dozens of works on the subject that have appeared of late. The common message of these books is not subtle: the rich have manipulated the political system to lay claim to wealth they have not earned and do not deserve, and they have done so at the expense of everyone else.

In the past, those who wrote about inequality focused on poverty and the challenge of elevating the poor into the working and middle classes. No more. Today they are preoccupied with the rich and with schemes to redistribute their wealth downward through the population. Many of the new egalitarians – professors at Ivy League universities, well-paid journalists, or heirs to family wealth – are well-off and comfortable by any reasonable standard. In interpreting their complaints about "the rich" or the top "1 percent," one naturally thinks of Samuel Johnson's barbed comment about the reformers of his day: "Sir," he said, "your levelers wish to level down as far as themselves; but they cannot bear leveling up to themselves." There is a sense in this controversy that we are watching members of the top 2 percent or 3 percent of the income distribution perform class warfare against the top 1 percent, while everyone else looks on from a distance, apparently convinced that the new class struggle has little to do with their own circumstances.

THE PIKETTY BUBBLE

The controversy over inequality gathered additional steam in recent weeks with the publication of Thomas Piketty's new book, *Capital in the Twenty-First Century* (Belknap/Harvard University Press), a dense and data-filled work of economic history running to nearly 700 pages that makes the case against inequality far more extensively and exhaustively than any work that has appeared heretofore. His book, published in March 2014, climbed to the top of the best-seller lists by mid-April, where it remained for several weeks thereafter. Bookstores in New York City, Washington, D.C., and Boston quickly sold out of copies, and even Amazon could not keep up with public demand for the book. The Piketty "phenomenon" arrived as a surprise to just about everyone, most especially to the publisher. "We've printed and printed and printed, and the market soaks up whatever we print," the book's editor at Harvard University Press said in April, just a few weeks after the publication date. "The American reception of the book has re-energized interest in France. Now the French edition is sold out." The editor was not complaining; this is the kind of problem publishing houses like to have.

All this attention quickly turned Piketty, a scholarly-looking professor at the Paris School of Economics, into something of a literary celebrity and his treatise into a rallying point for those favoring income redistribution and higher taxes for the rich. *The New York Times* called the author "the newest version of a now-familiar specimen: the overnight intellectual sensation whose stardom reflects the fashions and feelings of the moment." Paul Krugman, in a review essay in *The New York Review of Books*, called the book "magnificent" and "awesome." Martin Wolf of the *Financial Times* described it as "extraordinarily important," while a reviewer for *The Economist* suggested that Piketty's book is likely to change the way we understand the past two centuries of economic history. A columnist for the *Financial Times* called the mass of commentary surrounding the book a "Piketty bubble." Meanwhile, *The Spectator* in London helpfully offered tips to people wishing to bluff their way to appearing well informed about the book without having taken the trouble to read it. Not since the 1950s and 1960s, when John Kenneth Galbraith published *The Affluent Society* and *The New Industrial State,* has an economist written a book that has garnered so much public attention and critical praise.

But the furor might have been anticipated in light of the effective way that the book taps into pre-existing worries about economic inequality. Liberals and progressives of all stripes have hailed it as the indictment of free-market capitalism they have been waiting decades to hear. The market revolutions of the past three decades have placed them on defense in public debates over taxation, regulation, and inequality, and Piketty's book provides them with the intellectual ammunition with which to fight back. It documents their belief that inequalities of income and wealth have grown rapidly in recent decades in the United States and across the industrial world, and it portrays our era as a new "gilded age" of concentrated wealth and out-of-control capitalism. It suggests that things are getting worse for nearly everyone, save for a narrow slice of the population – the "1 percent" – that lives off exploding returns on capital, and it pointedly supports their agenda of redistributive taxation.

Is Piketty a Marxist?

Some have compared *Capital in the Twenty-First Century* to Karl Marx's *Das Kapital* both for its similarity in title and its updated analysis of the historical dynamics of the capitalist system. Though Piketty deliberately chose his title to promote the association with Marx's tome, he is not a socialist or a Marxist, as he reminds the reader throughout the book. He does not endorse collective ownership of the means of production; historical materialism; class struggle; the labor theory of value; or the inevitability of revolution. He readily acknowledges that communism and socialism are failed systems. He wants to reform capitalism, not destroy it.

At the same time, he shares Marx's assumption that returns on capital are the dynamic force in modern economies, and, like Marx, he claims that such returns lead ineluctably to concentrations of wealth in fewer and fewer hands. For Piketty, like Marx, capitalism is all about "capital," and not much more. Along the same lines, he also argues that there is an intrinsic conflict between capital and labor in market systems so that greater returns on capital must come at the expense of wages and salaries. In this sense, rather like Marx, he advances an interpretation of market systems that revolves around just a few factors: the differential returns on capital and labor and the distribution of wealth and income through the population.

Though he borrows some ideas from Marx, Piketty writes more from the perspective of a modern progressive or social democrat. His book, written in French but translated into English, bears many features of that ideological perspective, particularly in its focus on the distribution rather than the creation of wealth, in its emphasis upon progressive taxation as the solution to the inequality problem, and in the confidence it expresses that governments can manage modern economies in the interest of a more equal distribution of incomes. He is worried mainly about equality and economic security, much less so about freedom, innovation, and economic growth.

His book has some admirable features. It is, first of all, a work of economic history, a field that economists have abandoned over the past several decades in favor of building statistical models and formulating abstract theories.

Piketty takes academic economists to task for the irrelevance of much of their work to the pressing problems of the day and for ignoring the lessons that history has to teach. The author takes seriously the history of economic ideas, mining the works of Adam Smith, David Ricardo, Thomas Robert Malthus, Karl Marx, and John Maynard Keynes in search of insights into the operation of the market system. He demonstrates that these theorists still have much to tell us about ongoing economic controversies, despite the fact that few economists today bother to read their works. There is much in this book to digest and reflect upon, even for those who do not share the author's point of view.

The popularity of his book is another sign that established ideas never really die but go in and out of fashion with changing circumstances. Liberals, progressives, and social democrats were shocked by the comeback of free-market ideas in the 1980s after they assumed those ideas had been buried once and for all by the Great Depression. In a similar vein, free-market and "small government" advocates are now surprised by the return of social-democratic doctrines that they assumed had been discredited by the "stagflation" of the 1970s and the success of low-tax policies in the 1980s and 1990s. Piketty's book has garnered so much attention because it is the best statement we have had in some time of the redistributionist point of view.

Despite the attention and praise the book has received, it is a flawed production in at least three important respects. First, it misjudges the era in which we are living and those through which we have passed. Second, it misunderstands the sources of the "new inequality." Third, the solutions it proposes will make matters worse for everyone – the wealthy, the middle class, and the poor alike. The broader problem with the book is that it advances a narrow understanding of the market system that singles out returns on capital as its central feature but in the process ignores the really important factors that account for its success over an extended period of 2½ centuries.

THE "IRON LAW" OF CAPITALISM

Piketty organizes his book around an old question dating back to the 19th century: Does the capitalist process tend to produce over time a growing equality or inequality in incomes and wealth? In doing so he assumes without argument that equality rather than some other measure or mix of measures – such as growth, innovation, living standards, or freedom – is the basic standard according to which the system should be judged.

The dominant view throughout the 19th century was that rising inequality was an inevitable by-product of the capitalist system. In the United States, Thomas Jefferson tried to preserve an agricultural society for as long as possible in the belief that the industrial system would destroy the promise of equality upon which the new nation was based. In Great Britain, David Ricardo, writing in the early 19th century, argued that because agricultural land was scarce and finite, landowners would inevitably claim larger shares of national wealth at the expense of laborers and factory owners. Ricardo did not foresee that land prices in Great Britain would level off due to free trade and technological innovations that increased the supply and reduced the price of food.

Later, as the industrial process gained steam, Marx argued that because of competition among capitalists, ownership of capital in the form of factories and machinery would become concentrated in fewer and fewer hands, while workers continued to be paid subsistence wages.

Marx did not foresee that productivity-enhancing innovations, allied perhaps with the unionization of workers, would cause wages to rise and thereby allow workers to enjoy more of the fruits of capitalism.

The perspective on the equality-inequality issue changed in the 20th century due to the rise in incomes for workers, continued improvements in worker productivity, the expansion of the service sector and the welfare state, and the general prosperity of the postwar era. In addition, the Great Depression and two world wars tended to wipe out the accumulated capital that sustained the lifestyles of the upper classes. In the 1950s, Simon Kuznets, a prominent American economist, showed that wealth and income disparities leveled out in the United States from 1913 to 1952. On the basis of his research, he proposed the so-called Kuznets curve to illustrate his conclusion that inequalities naturally increased in the early phases of the industrial process but then declined as the process matured, as workers relocated from farms to cities, and as human capital replaced physical capital as a source of income and wealth. His thesis suggested that modern capitalism would gradually produce a middle-class society in which incomes did not vary greatly from the mean. This optimistic outlook was nicely expressed in John F. Kennedy's oft-quoted remark that "a rising tide lifts all boats."

From the perspective of 2014, Piketty makes the case that Marx was far closer to being right than Kuznets. Kuznets, in Piketty's view, was simply looking at data from a short period of history and made the error of extrapolating his findings into the future.

Piketty argues that capitalism, left to its own devices and absent government intervention, creates a situation in which returns on capital grow more rapidly than returns on labor and the overall growth in the economy.

This is Piketty's central point, which he takes to be a basic descriptive theorem of the capitalist order. He tries to show that when returns on capital exceed growth in the economy for many decades or generations, owners of capital disproportionately accrue wealth and income, and capital assets gradually claim larger shares of national wealth, generally at the expense of labor. This, he argues, is something close to an "iron law" of the capitalist order.

He estimates that since 1970, the market value of capital assets has grown steadily in relation to national income in all major European and North American economies. In the United States, for example, the ratio increased from almost 4 to 1 in 1970 to almost 5 to 1 today, in Great Britain from 4 to 1 to about 6 to 1, and in France from 4 to 1 to 7 to 1. Measured from a different angle, income from capital also grew throughout this period as a share of national income. From 1980 to the present, income from capital grew in the United States from 20 percent to 25 percent of the national total, in Great Britain from 18 percent to nearly 30 percent, and in France from 18 percent to about 25 percent. While these do not appear to be earthshaking changes, they weigh heavily in Piketty's narrative that stresses the outsize role that capital has seized in recent decades in relation to labor income.

The weak patterns in the data summarized above suggest that Piketty may have overstated the claims for his iron law. There is nothing particularly original or radical in the proposition that returns on capital generally exceed economic growth. Economists and investors regard it as something of a truism, at least over the long run. For example, the long-term returns on the U.S. stock market are said to be about 7 percent per annum (minus taxes and inflation), while real growth in the overall economy has been closer to 3 percent. This is generally thought to be a good thing, since returns on capital encourage greater investment, and this in turn drives innovation, productivity, and economic growth. John Maynard Keynes was not alone among prominent economists in asserting that the accumulation of capital is a measure of economic progress.

But it does not follow from this that returns on capital, even if they are greater than overall growth in incomes, must be concentrated in a few hands instead of being distributed widely in pension funds, retirement accounts, college and university endowments, individual savings, dividends, and the like. Nor is it true that greater returns on capital must come at the expense of labor, since growing productivity advances the standard of living for everyone and workers benefit along with everyone else when their savings or pensions grow with increasing returns on capital. The low and still-falling interest rates of recent decades suggest that returns for at least some forms of capital are similarly falling. It is even questionable whether wealth is in fact growing faster than incomes in the U.S. economy, as Piketty's iron law says it must do. Martin Feldstein, writing in *The Wall Street Journal*, pointed out that since 1960, household wealth in the United States has grown by 3.2 percent per year while incomes have grown at a rate of 3.3 percent per year. The reason wealth does not continue to grow permanently at a compound rate is because owners die sooner or later, at which time their assets are disbursed through estate taxes, charitable gifts, and bequests to heirs.

But why, then, has capital grown in recent decades as a share of national income and in relation to labor income? The answer is to some extent embedded in Piketty's definition of *capital*. He defines *capital* in a broad way to include not only inputs into the production process – like factories, equipment, and machinery – but also stocks, bonds,

personal bank deposits, university and foundation endowments, pension funds, and residential real estate, all assets
that are subject to substantial year-to-year fluctuations in
market value. In his measure of capital, then, Piketty is
undoubtedly incorporating the explosion in asset prices
that has taken place since the early 1980s, especially in
stocks and to some degree in real estate as well.

Inequality and New Taxes

If *Capital in the Twenty-First Century* is known for anything,
it is for its documentation of rising inequality and its call
for new and higher taxes on the wealthy. Every major
review of the book has dwelled at length on these two
subjects, often without linking them to Piketty's larger
themes about the iron law of capitalism, the increasing
returns on capital, and the competition between labor and
capital for shares of national income. Piketty sees inequality as an inevitable by-product of modern capitalism and
sees substantially higher taxes as the only means of rem-
edying it.

There are two central chapters in the book in which he
traces the distribution of wealth and incomes in the United
States and Western Europe from the late 19th century to
the present day. His analysis yields a series of U-shaped
charts showing that the shares of wealth and income
claimed by the top 1 percent or 10 percent of households
peaked from 1910 to 1930, then declined and stabilized
during the middle decades of the century, and then began
to rise again after 1980.

In the United States in the decades before the Great
Depression, the top 1 percent received about 18 percent of
total income and owned about 45 percent of total wealth.
Those figures fell to about 10 percent (share of income)

and 30 percent (share of wealth) in the five decades from 1930 to 1980, at which point these shares started to grow again. As of 2010, the top 1 percent in the U.S. received nearly 18 percent of total incomes and owned about 35 percent of the total wealth. The pattern is similar for the top 10 percent of the income and wealth distributions. Before the Great Depression (from 1910 to 1930), this group claimed about 45 percent of national income and about 80 percent of the wealth; from 1930 to 1980, those shares fell to roughly 30 percent (income) and 65 percent (wealth); and from 1980 to 2010 their shares increased again to between 40 percent and 50 percent (income) and 70 percent (wealth). Piketty also shows that the "super-rich," the top one-tenth of 1 percent of the income distribution (about 100,000 households in 2010) increased its share of national income from about 2 percent in 1980 to close to 8 percent in 2010. The patterns are similar in the other Anglo-Saxon countries – Great Britain, Canada, and Australia – but very different in continental Europe, where the wealthiest groups have not been able to reclaim the shares of income and wealth that they enjoyed before World War I.

There is little mystery as to the sources of the U-shaped curves in income and wealth distribution in the United States and the flatter curves in continental Europe. In Europe in particular, the two great wars of the first half of the century, combined with the effects of the Great Depression, wiped out capital assets to an unprecedented degree, while progressive taxes enacted during and after World War II made it difficult for the wealthiest groups to accumulate capital at earlier rates. In the United States, the Depression wiped out owners of stocks, and high marginal income-tax rates (as high as 91 percent in the 1940s and 1950s) similarly made it difficult for "the rich" to accumulate capital. Obviously, wars, depressions, and confiscatory taxes are not beneficial to anyone, perhaps least of all to owners of capital. Beginning in the 1980s, as rates were reduced on incomes and capital gains, especially in the United States and Great Britain, those old patterns began to reappear.

Piketty highlights a new element in the situation, which is the dramatic rise in salaries for "super-managers" since the 1980s, particularly in the United States. These are, as he writes, "top executives of large firms who have managed to obtain extremely high and historically unprecedented compensation packages for their labor." This group also includes highly compensated presidents and senior executives of major colleges, universities, private foundations, and charitable institutions who often earn well in excess of $500,000 per year. Surprisingly, then, "the rich" today – the members of the top 1 percent – are salaried executives and managers rather than the "coupon clippers" of a century ago who lived off returns from stocks, bonds, and real estate. They are, in other words, people who work for a living and earn their incomes from salaries.

Piketty doubts that the new super-managers earn these generous salaries on the basis of merit or contributions to business profits. He also rejects the possibility that these salaries are in any way linked to the rapidly growing stock markets of recent decades. He points instead to cozy and self-serving relationships that executives establish with their boards of directors. In a sense, he suggests, they are in a position to set their own salaries as members of a "club" alongside wealthy directors and trustees.

To remedy the growing inequality problem, Piketty advocates a return to the old regime of much higher marginal tax rates in the United States. He thinks that marginal rates could be increased to 80 percent (from 39.5 percent today) on the very rich and to 60 percent on those with incomes between $200,000 and $500,000 per year without reducing their effort in any substantial way. Such taxes would hit the so-called super-managers who earn incomes from high salaries, though it would not get at the owners of capital who take but a small fraction of their holdings in annual income.

He advocates a global "wealth tax" on the "super-wealthy," with that tax levied against assets in stocks, bonds, and real estate – though he admits that such a tax has little chance of being enacted. Wealth taxes are notoriously difficult to collect, and they encourage capital flight, hiding of assets, and disputes over the pricing of assets. They require individuals to sell assets to pay taxes, thereby causing asset values to fall. The United States has never had a wealth tax; indeed, the U.S. Constitution, while authorizing taxes on income, does not allow for taxes on wealth. Several European countries – Germany, Finland, Sweden, and others – had such a tax in the past but have discontinued it. France currently has a wealth tax that tops out at a rate of 1.5 percent on assets in excess of €10 million (or about $14 million).

Under Piketty's scheme, the tax would be imposed on a sliding scale beginning at 1 percent on modest fortunes (roughly between $1.5 million and $7 million) and perhaps reaching as high as 10 percent on "super fortunes" in excess of $1 billion. The purpose of the tax is to reduce inequality, not to spend the new revenues on beneficial public purposes. Wealthy individuals like Bill Gates and Warren Buffett, with total assets in excess of $70 billion each, might have to pay as much as $7 billion annually in national wealth taxes under such a scheme. A capital tax, according to Piketty, would have to be global in nature to guard against both capital flight and the hiding of assets in foreign accounts. It would also require a new international banking regime under which major banks would be required to disclose account information to national treasuries. In the United States, with household wealth currently at about $80 trillion, such a tax, levied even at modest rates of 1 percent or 2 percent, might yield as much as $500 billion annually.

Piketty implies that reductions in taxes over the past three decades have allowed the rich to accumulate money while avoiding paying their fair share of taxes. Nothing could be further from the truth. As income taxes and capital-gains taxes were reduced in the United States beginning in the 1980s, the share of federal taxes paid by "the rich" steadily went up. From 1980 to 2010, as the top 1 percent increased their share of before-tax income from 9 percent to 15 percent, their share of the individual income tax soared from 17 percent to 39 percent of the total paid. Their share of total federal taxes more than doubled during a period when the highest marginal tax rate was cut in half, from 70 percent to 35.5 percent. The wealthy, in short, are already paying more than their fair share of taxes, and the growth in their wealth and incomes has had nothing to do with tax avoidance or deflecting the tax burden to the middle class.

A Different Look

Piketty's estimates of wealth and income shares over the decades are probably as reliable and accurate as he or anyone else can make them, but even so, they are estimates based upon imperfect and highly inexact data often interpolated or extrapolated from entries in government records. This is especially true of his information on wealth, since governments have long maintained records on incomes (to collect taxes on them) but not on individual wealth.

Following the publication of the book, Chris Giles of the *Financial Times* double-checked some of the information on the website that Piketty maintains and in the process discovered several material errors both in the data and in Piketty's analysis. Giles writes, for example, "Professor Piketty cited a figure showing the top 10 per cent of British people held 71 per cent of total national wealth (in 2010). The Office for National Statistics' latest Wealth and Assets Survey put the figure at only 44 per cent." That is a substantial discrepancy that undercuts the claim of growing inequality in Great Britain. Giles discovered additional errors and unexplained inferences in Piketty's data on the distribution of wealth in the United States that similarly undermine his conclusions about inequality in this country. It will take some time to sort out these criticisms, as other researchers attempt to replicate his analysis and as Piketty himself replies to his critics. In the meantime, cautious readers will be justified in regarding as tentative Piketty's conclusions about rapidly growing inequalities in wealth in Great Britain and the United States.

Even where Piketty's numbers may be accurate and not subject to the above criticisms, they could still produce misleading conclusions. As some have pointed out, he uses statistics on national income as denominators for his calculations of shares of income claimed by various groups of the population, but these figures exclude transfers from the government such as Social Security payments, food stamps, rent supplements, and the like, which constitute a growing portion of income for many middle-class and working-class people. If those transfers were included in the calculations, then the shares of income claimed by the top 1 percent or 10 percent would undoubtedly decline, and the shares of other groups would increase by corresponding amounts.

Leaving this controversy aside and accepting his data as valid for the time being, there are nevertheless good reasons to question his basic conclusions about capitalism in the 20th century. Piketty claims that inequality has increased since 1980, especially in the United States and Great Britain, that this kind of inequality is built into the nature of capitalism, and that it has been exacerbated by new tax policies that have cut the levies on high incomes and great wealth. These claims are greatly exaggerated.

The inequality that he measures is essentially a by-product of the stock-market boom of the past three decades. Since the early 1980s the U.S. stock market, measured by the Dow Jones Industrial Average, has grown twentyfold, the British stock market, as measured by the FTSE 100, by nearly tenfold, and the German market (measured by the DAX 30) by more than fifteenfold. The capitalization of world stock markets has grown from about $2 trillion in 1980 to about $60 trillion today. We have lived through an unprecedented three-decade-long bull market in stocks that no one foresaw in the 1970s. It would be surprising if such an escalation in market prices did not have a significant influence on the distribution of wealth and incomes, and it would be hazardous to forecast that such a pattern must continue indefinitely into the future.

The chart on page 34 makes the point more clearly that rising inequality is closely linked to stock-market returns. The chart illustrates the strong association from 1957 to 2012 between shares of income claimed by the top 1 percent in the United States and parallel changes in the Dow Jones Industrial Average and the Standard and Poor's 500 Stock Index. The income data are taken from a paper published by Piketty and Emmanuel Saez and posted on

Saez's website; the stock-market data are taken from tables published by the St. Louis Federal Reserve Bank. For ease of illustration and comparison, the three measures are indexed to 100 in 1957; the values for the top 1 percent are shown on the left axis and the stock-market values are on the right. The top line – the solid black line – charts the growth in income shares of the top 1 percent, while the gray line measures changes in the S&P 500, and the dotted line changes in the Dow Jones Industrial Average.

The key point is that all three lines move along the same pattern, remaining roughly flat and stable from 1957 to 1982, then moving upward in tandem thereafter with peaks and valleys occurring simultaneously with booms and busts in the stock markets. The changes in inequality began to tick upward after 1980 and accelerated in the 1990s, as the stock markets gained steam. As the chart shows, income inequality dropped most rapidly and dramatically when the stock markets faltered, as they did in 2000 with the technology bust and, more spectacularly, in 2008 with the financial crisis. Measured statistically, there is a 0.95 correlation between changes in the income shares of the top 1 percent and changes in the S&P 500, and there is a 0.96 correlation with changes in the Dow Jones Industrial Average. These patterns strongly suggest that changes in inequality in the United States have been closely linked to the three-decade-long boom in world stock markets. When inequality rises as a result of a boom of this kind, it is far less socially damaging than when it is caused by a bust, as in the Great Depression.

Piketty argues that the increased compensation for super-managers in recent decades is unrelated to the impressive returns on stocks. That is a doubtful proposition, if we bear in mind that many outsize compensation packages for business executives are paid in the form of stocks and stock options. This practice was hailed a few decades ago as a means of linking an executive's performance to the success of the company, but now it is attacked because it contributes to income inequality.

One could raise the question as to why the financial markets in the United States and elsewhere suddenly took off in the early 1980s and continued their upward movement for three-plus decades. It is beyond the scope of this Broadside to offer a detailed answer to such a question. Nevertheless, a few propositions suggest themselves. The period that began in 1981 or 1982 has been one of falling interest rates and disinflation, two developments that are especially beneficial to stock and real estate prices. The elimination of trade barriers; the end of the Cold War; and the entry of China, India, and various Asian countries into the world economy were also beneficial developments that reinforced the booming stock markets but perhaps disadvantaged American workers who were now forced to compete in a global marketplace. The end of the gold standard paved the way for a rapid expansion of credit and debt in the 1980s. Cuts in tax rates played but a minor role in comparison with these more important developments.

We could, of course, "solve" the inequality problem in the same way that it was "solved" in the 1930s – by erecting trade barriers, shutting down international trade, and crashing the stock markets. Piketty does not endorse any such result – but it is one toward which his analysis indirectly points.

Gilded Age or Golden Age?

Professor Piketty claims – in the broader message of his book – that we are living through a new "gilded age" of extravagant wealth and lavish expenditures enjoyed by a narrow elite at the expense of everyone else. As with the original "gilded age" of the late 19th century, the wealth accrued by the few gives the illusion of progress and prosperity but conceals growing hardships and economic difficulties endured by the rest of the population. Much of his thesis rests upon this proposition: our era is one of *faux* prosperity, a claim that is manifestly untrue.

Piketty divides the history of modern capitalism into three phases: first, the original gilded age, running in Europe from roughly 1870 to the outbreak of World War I in 1914 (he often refers to it as the *Belle Époque*) and in the United States from the end of the Civil War to the stock-market crash in 1929; second, the golden age of social democracy from 1930 to 1980, when progressive tax regimes and welfare programs were installed in most industrial countries; and, third, the new gilded age beginning in 1980 and running to the present, during which these tax regimes were dismantled, marginal rates and capital-gains taxes were reduced, and wealth and income began to flow once again to the very rich. He documents these three historical phases with data and charts showing that the shares of wealth and income claimed by the top 1 percent or 10 percent of households peaked in the early decades of the 20th century, then declined and stabilized in the middle decades of the century, and then began to rise again after 1980.

This argument makes sense only if one accepts the one-eyed premise that these multifaceted regimes can be assessed on the basis of the single criterion of wealth and income distribution or that the essence of the capitalist order is found solely in returns on capital and in the distribution of wealth and incomes rather than in rising living standards, innovation, and the spread of modern civilization. In each of these three eras, there was much more going on than simply the rearranging of wealth and incomes.

No less an authority than John Maynard Keynes looked back upon the prewar era in Europe as a golden age of capitalism. "What an extraordinary episode in the economic progress of man that age was which came to an end in August, 1914," he wrote in 1919 in *The Economic Consequences of the Peace*. He marveled at the economic progress made across the continent after 1870 following the unification of Germany. Industry and population grew steadily as trade across the continent accelerated, widening the sphere of prosperity and the reach of modern comforts. In the United States, rapid growth, stable prices, and high real wages drew millions of immigrants from Europe to build railroads, work in factories, and industrialize the country. Far-reaching innovations – electricity, the telegraph, mass-produced steel, and motored cars – drove the industrial process forward and made a few people very rich. It was the first era of globalization and open trade. These three factors – innovation, migration toward emerging centers of wealth, and widening circles of trade – have been key elements of "golden ages" throughout history and especially in the modern age of capitalism. This particular golden age ended in 1914 in Europe and in 1929 in the United States.

The so-called golden age of social democracy has much to commend it; one should not gainsay the genuine economic and social progress achieved in the United States and elsewhere during the middle decades of the century. Nevertheless, the virtues of that era can be overstated. As Piketty acknowledges, much of the accumulated capital of the preceding era was wiped out by war and depression. The confiscatory tax rates of that era, with marginal rates as high as 91 percent in the U.S. in the 1940s and 1950s, played a secondary role in the relative equalization of wealth and incomes. The impressive growth rates of the 1950s and 1960s developed from a depressed base and by building out innovations from the earlier period. Labor unions grew and won impressive wage gains for members, but mainly because (in the United States) they were bargaining with domestic oligopolies in industries that included auto, steel, railroad, and aluminum. The structure of American industry was highly concentrated, which, in the opinion of some, impeded innovation. Economist Galbraith wrote that cartelization was a permanent feature of the U.S. economy. There was little immigration into the United States and Western Europe from 1930 to 1970. Most important for the distribution of wealth, the U.S. stock market barely moved in real terms from 1930 to 1980; in 1980, the Dow Jones Industrial Average was at a lower level (adjusted for inflation) than at its peak in 1929.

The high tax regime of that era collapsed in the 1970s, not because "the rich" dismantled it but because government spending and regulation brought with them more crime, dependency, and disorder, along with simultaneously growing rates of unemployment and inflation. It was Jimmy Carter who first led the charge to deregulate the airline, railroad, trucking, and communications industries. Democrats and Republicans alike agreed that the U.S. economy was suffering from a shortage of capital – and that tax rates should be reduced to promote capital formation. That approach succeeded, as we have seen. At the same time, U.S. leaders pushed successfully for the elimination of trade barriers and a more open international trading system.

One might echo Keynes's comments about the prewar era in Europe in reflecting upon the era through which we have lived from the 1980s to the present. Far from being a gilded age, it appears from a broader perspective to have been new golden age of capitalism, marked by life-changing innovations in technology, globalized markets, and widening circles of trade; unprecedented levels of immigration into centers of prosperity; the absence of major wars; rising living standards around the world; falling inflation and interest rates; and a 30-year bull market in stocks, bonds, and real estate. At the same time, the boom in financial assets and real estate has also enriched the endowments of colleges, universities, and foundations, along with pension and retirement funds upon which millions of households depend.

These developments broke up the concentrated structure of the U.S. economy, making it more open, competitive, and innovative. At the same time, corporate profits are far higher now than in the age of industrial concentration and oligopoly. The end of the Cold War and the entrance of China into the world economy similarly broke open the structure of world politics and finance that dominated the middle decades of the century. Meanwhile, global levels of poverty and inequality have declined dramatically over the past three decades. Though some have won incredible riches in this new age of capitalism, they have done so by developing new products and technologies that benefit everyone or by investing in enterprises that earn profits by satisfying customers.

Keynes once remarked that the challenge in such a situation is to keep the boom going, not to bring it to a premature end out of a superstition that those who have prospered must be punished. That error has been made at various times in the past, most recently in the 1930s. It may be inevitable that our "golden age" will end sooner or later – but it will be much sooner if Professor Piketty and his supporters have their way.

CLAUDIA ROSETT

WHAT TO DO
ABOUT THE U.N.

Under the new presidential administration, the United States has launched a vigorous attempt to address the failings of the United Nations. President Donald Trump's ambassador, Nikki Haley, has called out the U.N. for its waste, abuses, bigotry, and tilt toward dictators. The United States has announced that it will withdraw from UNESCO (the United Nations Educational, Scientific and Cultural Organization) rather than carry on as the chief contributor to a U.N. agency that wields its franchise to the detriment of America and one of our closest democratic allies, Israel. Diplomatically, and financially, the US is now pressuring many elements of the U.N. to mend their worst ways.

These efforts have for now blunted the urgency of calls for a broader solution. But the basic problem remains. The U.N. stands as a remnant of the ruinous collectivist experiments of the past century: It is largely unaccountable, morally corrupt, ever expanding, and prone by its basic design to erode rather than fortify the foundations of a free and peaceful world order. America's true interests do not lie in preserving the U.N. but in supplanting it with coalitions and institutions better designed to defend the cause of freedom and individual human dignity in the twenty-first century.

WHEN PRESIDENT BARACK OBAMA during his final weeks in office abandoned Israel to the edicts of the United Nations Security Council, he touched off a furor about the failings of the U.N. itself. The 15-member council, tasked with securing peace for the world, stood exposed as a collection of bigots and hypocrites bent on punishing the only democracy in the Middle East. This has inspired renewed calls from Congress and the American public to reform the U.N., defund the U.N., withdraw from the U.N. – calls for something salutary to be done.

The advent of a new administration opens the door to a broader and urgently needed debate over how, precisely, America in our time should deal with the U.N. Created in 1945 by the victors of World War II with a charter mission to "save succeeding generations from the scourge of war," the U.N. has evolved into an organization notorious not only for its waste but also for its abuse, fraud, bigotry, mendacity, and predilection for actions (or choreographed inactions) that make war more likely, not less.

The need for remedies goes way beyond the need to defang the Security Council's Resolution 2334 savaging Israel, a resolution that is both damaging and disingenuous. In the name of peace, and in the guise of condemning settlements, this resolution invites the world to further undermine an already beleaguered Jewish state. That's a road to war, not peace.

This diplomatic lynching is all the more alarming because it is no random act of prejudice, no appalling vice of an otherwise benevolent institution. It springs from a fundamental U.N. flaw that continually undermines not only Israel but the rest of the free world: the U.N.'s inherently corrupt moral compass. Combined with the U.N. system's privileges, immunities, proliferating ambitions, and ever-expanding overreach, this moral rot is a growing menace to America itself.

America's leaders have many means available to fight back, if they have the will to use them. But if they confine their mission to yet another attempt to fix the U.N., they will fail. The desire to reform the U.N. rather than simply reject it, or at the very least work around it, springs from a worthy set of impulses, among them a basic prudence about being careful what you discard. However, there is by now a record of U.N. reform efforts stretching back decades – and it is horrifying. Among the more recent episodes was a big push in 2005–2006 to clean up the U.N. following the Oil-for-Food corruption scandal in Iraq, as well as congressional efforts in the 1990s to inspire better U.N. behavior by adding an internal audit department and withholding U.S. funds (a reform effort that failed to forestall the Oil-for-Food debacle).

Each time, the U.N. has emerged not only unreformed in character but bigger in scale, broader in reach, and at least as perverse, if not more so, in its influence and many of its activities. Emblematic of this pattern is the case of the old Commission on Human Rights, which the U.N. set up in 1946 "to weave the international legal fabric that protects our fundamental rights and freedoms." The commission became a magnet for human rights abusers among the U.N.'s member states, less interested in weaving the promised fabric than in redefining it to suit themselves. By 2003, the commission was packed with despotisms, focused chiefly on condemning Israel, and was chaired by Libya. The U.N.'s Potemkin remedy, in 2006, was to dissolve the commission and in its place set up the current Human Rights Council. A skeptical Bush administration steered clear of the new council, whereas Europe embraced it and Spain celebrated its nascence by donating a $23 million artwork ceiling, entailing more than 30 tons of paint, for its meeting chamber in Geneva. In 2009, despite evidence that the new council was already reverting to the vices of the old commission, the U.S. became a member under Obama's policy of engagement, proposing to work aggressively from within to make the council a world-class forum for advancing human rights. Today — you guessed it — the council is packed with human rights abusers fixated on condemning Israel.

It is time to consider quite seriously whether America should step clear of the U.N., withdrawing both U.S. money and the huge degree of legitimacy that America's founding membership and participation confers on the institution. The logistics of any such move might appear daunting, and the attendant uncertainties frightening. But for years, like the proverbial frog in a pot of water coming to a boil, America has been the mainstay of a U.N. at which venally corrupt and morally malign behavior is a chronic near-certainty on an amplifying scale. That ought to qualify as even more daunting and frightening.

The clarifying question, too often ignored, is one of opportunity cost. If we did not have the U.N., what system, or set of coalitions, might America choose today to create in its place? What opportunities for life, liberty, and the pursuit of happiness have been choked off, around the globe, because the U.N. — thanks to the configuration of forces in 1945 — gave veto power on the Security Council to Stalin's Soviet Union, a privilege since inherited by an increasingly despotic and aggressive post-Soviet Russia?

For instance, would America, starting with a fresh slate, really invent or endorse as the world's leading human rights body an outfit that — à la U.N. Human Rights Council — routinely welcomes such members as Russia, China, Saudi Arabia, and Venezuela?

The task of unwinding the U.S. from its involvements in the U.N. might seem formidable. But at least for the sake of making informed judgments about the future of U.S. sovereignty, security, and foreign policy, surely it's worth working out how that might be done and what opportunities it might open up. There's little in the modern public domain to suggest that anyone versed in the byways of the U.N. has ever tackled the task of charting a full roadmap for such an exit.

It bears noting that the U.N. charter itself is hazy on such matters. The U.N.'s founders, mindful of the disintegration of its predecessor League of Nations, made no provision for the withdrawal of a member state. (Indonesia tried it in 1965, and then went back.) In principle, member states can be expelled. But that has not been the practice, although the U.N. charter's Chapter II, Article 6, states, "A Member of the United Nations which has persistently violated the Principles contained in the present Charter may be expelled from the Organization by the General Assembly upon the recommendation of the Security Council." That raises the question of why the likes of Iran, Sudan, and North Korea have not been kicked out. Surely they all qualify as being in violation of the charter obligations regarding "respect for human rights," and their commitments to any rational definition of peace are at best doubtful. If the U.N. doesn't take its own charter principles seriously, just how seriously should America take the U.N.?

These are matters ever more deserving of debate and in-depth exploration. President Trump and a number of Republican lawmakers are now pursuing ways of reducing America's support for the U.N. But among the policy elite of Washington and New York, any talk of actually leaving or massively defunding the U.N. has long been a no-go zone. It's been 34 years since the Cold War diplomatic fracas of the Reagan era in which Ambassador Jeane Kirkpatrick's deputy, Charles Lichenstein, dared to tell U.N. members that if they did not like the way America was treating them, they and the U.N. were welcome to leave; not only that but "the members of the U.S. mission to the United Nations will be down at the dockside, waving you a fond farewell as you sail off into the sunset."

Today, in the wood-paneled realms of America's foreign-policy shamans, the 72-year-old U.N. ranks as a totem of international order, a permanent fixture, and – among select inner circles both within and surrounding the U.N. – a font of jobs, consulting contracts, influential connections, and per diems. Any attempt to suggest the U.N. might be past its shelf date invites being elbowed off the stage. The usual argument is that the U.N. may be imperfect, but it's all we've got.

The imperfections are by now so acute that the retort ought to be, If the U.N. is all we've got, it's time we came up with something else.

Long gone is the heady post–Cold War glow of the early 1990s, and gone with it should be any illusions that the U.N. is the vehicle to carry a post-Soviet brotherhood of man into a new golden age. That notion was eclipsed in short order by the genocidal slaughters of the mid-1990s, while U.N. peacekeepers looked on, in Rwanda and at Srebrenica. Any lingering faith in the U.N. as a guardian of world integrity should have been smothered by the global cloud of graft that mushroomed out of the U.N.'s 1996–2003 Oil-for-Food relief program for Saddam Hussein's U.N.-sanctioned Iraq.

Among the arguments today for carrying on with the U.N. is the idea that it was founded at the end of World War II with the main mission of averting another world war. And lo! In the 72 years since its founding there has been no global conflagration. Ergo, argue U.N. advocates, the U.N. prevents world war. There's a strong counterargument that the U.N. is stealing credit from its oftenreviled chief patron, the U.S. – the real mainspring of post–World War II peace and prosperity. The U.N.'s existence has coincided with that of the Pax Americana, in which the U.S. democratic superpower has stood – at least until recently – as leader of the free world, a bulwark of liberty, fighting a number of regional wars against aggressive tyrannies, quite plausibly deterring others, and winning the Cold War against a Soviet Union which, with considerable support inside the U.N., aspired to extend its communist blight around the globe. Arguably, America – and the NATO military alliance – won the Cold War despite the U.N., not because of it.

Obama, during his two terms as president, actually bolstered the case for American leadership and against the U.N.-as-world-peacekeeper, though presumably that was not his aim. For eight years, Obama effectively ordered America to stand down while he gave the U.N. every chance to display its prowess. Striving to place the U.N. at the center of America's foreign policy, he declared in a 2009 speech to the U.N. General Assembly that "no one nation can or should try to dominate another nation." He downsized the United States' role around much of the globe, gutting the U.S. military, pulling out of Iraq, deferring to Russia, bowing to China, inertly bearing witness to mass protests in Iran, erasing his own red line in Syria, and responding to videotaped beheadings by ISIS with the assurance that America stands "shoulder-to-shoulder" with the "international community."

Via the U.N., Obama led from behind on Libya, awaited U.N.-assisted diplomatic remedies as revolt in Syria exploded into all-out war, and on the way out of office capped his backseat endeavors by declining to wield the U.S. veto while the Security Council had its way with Israel. Obama also exalted the preferences of the U.N. over those of Congress, enlisting the U.N.'s eager help to clinch in the eyes of the "international community" such domestically unpopular "legacies" as the feckless Iran nuclear deal and the costly Paris climate agreement. In neither case did Obama submit his grand international bargain as a treaty, to be ratified by the Senate. Rather, he defaulted to the U.N., as an end run around the U.S. Constitution's system of checks and balances. In doing this, Obama provided a superb case study in how the U.N. allows national leaders to abuse their powers – supplanting even democratic process with the approval of a vast multilateral collective, accountable in theory to all nations and in practice to no one.

The results by now of letting the U.N. take the lead range from damaging to catastrophic. Around the world, according to Washington-based Freedom House, freedom is in its 10th straight year of an accelerating slide. Led-from-behind Libya has collapsed into a terrorist-infested failed state. In Syria's war, more than 400,000 people have died while refugees have swamped Europe and the ISIS "J.V." team has expanded into a global network engendering terrorist butcheries in venues such as – to name just a few – a Paris concert hall, a Brussels airport, and a San Bernardino Christmas party. Missile-testing, terrorist-sponsoring Iran is extending its reach in the Middle East. Russia has ripped the basic fabric of international order by snatching Crimea (and gotten away with it) and threatens the rest of Ukraine. China is inventing territorial claims along vital shipping routes in the South China Sea. North Korea, despite a growing stack of U.N.

sanctions and Obama's chairing of a "historic" 2009 U.N. Security Council meeting envisioning a world without nuclear weapons, has been openly building and testing nuclear weapons.

All these opportunistic players find at the U.N. a clubhouse convenient to their common antidemocratic, anti-American cause. In matters as troubling as nuclear proliferation or ballistic missile testing by rogue states, Russia and China make use of their veto power on the Security Council not for peace but for their own benefit. They either run interference for such client states as Iran and North Korea or extract concessions from the U.S. in exchange for approving sanctions that they then disregard – leaving it to the U.S. to chase after their illicit traffic. All the while, the entire U.N. enterprise is lavishly bankrolled and legitimized by the world's leading democracies, above all by the U.S., in the utopian hope that U.N. programs will bring prosperity and its powwows will bring peace.

In sum, welcome to the U.N. world order.

American voters seem less than delighted with these trends. Donald Trump won the presidency with a campaign that included a highly skeptical view of the U.N., blaming the organization for causing problems rather than solving them. He has criticized the U.N. as "just a club for people to get together, talk and have a good time." He has warned that unless the U.N. lives up to its "huge potential," it is "a waste of time and money."

That's a dramatic improvement over Obama's approach. But the U.N. does plenty of things far more pernicious than simply wasting time and money. And we should all be wary of the idea that the U.N., if only it could get its act together, has "huge potential." That's the endless *Through the Looking Glass* promise of jam tomorrow but – somehow – never jam today. It's an enticing view, especially for folks who might be too busy with their day jobs to pay much attention to the inner workings of the U.N. Many Americans are worried by the U.N.-adopted Iran nuclear deal, which paves Iran's path to the bomb and pads its pockets en route. But many also cherish childhood memories of collecting Halloween coins for UNICEF, the U.N.'s agency for children. The temptation is to figure that like most large families, the U.N. has its shortcomings, but at least it cares for children.

Yes, UNICEF, with its annual revenues of roughly $5 billion, does do some good for children. But what else goes on? The agency has a record of being close to tyrants and loose in its financial practices. For instance, among the 36 U.N. member states currently on the executive board, or governing body, of UNICEF is Iran – which still engages in juvenile executions (hanging being Tehran's preferred method). In 2009, UNICEF's Iran website featured a fundraising appeal for the children of terrorist-run Gaza, in which donors were invited to send money via an Iranian bank then under U.N. sanctions for its role in Iran's nuclear and missile programs. When I inquired at the time about this financial arrangement, UNICEF would not disclose what was going on with that bank account. Also on the current UNICEF board are such human rights abusers as Belarus, Russia, Saudi Arabia, Cuba, and China – home until just last year to a longtime one-child policy that included fines and forced abortions.

If America wants to help the world's children, a highly relevant question is whether there might be better ways to do it than via an opaque U.N. agency with dictators serving on its board. Were a private American charity to try transferring funds to terrorist-run Gaza via a bank blacklisted as a conduit for illicit nuclear and missile traffic, it's likely that someone would land in jail. But when the U.N. does it, it's just another day raising money for children.

That's pretty much how it works across the entire U.N. system, where UNICEF's despot-infested board is basically business as usual. Iran, in all its misogyny, also currently sits on the executive board of U.N. Women and in 2009 chaired the board of the U.N.'s flagship agency, the U.N. Development Programme. From 2012 to 2016, despite being under U.N. sanctions for most of that stretch, Iran chaired the second-largest voting bloc in the General Assembly: the 120-member Non-Aligned Movement (NAM). Last year Venezuela succeeded Iran as head of NAM, hosting a party at which only a handful of political eminences showed up, but among them were the presidents of Iran, Zimbabwe, and Cuba; the titular head of state of North Korea, Kim Yong-nam; and the head of the Palestinian Authority, Mahmoud Abbas.

The assembly's largest voting bloc, the development-themed 134-member group known as the G-77, distinguished itself in 2009 by choosing as its chair the ambassador of Sudan. Sudan's president, Omar al-Bashir, had been charged four years earlier by the International Criminal Court for genocide and crimes against humanity (al-Bashir, still Sudan's president, has never been arrested). Secretary-General Ban Ki-moon sent Sudan's ambassador his best wishes, and Sudan celebrated its ascent to the head of the G-77 by throwing a party in the U.N. Delegates' Dining Room, replete, as reported by *Inner City Press*, with ice sculptures, lobster, and chocolate-covered strawberries.

All of which brings us to the core design flaws of the U.N. itself.

To the casual visitor, the U.N. might look and sound like a grand experiment in global democracy, dedicated to liberty and justice for all. Under the 1945 charter, with its talk of peace and freedom, the U.N. holds elections. Its 193-member General Assembly votes, upon recommendation of the Security Council, for a secretary-general who routinely makes way for a successor, after serving one or two five-year terms. The 15-member Security Council often holds votes, albeit with five permanent members – Russia, China, France, Britain, and the U.S. – wielding the power to veto any resolution.

But the U.N. is not a democratic polity. Its leaders, or officials, are not accountable to those truly affected by its actions. It is a huge collective of governments, which in effect reports to itself. There is no constituency of ordinary people who can vote its officials out or hold them directly responsible for what they do. There is no equivalent of public confirmation hearings for the appointment of senior officials. There is no provision for draft Security Council resolutions to be disclosed to the public before they are introduced for a vote.

To make matters worse, the U.N. was created with a shield of diplomatic privileges and immunities. That has its conveniences for the U.N., but for the rest of us it means there is no way to legally hold its offices, personnel, or programs to account. Were the U.N. merely a talking shop, these immunities might be reasonable. There is a long tradition of envoys enjoying immunity to come parley. But the U.N. long ago outgrew the role of a mere council. Today it more closely resembles a neocolonial empire, with overlapping and intersecting offices, programs, peacekeepers, special initiatives, and ambitions to try to engineer development and regulate the climate of the planet. This goes on around the globe, across borders and legal jurisdictions, swaddled in laissez-passer privilege and diplomatic immunities. This arrangement fosters what a U.N. internal auditor neatly summarized back in 2006 – while investigating massive corruption in U.N. peacekeeping contracts – as a "culture of impunity." The secretary-general has the power in special circumstances to waive immunity, but such instances are rare.

In other words, while proposing to act as moral arbiter and shepherd of peace and prosperity for the planet, the U.N. is itself exempt from law and justice. These immunities also translate into a considerable degree of secrecy at the U.N., which cranks out endless information on its labors for humanity but has no compelling incentive to answer questions it doesn't like. In 2006, following a number of huge bribery scandals involving senior U.N. staff, the U.N. Secretariat rolled out an "ethics" reform involving financial disclosure by senior U.N. officials – with the intriguing feature that these officials could opt not to disclose their disclosures to the public.

To make it still worse, within this secretive and diplomatically immune collective, the majority of member states are not free polities. They bring with them an antidemocratic tilt that permeates the U.N. According to a 2016 report by Freedom House, only about 40 percent of the world's population and 44 percent of its countries rank as free – a database that roughly duplicates the membership of the U.N. The rest of the world lives under governments that range from "partly free," such as Guatemala or Pakistan, to "not free," such as Cuba or North Korea. That's the voting majority in the General Assembly.

At the U.N., the effect of this mix of dictatorships and democracies is to create a rough set of double standards regarding who takes seriously the U.N.'s edicts and ground rules and who doesn't. American administrations, bound by American law and answerable to voters, pretty much have to keep their official bargains with the U.N., or justify to the satisfaction of those back home why they didn't. Dictators, when they're at home, get to call the shots, and tend to silence anyone who dissents. They are much freer to pick and choose which U.N. constraints they will honor and which they won't. The upshot is that while law-abiding, free societies bear the full cost of whatever they agree to at the U.N., dictatorships have every incentive to manipulate and exploit the U.N. system to the hilt.

Thus, for instance, the U.S. may woo and reward China's agreement to approve a U.N. sanctions resolution meant to stop North Korean nuclear tests. But when it comes to enforcing those sanctions, different rules seem to apply. America tends to prosecute violators. China, for all its amazing surveillance apparatus, can't locate them.

There's yet another layer to this setup, fraught with yet more perverse incentives, concerning the matter of legitimacy. U.N. membership confers a seat and one vote in the General Assembly on all countries alike, whether they are democracies or dictatorships. For democratic governments, which derive their legitimacy from voters back home, this is useful but not necessarily earthshaking. Dictators, however, who tend to rule through a mix of force and propaganda, are forever in search of a legitimacy they do not actually enjoy at home. U.N. membership dignifies them with seats alongside the world's freely elected governments and treats them all as equals. When tyrants or their ministers parade across the U.N. stage in New York at the General Assembly opening every September, sandwiched between the speakers from America, Britain, and Japan, before a golden backdrop, one of the implicit messages to their oppressed populations back home is that their rulers, in the eyes of the world, are legitimate. An epitome of this moral equivalence was the U.N.'s decision in 1991 to admit simultaneously as members the countries of North and

South Korea – welcoming as twins a totalitarian state and a vibrant developing democracy.

Advocates of the U.N. like to argue that it provides the U.S. with a brand of global legitimacy and latitude it would not otherwise enjoy. Actually, it's the other way around. It is primarily the U.S. that confers legitimacy on the U.N. On balance, the U.N. offers far more benefits at the margin to despotisms than it does to its democratic chief patrons. The U.N. effectively serves as a vehicle for the transfer of legitimacy from democratic to unfree regimes, dignifying the dictators and tainting the complicit democrats. Presumably that's at least one of the reasons why, when Deputy Ambassador Lichenstein in 1983 invited the U.N. (and the Soviet delegation in particular) to sail off into the sunset, nobody sailed.

Into this stew of self-dealing member states, the taxpayers of the world's leading democracies pour tens of billions every year. America is by far the largest contributor, paying for 22 percent of the General Assembly's annual budget and more than 28 percent of the peacekeeping budget, for a combined sum that currently comes to roughly $3 billion. You might suppose that America's billions buy plenty of influence over how that money gets spent. But long custom at the U.N. has largely turned America's outsized contributions into an entitlement. A telling moment came during a General Assembly debate in December 2007 over the assembly's proposed budget, to which the U.S. had some objections. These budgets are usually passed by consensus, but on this occasion, the U.S. asked for a vote. Following an all-night debate, during which some members left, the assembly approved the budget, by a vote of 142 to 1. That lone dissenting vote was cast by the biggest donor in the room, the United States.

Most debates about funding or defunding the U.N. tend

to focus on the U.S. dues to the General Assembly and peacekeeping. But that $3 billion is just a fraction of the lucre that the American government gives to the wider U.N. system. Some years ago, during a bout of U.N. reform following the Oil-for-Food scandal, Congress began requiring the administration's Office of Management and Budget (OMB) to provide yearly reports on total U.S. contributions to the U.N., across the entire federal government. These reports were illuminating, showing U.S. tax dollars flowing to the U.N. not only via the State Department but from 10 other departments, including Agriculture, Commerce, Energy, and Health and Human Services, plus outfits such as the Environmental Protection Agency. For fiscal year 2010, the total reported by OMB was $7.69 billion – billions more than the dues for the General Assembly's "core" budget and peacekeeping.

Regrettably, the congressional requirement for these OMB reports expired some years ago, and after 2011 the Obama administration stopped releasing them. Fiscal year 2010 is the most recent for which these official compilations of total U.S. contributions to the U.N. are publicly available. But some information can be gleaned from the U.N. website, where the most recent available figures show that by 2014, total U.S. contributions totaled $10 billion (more than three times the amount America contributes to the "core" U.N. budget plus peacekeeping). That $10 billion represents about one-fifth of the U.N.'s system-wide revenues for 2014, which, as reported on the same U.N. website, totaled a staggering $48 billion.

It's hard to know how reliable or genuinely comprehensive these U.N. numbers are, or what lags might be reflected in the figures. The U.S. reports in fiscal years, the U.N. in calendar years. For fiscal year 2010, the U.S. administration reported giving the U.N. a few billion more ($7.69

billion) than the U.N. says it received from the U.S. government for either calendar year 2010 ($5.0 billion) or calendar year 2011 ($4.6 billion). In early January, the U.N. website showed total systemwide revenues spiking in 2012 by tens of billions for a total of $83.7 billion; when I queried the U.N. spokesman's office about that amount, the U.N. revised the figure on its website down to $42.3 billion, attributing the much higher sum shown earlier to "data not displaying correctly."

Errors and discrepancies are nothing unusual in matters involving U.N. financial reporting. A U.N. system that began as a club of dues-paying governments has become a global fundraising franchise so complex that the U.N. itself seems to have trouble keeping track. There are voluntary donations from governments, donations from nongovernmental organizations, donations in kind, public-private partnerships, and a welter of obscure trust funds and special appeals – along with those coins collected for UNICEF.

Whatever the actual sums, it's safe to say that many billions of U.S. dollars flow annually into the vast global conglomerate that is the U.N. system, with its dictator-laced governing boards and biases and its diplomatically immune personnel and ventures. For the U.N., the incentive is to keep discovering new roles for itself, conducive to yet more fundraising, chiefly from governments. The U.N. is flagrantly failing in such charter missions as ending war in the Middle East or preventing nuclear proliferation by North Korea. But it has done quite well for itself out of proposing to regulate the climate of the planet, at some date in the misty distant future, to within a few decimal points centigrade of some bureaucratically beatified target temperature.

There are plenty of caveats about how well the U.N.'s

ever-expanding galaxy of programs serves the U.N.'s officially chosen beneficiaries, such as the children guarded by peacekeepers or underwritten by UNICEF. But there is little doubt that for a privileged few, the U.N.'s franchise as prime official guardian of the world order translates into a U.N. gravy train, transferring wealth (and jobs) from ordinary taxpayers to officials of the U.N. and their counterparts within the policy elites of the U.N. member states.

To help keep U.S. funds flowing in, the U.N. maintains an information office in Washington, surrounded by a growing cluster of U.N. agency liaison offices, all located on or near Washington's K Street – a venue famous for its lobbyists and close to the wellsprings of congressional appropriations and administration approval. Officially these U.N. offices are in Washington to provide information, taking their cue from the 1946 founding mission of the U.N.'s Department of Information: "to promote global awareness and understanding of the work of the United Nations." In practice, the U.N. tends to hire former U.S. State Department and congressional staffers to run these offices, whence they can elaborate to their former colleagues and connections, both on the Hill and at the State Department, on the U.N.'s self-described virtues and need for ever more U.S. tax dollars.

As a rule, the U.N. does not like to promote awareness of the incentives driving its own Department of Information. But in trying to winnow U.N. facts from fiction, it can be useful to keep in mind that the U.N.'s information department reports to the General Assembly's Committee on Information, which includes among its 115 members such paragons of propaganda as North Korea, China, Syria, Sudan, and Cuba, with Iran currently serving – and not for the first time – as the committee's rapporteur. The information department, overseen by this committee, is funded out of the General Assembly budget to the tune of roughly $100 million per year, with 22 percent of that money coming from the United States. In sum, money being fungible, this means that the U.N., via information offices overseen in part by some of the world's worst regimes, spends American money to lobby in Washington for yet more American money.

Out of the U.N. murk, scandals routinely arise, many of them appalling in their dimensions but quickly gone from the headlines. U.N. secrecy, spin, and immunities often mean that the full story never gets aired and no one gets called to account. More than a decade after the U.N. proclaimed a policy of "zero tolerance" for peacekeepers raping children they are sent to protect, the U.N. has still not managed to stop such abominations – though these days it does provide generic statistics on the problem. Meantime, peacekeepers are dispatched to places where there is no peace to keep, such as South Sudan. Or, like the peacekeepers of the U.N. Interim Force in Lebanon (UNIFIL) watching the terrorists of Hezbollah truck in weapons – again – for the next war against Israel, the U.N.'s blue berets provide a facade of control while under their gaze the preparations proceed for slaughter.

For a saga that showcased myriad U.N. failings, it's worth revisiting the 2007 scandal that became known as Cash for Kim. That geyser of sleaze erupted out of the Pyongyang office of the U.N.'s flagship agency, the U.N. Development Programme (UNDP). A whistleblower who worked in that office tipped off U.S. authorities that in North Korea the UNDP, in violation of the U.N.'s own rules, had developed much too cozy a relationship with the tyrannical regime of North Korea. As it turned out, the UNDP office was dishing out funds to the North Korean government, importing

U.S.-government-controlled items that could be put to dual use for weapons technology, allowing North Koreans to handle the UNDP's bank account, transferring funds to proliferation-connected business entities in Asia, and keeping counterfeit U.S. $100 bills in its office safe. There was a U.N. inquiry, and for a while the UNDP office in Pyongyang was shut down. But the only person punished was the whistleblower, who lost his job.

This took place under the aegis of a U.N. agency tasked with "development," which brings us to yet another piece of the U.N. problem. Presumably there are some good intentions behind such U.N. cross-agency grand plans for the planet as the 2030 Agenda for Development, with its "17 Sustainable Development Goals." But if there's a whiff of the old Soviet five-year plans to this lingo, it's no accident. These huge U.N. programs, laying out blueprints for the erstwhile benefit of humanity, basically amount to central planning. It's entirely fitting that the U.N. chose as its new secretary-general António Guterres, who has not only served as a prime minister of Portugal and head of the U.N.'s refugee agency, but whose credentials also include a six-year stint as head of the Socialist International. This does not bode well.

The experiments of the last century should have taught us that central planning is a recipe not for development but for poverty and authoritarian rule. The real remedy is freedom: democracy, under decent and impartial law, coupled with free markets. But that goes against the grain of the U.N. character described above, and for the fundraising purposes of the U.N., there's not much money in it. So the U.N.'s grand plans continue to multiply, often to the benefit of the rotating arrays of dictatorships that sit on the U.N.'s governing bodies. It is perhaps telling that at the time of the UNDP's Cash for Kim scandal, North

Korea had a seat on the UNDP executive board, and the U.N. was paying to fly North Korea's envoys, business class, to the UNDP's board meetings in New York.

Likewise, the U.N.'s enormous agenda focused on "climate change" boils down, in economic terms, to a grab for control of the vast energy sector of the world economy, or at least a big say in how it works. Whatever your views on climate change, the further question ought to be whether the U.N. – immune, opaque, and unaccountable – is remotely qualified to regulate anything. This is an institution that can't keep track of its own money, and based on the record sometimes prefers not to.

For America's leaders, the temptation is simply to live with the failings of the U.N. (imperfect, but all we've got) or to try to address the worst of them, case by case, again and again. The results, on balance, just keep getting more dangerous, more corrupt, more ruinous. It's time to look for alternatives. The essence of freedom is choice. A basic element of the democracy and capitalism that made America great is competition. Are things really that different in world affairs?

It's time to end the U.N.'s 72-year monopoly as the world's leading multilateral body. How that might be done needs serious study. But the first step is to bring the question fully into the debate. Where to begin?

The first priority should be to scrap the Washington taboos, by asking not whether America should pull down the pillars of the U.N. but how that might most beneficially be done and what better could be built or devised in its place. Some inspiration could perhaps be taken from John F. Kennedy's famous line about choosing to do such things as go to the moon "not because they are easy, but because they are hard."

For an exit plan from the U.N. to succeed, there must

be – to begin with – a plan. This is something that men of good will could surely come up with. It would help to hear from experts versed in the ways of the U.N. and Washington but not invested in them. It would also help to have a genuine debate about what America would need, and could create, were it to jettison the U.N., in order to navigate an increasingly dangerous 21st century.

To better inform any such planning, it would help to have current information, in full, on what the U.S. actually provides to the U.N. The Trump administration could revive the practice of releasing comprehensive OMB reports on all U.S. contributions, and provide to Congress and the public the information that has gone unreported from fiscal year 2011 to the present. Congress, for its part, could revive its requirement for such reports.

It would also be useful to have a clearer window on the U.N. itself, with an eye to asking if there are better ways to help the world than via the likes of UNICEF, the UNDP, and the General Assembly. In 2007, when the Cash for Kim scandal hit the headlines during Ban Ki-moon's first month as secretary-general, Ban's immediate reaction was to promise, via his press office, that he would "call for an urgent, system wide and external inquiry into all activities done around the globe by the U.N. funds and programs." Within days, Ban scrapped that promise. The urgently needed global, independent audit of the U.N. system never took place. It is a pledge that his newly arrived successor, Guterres, should be asked to redeem (with a truly independent audit of the U.N. Secretariat thrown in). Trump, who has now taken ownership of America's relations with the U.N., would be wise to insist on it. If Guterres and his U.N. colleagues say no, then that too is informative.

The U.N. is swift to tout its own achievements, real or imagined. But there is plenty in the record to suggest that the more we understand about the true workings of the U.N., the stronger the case for consigning it to the heap of failed collectivist experiments of the 20th century and for designing better alternatives. Either this task gets done in the not-so-distant future because men of vision and good will put their minds to finding ways to do it, or it waits upon the aftermath of some cataclysm, toward which the U.N., as now configured, increasingly impels us.

AVIK ROY

HOW MEDICAID
FAILS THE POOR

Republicans have struggled to repeal and replace Obamacare because there are deep divisions about what conservatives' goals should be on health care. The phrase "repeal and replace" is so appealing to Republicans in part because it leaves unanswered the question "Replace with what?"

Many conservatives believe that the American health care system was a free-market one before Obamacare was passed in 2010. But the federal takeover of American health care didn't take place in 2010 as they think. It took place in 1965, when Lyndon Johnson signed the Medicare and Medicaid bills into law. Those bills – technically, amendments to the Social Security Act – are the principal drivers of the federal debt today, and the principal reason American health care is the costliest in the world. And those high costs are why twenty-seven million Americans go uninsured.

Worse still, the seventy-five million who are insured by Medicaid – our primary health insurance program for the poor – get substandard coverage, with health outcomes no better than they are for those with no insurance at all. In How Medicaid Fails the Poor, *I describe how Medicaid's haphazard design – unchanged since the 1960s – has driven doctors out of the program, making it difficult for Medicaid enrollees to gain access to care.*

Americans have always wanted every citizen to have access to adequate health coverage and care. "No one in this country should be denied medical care for lack of funds," said Ronald Reagan in 1964 while campaigning for Barry Goldwater. But the conventional wisdom that more government intervention is needed to cover the poor is the point the theory gets wrong. Government intervention is what has caused American health care to be unaffordable in the first place.

The Reagan approach to health care reform is worth revisiting. It could involve a robust and voluntary system of tax credits and health savings accounts to help the poor afford the coverage and care that they need, instead of them being forced to depend on single-payer programs like Medicaid. And it would roll back federal subsidies for those who don't need them.

A coherent Reagan-style reform could dramatically reduce federal spending and taxes, especially over the long term, by focusing our expenditures on those who are truly in need. Republicans should expand their health reform ambitions, from solely focusing on Obamacare to addressing the larger set of ways in which the federal government has distorted health care, of which Obamacare is merely the most recent part.

Most importantly, reform would require a Reaganesque commitment to the principle that helping the needy afford health care is a legitimate and desirable policy goal. It's a goal that most Americans share, and one that is entirely compatible with conservatives' allegiance to limited government and free markets.

Indeed, the only way conservatives will ever be successful at gaining public support for market-oriented health reform is by deploying it to improve coverage and care for the poor and vulnerable. Either we believe free enterprise can achieve that outcome or we're not true believers in free enterprise. It's time to choose.

THE PLIGHT OF American health care is best told through the eyes of a seventh-grader named Deamonte Driver.

Deamonte was born on the wrong side of the tracks, in Prince George's County, Md. Prince George's was founded in 1696 and was named for the Danish prince who married Queen Anne of Great Britain. In 1791, a chunk of the county was ceded to help create the District of Columbia.

Today, Prince George's sits directly east of the nation's capital. Aided by the decades-long expansion of federal spending, Prince George's is now the wealthiest county in America in which the majority of the population is black. But Deamonte was not one of the wealthy ones. He was an African-American child on welfare. He was raised by a single mother. He spent his childhood in and out of homeless shelters. He died in 2007, at the age of 12.

Deamonte, however, did not die in a drive-by shooting, or in a drug deal gone bad. He died of a toothache.

In September 2006, Deamonte started complaining to his mother, Alyce, that his teeth hurt. Alyce started calling around, looking for a dentist who would see him. But every dentist she called said no. Months later, after she had made several dozen phone calls, she found one.

The dentist she finally found told her that her son had six abscessed teeth, and he recommended that Deamonte see a surgeon to take them out. That took another round of phone calls. It took another several months for Alyce to find Deamonte an oral surgeon who was willing to take the job.

Within a week of the long-anticipated surgical appointment, Deamonte told his mother that his head ached. It turned out that the infection from one of his abscessed teeth had spread to his brain. Deamonte was taken to the hospital, where he underwent emergency brain surgery. He got better for a while but began to have seizures and was operated on again. Several weeks later, Deamonte was dead.

According to Ezra Klein of the *Washington Post*, Deamonte Driver's story shows us why it would be immoral to repeal the Affordable Care Act, a.k.a. Obamacare, a law that strives to expand health insurance coverage to the uninsured. "To repeal the bill without another solution for the Deamonte Drivers of the world? And to do it while barely mentioning them? We're a better country than that. Or so I like to think."

But Deamonte Driver did not die because he was uninsured. Indeed, Deamonte Driver died because he *was* insured – by the government. It turns out that Deamonte was on Medicaid.

* * *

Obamacare does not offer better health care to the Deamonte Drivers of the world. Under Obamacare, if Deamonte were still alive today, he would still be stuck with the same dysfunctional Medicaid coverage that he was stuck with before. Indeed, Medicaid is likely to get much worse. According to the Congressional Budget Office, Obamacare will shove 17 million *more* Americans into Medicaid, the developed world's worst health care system.

There are many problems with Obamacare. But the law's cruelest feature is what it will do to low-income Americans who are already struggling. Study after study shows that patients on Medicaid do no better, and often do worse, than those with no insurance at all.

There is a way to provide high-quality health care to the poor, one that would spend substantially less than Medicaid while ensuring that low-income Americans are protected against costly medical bills. But to understand the solution, we must first understand what went wrong.

* * *

It may seem strange to say this, but Medicaid – a program that in 2013 cost taxpayers more than $450 billion – started out as an afterthought. In the 1930s, '40s, and '50s, American progressives believed that the most politically palatable way to expand government sponsorship of health care was to begin with the elderly.

After all, the elderly were a far more sympathetic group in the public's eyes. Older Americans had less opportunity to earn their own money in order to fund their health care and were therefore generally poorer than other Americans, along with being less healthy. Being both relatively poor and relatively unhealthy, they were, in turn, also less likely to have health insurance. And policymakers believed that the model of Social Security as a "self-financed" program for the elderly, paid for with a dedicated payroll tax, could easily be extended to health insurance.

For many years, however, these efforts to expand government-sponsored health insurance were successfully opposed by a coalition in Congress of Republicans and conservative Democrats. They were also opposed by the organized force of American doctors, who feared that socialized medicine would restrict their freedom to serve their patients as they thought best.

In 1961, the American Medical Association (AMA) organized an early attempt by progressives to erect a universal, single-payer health-insurance program for the elderly. "Operation Coffee Cup," as the AMA called it, involved asking doctors' wives to organize coffee klatches in order to persuade their friends to write letters to Congress opposing the single-payer bill. At the meetings, the wives would play a recording narrated by an actor named Ronald Reagan, who warned that the single-payer bill "was simply an excuse to bring about what [progressives] wanted all the time: socialized medicine." The bill was defeated.

This dynamic, in which the AMA and congressional conservatives blocked government-sponsored health care, shifted dramatically in 1964, when Barry Goldwater challenged Lyndon Johnson for the presidency.

It would have been tough for any Republican to beat LBJ that year. Johnson, John F. Kennedy's vice president, had gained a substantial measure of sympathy after Kennedy was assassinated in November 1963. "In your heart, you know he's right," said a campaign ad for Goldwater the following year. But after Goldwater proclaimed that "extremism in the defense of liberty is no vice," Johnson's campaign retorted, "In your guts, you know he's nuts."

Democrats gained 36 seats in the House of Representatives – giving them an astonishing 155-seat majority – and increased their already huge Senate majority by two seats, nudging them up to a 36-seat majority. (By comparison, the substantial majorities Democrats held after the 2008 election were merely 79 seats in the House and 20 seats in the Senate.) Even taking conservative-leaning Democrats into account, liberals were utterly in control of Washington in 1965.

Suddenly, Democrats found themselves with a mandate to enact far-reaching reforms, and they did not waste the opportunity. Wilbur Mills, a conservative Democrat who chaired the key House Ways and Means Committee, had been a reliable obstacle to progressive legislation. After the 1964 election, he decided to shepherd LBJ's bill through Congress.

The first bill of the 1965 congressional session – H.R. 1 in the House and S. 1 in the Senate – was titled "Hospital Insurance for the Aged Through Social Security." The focus on hospital insurance reflected the fact that hospitalization costs represented the greatest financial burden on the elderly at the time.

As the "Medi-care" Bill zipped through Congress, Republican leaders, still reeling and disoriented from their painful defeat, criticized the proposal from the left, arguing that the legislation was inadequate because it covered neither physician services nor prescription drugs and because it offered equal subsidies to seniors regardless of income. Mills called their hand and raised them, creating a new program for physician services called Medicare Part B – and a separate health care entitlement for the poor, regardless of age, called Medicaid.

President Johnson signed the Medicare and Medicaid provisions into law, amending the Social Security Act on July 30, 1965. Johnson gave former President Harry Truman the first Medicare card. The AMA and its physician members eventually reconciled themselves to Medicare. The program, in its early decades, let doctors charge whatever they wanted, creating a kind of unlimited slush fund for physicians that was funded by taxpayers. Costs skyrocketed.

Medicaid, on the other hand, was to be jointly funded by state governments along with Washington. State governments, with their balanced-budget amendments, borrowing restrictions, and limited funds, did not have the latitude to absorb runaway costs.

"Though adopted together, Medicare and Medicaid reflected sharply different traditions," wrote Paul Starr in *The Social Transformation of American Medicine.* "Medicare was buoyed by popular approval and acknowledged dignity of Social Security; Medicaid was burdened by the stigma of public assistance. While Medicare had uniform national standards for eligibility and benefits, Medicaid left the states to decide how extensive their programs would be. Medicare allowed physicians to charge above what the program would pay; Medicaid did not and participation among physicians was far more limited. The objective of Medicaid was to allow the poor to buy into the 'mainstream' of medicine, but neither the federal government nor the states were willing to spend the money that would have been required."

* * *

The fact that Medicaid is jointly funded by the states and the federal government has had a consequential role in its evolution. The share that states pay, relative to Washington, is determined by a formula called the Federal Medical Assistance Percentage (FMAP). Title XIX of the Social Security Act, which now contains the Medicaid program, specifies that the federal government will contribute no less than 50 percent of a state's Medicaid costs.

The actual percentage of Medicaid spending that the federal government will sponsor varies depending on the relative wealth of a given state. In the nation's poorest state, Mississippi, Washington provides 73 percent of the funds; in wealthier states, like Massachusetts and New York, Washington pays the minimum 50 percent. Today, the median state enjoys an FMAP of 60 percent.

That means that for every dollar a state spends on its Medicaid program, the federal government will kick in an additional $1.50. It's not every day that a state politician gets to spend one dollar of his constituents' money and gain credit for spending nearly $2.50 in return. But that's how Medicaid works. As a result, irresponsible officials in many states have ratcheted up their Medicaid spending, knowing that taxpayers in other states will be forced to foot a good chunk of the bill.

Even then, the money eventually runs out. But by that point, hundreds of thousands of poor state residents have enrolled in the program, and governments are loath to throw them off the rolls. The federal Medicaid statute specifically bars states from charging higher premiums or co-pays to Medicaid enrollees, which would normally be a very effective way to save money.

As a result, states have one option that they use more than any other to keep their Medicaid costs in check: they pay hospitals and doctors less to provide the same amount of care to the same number of patients.

"As in previous years, provider rate restrictions were the most commonly reported cost containment strategy," concludes an extensive 2012 review of state-based changes to Medicaid by the Kaiser Family Foundation. "A total of 39 states restricted provider rates in [fiscal year] 2011 and 46 states reported plans to do so in [fiscal year] 2012."

It has gotten so bad that in the average state, for every dollar that a private insurer pays a primary-care physician to care for a patient, Medicaid pays 52 cents. Of the 10 Medicaid states, including Washington, D.C., that pay doctors the least, nine are reliably blue states with left-leaning politics and expansive Medicaid programs: New York (where Medicaid pays 29 percent of what private insurers do), Rhode Island (29 percent), New Jersey (32 percent), California (38 percent), D.C. (38 percent), Maine (42 percent), Florida (44 percent), Illinois (46 percent), Minnesota (46 percent), and Michigan (47 percent).

Now imagine you're a primary-care doctor with a busy practice. Two people call asking for an appointment to see you today, and you have one slot open. Do you give that slot to the patient who has private insurance, or the one who has Medicaid?

* * *

Actually, we don't even have to imagine. Sandra Decker, an economist for the National Center for Health Statistics at the Centers for Disease Control, did the work of correlating Medicaid's low rates to the percentage of doctors who accept new Medicaid patients, on a state-by-state basis. She found that primary-care doctors were 73 percent more likely to reject Medicaid patients relative to those who are privately insured, and specialists were 63 percent more likely to reject Medicaid patients.

Unsurprisingly, the states with the worst Medicaid reimbursement rates also had the lowest rates of physician acceptance of new Medicaid patients. Worst of all was New Jersey, where 60 percent of physicians were unwilling to accept new Medicaid patients. Next was California (43 percent), then Florida (41 percent), Connecticut (39 percent), Tennessee (39 percent), and New York (38 percent).

The fact that physicians reject Medicaid patients has real, human costs. In 2011, doctors at the University of Pennsylvania conducted a study, in which researchers posed as the parents of kids on Medicaid with urgent medical problems like acute asthma attacks or a broken forearm. They would call doctors in the relevant specialty and ask for appointments. If the "parents" told the doctors that their kids were on Medicaid, they were denied an appointment 66 percent of the time, compared with only 11 percent if they said they had private insurance.

In addition, the authors reported in the *New England*

Journal of Medicine, at those clinics that accepted both Medicaid/SCHIP and privately insured children, the average wait time for an appointment was, on average, 22 days longer for those on Medicaid/SCHIP: 42 days vs. 20.

The health scenarios used in the study were all for kids with significant medical problems: persistent, uncontrolled asthma; acute depression; forearm fracture; new-onset seizures; type 1 diabetes; obstructive sleep apnea (diYculty breathing) and chronic ear infections; and severe atopic dermatitis (itchy rashes) that won't respond to conventional steroids. So, to put this in human terms: a mother whose child has persistent, uncontrolled asthma has zero or a near-zero chance of being rejected by a doctor if the child has private insurance. However, if the child is on Medicaid or its sibling, SCHIP, the child has a 55 percent chance of not being able to get an appointment.

"It's very disturbing," said Dr. Karin Rhodes, one of the authors of the study, to Denise Grady of the *New York Times.* "As a mother, if I had a kid who was having seizures or newly diagnosed juvenile diabetes, I would want to get them in right away."

It's disturbing, all right, but hardly shocking to people who've experienced Medicaid's dysfunction firsthand. "It's interesting to think you even need a study to prove that," said Dr. Stephen Stabile of the Cook County Hospital system in Chicago. "It's pretty much common knowledge."

This isn't just a problem for kids with significant medical problems but also for those who need routine care. The June issue of the journal *Pediatrics* contains another study from the *New England Journal* authors, using the same methodology, in which they surveyed the ability of mothers to obtain urgent dentist appointments for their kids. In that study, 64 percent of Medicaid/SCHIP beneficiaries were unable to get an appointment, compared with a 5 percent rejection rate for those with private insurance: a ratio of 14 to 1.

* * *

There's a massive fallacy at the heart of Medicaid, and therefore at the heart of Obamacare. It's the idea that health insurance equals health care.

It doesn't take a PhD in health economics to appreciate that if you have a card that says you have health insurance, but that card doesn't get you into the doctor's office when you need help, you're not going to get better health care. But in case you were wondering, PhDs – and MDs – have looked at this problem. In 2010, a group of surgeons at the University of Virginia asked this question: Does the type of health insurance you have make a difference in the outcomes of the care you receive?

To answer it, they evaluated 893,658 major surgical operations from 2003 to 2007. The results were jarring. Patients on Medicare who were undergoing surgery were 45 percent more likely to die before leaving the hospital than those with private insurance; the uninsured were 74 percent more likely; and Medicaid patients were 93 percent more likely. That is to say, despite the fact that we will soon spend more than $500 billion a year on Medicaid, Medicaid beneficiaries, on average, fared slightly worse than those with *no insurance at all.*

The most obvious rebuttal to the Virginia surgeons' findings is, "Well, of course Medicaid patients did worse. People on Medicaid are poor, and poor people tend to be in poorer health than wealthy people." But the UVa authors anticipated this criticism. They normalized their figures to take relevant factors into account: age, gender, income, geographic region, operation, and health status.

The UVa study wasn't the first to show that Medicaid patients fare poorly. Other studies had found similar results:

> ➤ A University of Pennsylvania study published in *Cancer* found that in patients undergoing surgery for colon cancer, the mortality rate was 2.8 percent for Medicaid patients, 2.2 percent for uninsured patients, and 0.9 percent for those with private insurance. The rate of surgical complications was highest for Medicaid, at 26.7 percent, compared with 24.5 percent for the uninsured and 21.2 percent for the privately insured.

> ➤ A Columbia-Cornell study in the *Journal of Vascular Surgery* examined outcomes for vascular disease. Patients with clogged blood vessels in their legs or clogged carotid arteries (the arteries of the neck that feed the brain) fared worse on Medicaid than did the uninsured; Medicaid patients outperformed the uninsured if they had abdominal aortic aneurysms.

> ➤ A study of Florida patients published in the *Journal of the National Cancer Institute* found that Medicaid patients were 6 percent more likely to have late-stage prostate cancer at diagnosis (instead of earlier-stage, a more treatable disease) than the uninsured; 31 percent more likely to have late-stage breast cancer; and 81 percent more likely to have late-stage melanoma. Medicaid patients did outperform the uninsured on late-stage colon cancer. (They were 11 percent less likely to have late-stage cancer).

> A University of Pittsburgh study of patients with throat cancer, published in *Cancer*, found that patients on Medicaid or without insurance were three times as likely to have advanced-stage throat cancer at the time of diagnosis, compared with those with private insurance. Those with Medicaid or without insurance lived for a significantly shorter period than those with private insurance.

> A Johns Hopkins study of patients undergoing lung transplantation, published in the *Journal of Heart and Lung Transplantation*, found that Medicaid patients were 8.1 percent less likely to be alive 10 years after their transplant operation, compared with those with private insurance and those without insurance. Medicaid was a statistically significant predictor of death three years after transplantation, even after controlling for other clinical factors. Overall, Medicaid patients faced a 29 percent greater risk of death.

You'd think that Medicaid's poor health outcomes would be a scandal on the left. You'd be wrong. After all, Obamacare puts 17 million more Americans into the Medicaid program. The law's supporters were placed in a bind: if Medicaid really does provide poor health outcomes, then they would have to admit that Obamacare is not all it was cracked up to be.

When Connecticut Senator Joe Lieberman said, in 2009, that he wouldn't support Obamacare if it expanded Medicare, the *Washington Post*'s Ezra Klein wrote, "Lieberman ... seems willing to cause the deaths of hundreds of thousands of people in order to settle an old electoral score." Government-sponsored health care, Klein asserted, would save hundreds of thousands of lives. Opposing such a program was the moral equivalent of sanctioning mass murder.

The argument that Medicaid was not making poor people healthier seemed so counterintuitive – especially to those who believe in the efficacy of government programs – that most progressives dismissed it entirely.

Others portrayed a discussion of Medicaid's poor outcomes as a conspiracy designed to *harm* the poor. "The right wing's attack on government insurance programs has taken a novel and brash twist," wrote Jonathan Cohn in a *New Republic* article titled "The Conservative Assault on Medicaid." "If you're a thirty-something mother making, say, less than $20,000 as a hotel housekeeper, some conservatives think you'd be better off uninsured – i.e., completely at the mercy of charity care, depending in many cases on emergency rooms even for routine treatment – than if you had the government's insurance policy for the poor."

Fortunately, a group of leading health economists – mainly based out of MIT and Harvard – took seriously the concerns about Medicaid's health outcomes and decided to design the definitive study that would prove that Medicaid made people healthier. The outcome of that study, published in 2013, would change the Medicaid debate forever.

* * *

The early 1990s were a heyday for progressive health reformers. Bill and Hillary Clinton famously campaigned for national health reform in 1992 and 1993; while that effort failed, a number of states led by Democratic politicians did their part to experiment with health-policy changes at the state level.

One of those states was Oregon. An emergency-room physician named John Kitzhaber, who also served in the Oregon State Senate, conceived of a plan to expand health coverage for the working poor, using the Medicaid program.

In 1993, before Kitzhaber's plan was approved by President Clinton, 240,000 Oregonians were on Medicaid. The following year, 120,000 additional residents enrolled. Spending on the program nearly doubled, from $1.33 billion in 1993-95 to $2.36 billion in 1999-2001.

The state budget buckled under the program's exploding costs. Something had to be done. So in 2003, the state passed a law closing the Medicaid program to new enrollees. That way, the rolls could gradually shrink over time, through attrition. In 2008, Oregon reopened the program to newcomers but limited the number of new spots to 30,000. Since nearly 90,000 Oregonians were on a Medicaid waiting list at the time, the state decided to hold a lottery to award the new Medicaid spots.

A group of economists from MIT and Harvard – including Kate Baicker, Amy Finkelstein, and Jonathan Gruber – realized that the problems in Oregon created an opportunity. For all the strengths of the Virginia study of surgical patients on Medicaid, that study had one all-too-common flaw: it was a *post hoc*, retrospective analysis of old patient records.

While such retrospective analyses can be useful, they run the risk of being infected with bias – the bias that hindsight is 20/20. The gold standard of experimentation, as with clinical drug trials, is a prospective, randomized experiment in which you study two populations, one with the desired treatment and one without, to see which fares better.

The Oregon lottery, the MIT and Harvard economists

figured out, could allow the researchers to conduct just this kind of prospective, randomized experiment on Medicaid. The state had randomly offered Medicaid coverage to 30,000 residents, leaving tens of thousands more still uninsured. By tracking these patients over time, the economists could assess whether or not Medicaid was making its enrollees healthier. Were they living longer than uninsured Oregonians? Did they have fewer incidences of heart disease, diabetes, and the like?

In 2011, months after John Kitzhaber's inauguration as the 37th governor of Oregon, the economists released their initial findings. While it was too early to measure Medicaid's effects on objective health measures, such as blood pressure or cholesterol, patients told the researchers that they felt better about their health.

This rather modest result led to a chorus of jubilation from liberal journalists. "Amazing Fact! Science Proves Health Insurance Works," read a headline from Ezra Klein. Wrote Matthew Yglesias: "A new rigorous study from Oregon confirms that Medicaid does, indeed, save lives." (The study did not, in fact, detect any change in mortality.) Oregon's result "suggests that having health insurance substantially improves health," wrote David Leonhardt of the *New York Times*. One of the authors of the study, Amy Finkelstein of MIT, cheered, "What we found in a nutshell is that having Medicaid makes a big difference in people's lives."

There were problems with the first-year Oregon data. In their research paper, the investigators noted that two-thirds of the improvement in patients' self-reported health took place "about 1 month after [Medicaid] coverage was approved" but before the patients had seen a single doctor or consumed any health care services. This strongly suggested that the "benefit" that patients were reporting was the insurance version of a placebo effect. But this subtlety didn't make the front pages.

When the following July came around and it was time to publish the two-year results of the study, the Oregon investigators were strangely silent. The 2012 presidential election came and went. The state-by-state debate on expanding Medicaid, under Obamacare, came and largely went. Finally, on May 1, 2013 – 10 months late – the *New England Journal of Medicine* published the second-year findings. Did Medicaid save lives? No. It "generated no significant improvement in measured physical health outcomes," including death, diabetes, high cholesterol, and high blood pressure.

What's almost as striking as this nonresult is how few Oregonians felt the need to sign up for this allegedly life-saving program. The authors report that of the 35,169 individuals who "won" the lottery to enroll in Medicaid, only 60 percent actually bothered to fill out the application. In the end, only half of those who applied ended up enrolling. Remember that this is a program on which we will be spending $7.4 trillion over the next 10 years, a program that Obamacare aims to throw 17 million more Americans into, because of the hundreds of thousands of lives that Medicaid will supposedly save.

Immediately, progressive bloggers went into overdrive to explain these results away. "The sample size was too small," they said, even though new medicines for diabetes, high cholesterol, and high blood pressure routinely show significantly improved health outcomes in much smaller trials. "Two years isn't long enough to show a significant benefit," they insisted, even though new drugs that failed to show any benefit in two years would be summarily rejected by the FDA and abandoned by their sponsors.

The Medicaid cohort reported that they felt better

about their health and their financial security as a result of enrolling in the program and were less depressed. We can presume that the 40 percent of Medicaid "winners" who didn't bother to fill out the application felt differently; they, however, were not surveyed.

Nonetheless, Medicaid's cheerleaders seized on this qualified bit of good news. "This is an astounding finding... a huge improvement in mental health," said economist Gruber. To which conservative blogger Ben Domenech responded, "I wonder whether we'd be better off replacing the [Medicaid] expansion with a program that hands out $500 in cold hard cash and a free puppy."

Austin Frakt of Boston University is a passionate Medicaid advocate who, for years, has disputed studies showing poor Medicaid outcomes. "That insurance... improves health and reduces mortality risk is as close to an incontrovertible truth as one can find in social science," Frakt averred in 2010. Frakt had been holding up the Oregon study as the gold standard for health-policy research. Now that its results were out, he veered in both directions: he highlighted, as Gruber had, the alleged benefit in mental health, while simultaneously insisting that the Oregon study was "far too small" to draw meaningful conclusions.

Paul Krugman, the cantankerous columnist for the *New York Times*, dismissed the Medicaid skeptics this way: "If health insurance is a good idea – and you are nuts if you let this study persuade you otherwise – Medicaid is cheaper than private insurance. So where is the downside?" After that argument went nowhere, Krugman abruptly shifted gears, arguing that Medicaid's health outcomes don't matter. "Fire insurance is worthless!" he snarked. "After all, there's no evidence that it prevents fires."

Unwittingly, Krugman had stumbled onto the answer. There is a way to provide health coverage to the poor that truly protects them from medical calamities. But to do so, we must first learn from the way we insure ourselves against fires.

* * *

Paul Krugman is right. Fire insurance doesn't prevent fires, and it isn't meant to. The purpose of fire insurance is to protect the policyholder from the catastrophic financial loss that occurs when one's home burns down. In every sector of the economy except health care, that's what insurance is for. We buy car insurance, for example, to protect ourselves from the financial cost of car accidents. Yet when it comes to health care, we expect health insurance to save lives and improve health, instead of expecting it merely to protect us from catastrophic medical bills.

We could easily apply the lessons of car insurance and fire insurance to health insurance. But we don't, because many people have been persistently and ideologically opposed to treating health insurance this way. Imagine if car insurance also paid for your gasoline and your car washes. You'd use premium gas all the time and get the deluxe car wash once a week. But your insurance rates would go up too, because your extra consumption – and everyone else's – would drive up the cost of coverage.

This, indeed, is the bottom line from the Oregon study: that protecting people against bankruptcy from medical bills is a good thing and that auto- and fire-like catastrophic coverage is a far less costly way to do that, compared with expanding an already failed entitlement program.

We should make one thing clear: while Medicaid costs too much, its principal problem is that it doesn't make

Medicaid patients healthier. It's not wrong to spend a large sum of money on health care for the poor. It is wrong to *waste* large sums of money on health care for the poor. There are so many market-based alternatives to Medicaid, alternatives that would offer uninsured, low-income Americans the opportunity to see the doctor of their choice and gain access to high-quality, private-sector health care.

Singapore, which has a universal system of catastrophic coverage and health-savings accounts, spends one-seventh of what we spend on health care, with comparable results. The HSA-catastrophic combination is meant to protect beneficiaries from large medical bills while giving them control over their own health spending. If we gradually replaced our $1.5 trillion-a-year health care behemoth with this approach, we could wipe out our budget deficit and permanently solve our entitlement crisis.

Indiana, under then-Governor Mitch Daniels, placed Medicaid patients on an inexpensive combination of high-deductible insurance and subsidized health-savings accounts. The program enjoyed a 98 percent approval rating among its participants. But the Obama administration has declined to renew Indiana's waiver to continue this program, insisting that it be replaced by traditional Medicaid.

But let's not tinker around the edges with Medicaid, like Indiana has had to. Let's build from scratch a new health program for low-income Americans, one that would actually offer better health care than many wealthy Americans receive.

* * *

It wouldn't be that hard. Start by paying a primary-care physician $80 a month to see each patient, whether he is healthy or sick. That's what so-called concierge doctors charge, and it would give Medicaid patients what they really need: first-class primary-care physicians to manage their chronic cardiovascular and metabolic conditions.

Dr. Lee Gross is a co-founder of an innovative company called Epiphany Health. He offers "concierge plans for the little guy." Epiphany is designed primarily for individuals and families who don't have traditional health coverage. Unlike Deamonte Driver's mom, Alyce, who had to call dozens of doctors to find just one who would see her son, Epiphany's doctors are on retainer. You pay $83 a month and receive primary care whenever you need it. Spouses cost $69 extra, while kids cost $49.

"The most common medical conditions can be successfully managed at the primary care level, meaning most people do not need to see specialists," Gross writes on his website. "There is also no reason to end up in the emergency room for minor illnesses or injuries because you have no other option."

That's the dirty secret of Medicaid. You might have heard the rumor that uninsured people are clogging emergency rooms because the law allows them to get free care there. But the unreported story is that it is *Medicaid* patients who clog the emergency rooms because they can't persuade regular doctors to see them.

So give every Medicaid enrollee the Epiphany plan. Then throw on top of that a $2,500-a-year catastrophic plan to protect the poor against financial ruin. The total annual cost of such a program would be $3,460 per person, 42 percent less than what Obamacare's Medicaid expansion costs. Heck, you could put the entire country on that kind of plan, along with giving people the opportunity to use health savings accounts to cover the rest.

As a result of the 2012 Supreme Court decision that upheld the constitutionality of Obamacare, states have the freedom to choose whether or not to participate in the law's expansion of the Medicaid program. Though the expansion is largely funded from federal tax dollars, every state will still have to spend a considerable sum of its money to sign on to the Medicaid expansion.

Patrick Colbeck, an aerospace engineer turned Michigan state senator, proposed just this combination – retainer-based primary care and catastrophic coverage – as a substitute for Michigan's Medicaid expansion. "We can use this as an opportunity to ... not only accomplish the stated objectives of Obamacare but [also to] establish Michigan as a destination state for employers seeking quality affordable healthcare for their employees," said Colbeck in the summer of 2013.

But Michigan opted to pass the 1965-vintage Obamacare version of Medicaid instead.

It was an unfortunate decision. At a time when middle-income Americans are being squeezed by the health law's hikes to private health-insurance premiums, the expansion takes money from them in order to fund a broken program that doesn't improve health outcomes. Instead, we could offer the poor real primary care and real catastrophic coverage.

Many conservative opponents of the Affordable Care Act are concerned that the law costs too much, that it represents too much government intrusion into the lives of ordinary citizens. But the law's true weakness is that it endorses and expands the humanitarian scandal that is today's Medicaid program. Instead of making sure that America never sees another case like Deamonte Driver's, Obamacare moves people out of privately sponsored coverage and into Medicaid. It's a senseless and cruel policy.

The good news is that all over America, innovative doctors and policy entrepreneurs like Lee Gross and Patrick Colbeck are coming up with ways to bring health care for the poor — and the middle class — into the 21st century, into the age of e-mails and iPhones and text messages. What these trailblazers need is the support of millions of Americans who can help turn their ideas into law. Americans like you.

ROBERT L. SHIBLEY

TWISTING TITLE IX

In the year since Encounter released Twisting Title IX, *one of the "what-ifs" I posed at the end of the work came to pass: Donald Trump was elected president. With this has come the opportunity to "untwist" Title IX, at least in part.*

On September 22, 2017, Education Secretary Betsy DeVos announced that the pseudoregulation in the "Dear Colleague" letter that is at the heart of Twisting Title IX *would be withdrawn and replaced with lawfully promulgated regulations. While this is a necessary step for correcting the problems I detail in this piece, the fight is far from over. Many of the schools with dramatically unfair policies have vowed to keep them in place, ensuring that, for now, the abuses described here will continue. Those who care about justice and civil liberties still have much work to do ensure that the policies implemented by the Department of Education are fair and that colleges and universities bring their policies in line with the fundamental principles of due process.*

DAVE WEBER (not his real name) knew he was in trouble. An underclassman at Stanford University, Dave, like many others, harbored ambitions of graduating and going on to success in Silicon Valley. But in February 2011, he received notice from Stanford that a female student had filed a sexual assault charge against him, alleging that a sexual encounter six weeks before had been, unbeknownst to Dave, nonconsensual.

How, one might ask, could someone unknowingly commit sexual assault? To Stanford, it was simple: both Dave and his accuser had been drinking. Stanford's policy at the time stated, "A person is legally incapable of giving consent ... if intoxicated by drugs or alcohol." This seemingly straightforward statement is far vaguer than it sounds, most importantly because it is not actually true. People who are merely intoxicated to some extent – in other words, people who have been drinking anything alcoholic at all – legally consent to sex all the time. California law, as with that of virtually every state, recognizes this, specifying that when it comes to the lack of ability to consent to sex, "[i]t is not enough that the victim was intoxicated to some degree, or that the intoxication reduced the victim's sexual inhibitions." Even the most intense crusader against campus sexual assault would be hard-pressed to defend the idea that sexual activity after *any* amount of alcohol or drugs constitutes rape.

So Dave thought he had a reasonable chance at his hearing. The policy had obviously been carelessly drafted, and Stanford campus tribunals, like the criminal justice system, required that disciplinary charges be proved "beyond a reasonable doubt." Dave hired a lawyer and was able to gather witness statements and other evidence for his hearing that, he thought, would demonstrate that even though his accuser had been drinking, she wasn't too drunk to consent. He received more good news in March, when the local district attorney informed Dave's attorney that no criminal charges would be filed. His campus hearing was scheduled for Apr. 11, 2011.

What Dave didn't know was that his hearing would come exactly one week too late, and that a fluke of scheduling would change the course of his life. Because on

Apr. 4, 2011, the U.S. Department of Education's Office for Civil Rights (OCR) issued a letter unlawfully mandating that the standard of proof in campus sexual misconduct cases be set at the lowest possible level: a "preponderance of the evidence," or a mere 50.01 percent likelihood of guilt. Stanford immediately applied this standard of proof to Dave, right in the middle of his case, leading to his "conviction" in a campus kangaroo court. As it turned out, this letter would serve as the starting whistle for a new age of federal intervention in academia – an era that would see OCR's actions destroy the academic careers (and, in some cases, the lives) of countless students like Dave accused of sexual misconduct, prompt administrators at nearly every American college and university to rush headlong toward censorship and grossly unfair treatment of students, and stand as one of the most unrepentant abuses of the regulatory system in recent times. All in the name of a 1972 law called Title IX.

WHAT IS TITLE IX AND WHERE DID IT COME FROM?

Title IX is the primary federal law intended to prohibit sex discrimination in federally funded education programs. The operative part of the law (which is followed by myriad exceptions) is a mere 37 words long:

> *No person in the United States shall, on the basis of sex, be excluded from participation in, be denied the benefits of, or be subjected to discrimination under any education program or activity receiving Federal financial assistance.*

Since federal funding includes ordinary grants to schools or school districts as well as student-directed funds such as Pell grants and Stafford loans, Title IX applies to all public schools, from the K–12 level all the way through graduate school, as well as to the overwhelming majority of private universities in the United States. The number of private universities that do not at least accept federal student loans may well be in the single digits. Since losing such funding would generally be a death sentence for all but the richest schools, Title IX and its interpretations have become the main cudgel with which federal bureaucrats beat colleges and universities into submission to their policy objectives. Compared to that threat, the once-substantial influence that the First Amendment and other constitutional principles had on private university policies has been vastly reduced.

Until quite recently, when most people thought of Title IX, it was generally in the context of college athletics. It is, most notoriously, the reason many colleges have more women's NCAA sports than men's. Because fielding a football team requires many substantial athletic scholarships, and because the current interpretation of Title IX effectively requires schools to provide athletic scholarships for men and women in numbers proportionate to their percentage of all students, female students can often receive athletic scholarships for nonrevenue sports like rowing or lacrosse when men cannot. Women have outnumbered men in college since 1979 and currently make up 57 percent of undergraduates (higher at some schools), so the seemingly easier access to scholarships for women has long been controversial.

Indeed, early discussions of Title IX in the press focused overwhelmingly on its impact on college athletics, as a search of the *New York Times* archive from the first half of the 1970s indicates. But it wasn't long before activists for women's issues found in the law a tool for combating a number of other social ills, starting with sexual harassment.

A FAMOUS FEMINIST'S PLAN

In the 1977 case of *Alexander v. Yale*, using a framework developed by then Yale law student (and later famed feminist activist and antiporn crusader) Catharine MacKinnon, a federal court found that colleges could be liable under Title IX not just for allowing overt discrimination but also for not responding to allegations of sexual harassment by professors. In that case, the issue that survived the preliminary pleadings was an allegedly straightforward offer by a professor to give student-plaintiff Pamela Price an *A* in exchange for sex. Price ultimately failed to prove at trial that the sexual proposition ever occurred, but the precedent was set: sexual harassment could now be considered discrimination and was thus within the province of Title IX.

The kind of harassment allegedly experienced by Pamela Price is called "quid pro quo" harassment. It was then, and is now, universally recognized as morally wrong behavior (even if the law had not yet caught up to that conception). It's also what most people think of when they think of sexual harassment. But at around the same time, a new kind of sexual harassment was beginning to be recognized by courts and government agencies: "hostile environment" sexual harassment. In 1980, the Equal Employment Opportunity Commission (EEOC), which administers the law known as Title VII banning sex discrimination in employment, passed regulations defining this new kind of sexual harassment as sexually discriminatory "conduct [that] has the purpose or effect of unreasonably interfering with an individual's work performance or creating an intimidating, hostile, or offensive working environment."

Such conduct did not need to be intentional. It didn't even have to come from a specific person or be aimed at making people uncomfortable. For instance, if workers at a factory commonly posted nude centerfolds in their workspace, under the new standard, this would likely create a hostile environment and therefore be considered sexual harassment even if there was no intent to make women uncomfortable and nobody was targeted.

As you might imagine, a standard of harassment that required neither intent nor a target struck many people as troublesome. The then chair of the EEOC, Eleanor Holmes Norton (who has since served 13 terms as the District of Columbia's representative in Congress), noted in the introduction to the new regulations that the EEOC had received a large number of comments pointing to the new hostile environment standard as the "most troublesome definition of what constitutes sexual harassment." She said, however, that the commission was convinced it was "necessary." And in 1986, the Supreme Court ratified the EEOC's concept of "hostile environment" harassment, at least in the workplace. (Catharine MacKinnon was involved in that case as well, co-writing the brief for the plaintiff in *Meritor Savings Bank v. Vinson.*)

A FULL-EMPLOYMENT PROGRAM
FOR THE SPEECH POLICE

If your workplace has a rule against dating other employees or your college prohibits instructors from dating students, the "hostile environment" standard is the reason. If your school or workplace tells you certain words are totally off-limits, this is why. The mandatory sexual harassment trainings that now feature in virtually every workplace – seminars that are run by an industry of amazingly well-paid "trainers" and are often mocked, frequently bizarre, and nearly always pretty awkward – are the direct result of the adoption of the idea of hostile environment sexual harassment. And the acceptance of the hostile environment doctrine by the Supreme Court turned out to be the inflection point that would change Title IX into a flexible tool used by activists to address any number of perceived societal ills that could arguably be linked to sex or gender.

With the table set from a legal perspective, the explosion of "political correctness" onto the scene in the 1990s led both the government and college administrators to put teeth into this expanded conception of Title IX. (Not coincidentally, that decade also saw the birth of FIRE, the Foundation for Individual Rights in Education, of which I am executive director, in 1999.) In 1994, OCR launched an investigation into Santa Rosa Junior College in California after two female students complained about "anatomically explicit and sexually derogatory terms" used in comments about them posted on an online college forum. OCR's conclusion was that this created a hostile environment for the students and ordered the college to adopt a clearly unconstitutional rule that would punish speech protected by the First Amendment – a "speech code." When the University of Massachusetts Amherst put in place a broad, unconstitutional speech code the following year, Chancellor David K. Scott suggested that the Department of Education now required it.

What would this mean in terms of administrators' attitudes toward free speech? The short answer is that it has resulted in nearly two decades of bad examples for college students of how to handle free speech in a free society.

THE CURIOUS CASE OF PROFESSOR KIPNIS

Laura Kipnis is a film professor at Northwestern University, near Chicago. One might think that a woman deemed a "provocative feminist" by the *Nation*, a leading liberal magazine, would have little trouble under a regime designed to put an end to sex discrimination on campus. But Kipnis quickly found out that, thanks to Title IX, expressing a controversial opinion is anything but safe on today's campuses.

Kipnis's "offense" was writing an article for the *Chronicle of Higher Education* (the primary trade publication for college faculty and administrators) titled "Sexual Paranoia Strikes Academe." The February 2015 article took as its launching point Northwestern's recent ban on faculty–student romantic or sexual relationships, relationships that, in earlier decades, were quite common. Kipnis wrote critically about the increasing regulation of sexual expression and behavior on campus. Observing that "students' sense of vulnerability is skyrocketing," Kipnis pointed out problems with various policies, including the university's sexual harassment policy, which banned "inappropriate jokes," remarking, "I'd always thought inappropriateness was pretty much the definition of humor – I believe Freud would agree."

Kipnis also related several other vignettes of faculty–student sexual interactions – including the facts of a well-known and widely publicized case of alleged sexual harassment of a student by a philosophy professor – and the various campus reactions to them. She concluded, "The new codes sweeping American campuses aren't just a striking abridgment of everyone's freedom, they're also intellectually embarrassing. Sexual paranoia reigns; students are trauma cases waiting to happen. If you wanted to produce a pacified, cowering citizenry, this would be the method. And in that sense, we're all the victims."

As if to prove her point, the reaction to this newspaper article was paranoid, swift, and over the top. Students held protests, dragging mattresses and pillows to the administration building, and filed a petition demanding that the university president officially condemn the article. Soon after, Kipnis was informed by Northwestern's Title IX office that two complaints had been filed against her for violating Title IX with her newspaper article and a subsequent single tweet. Among the charges were that Kipnis had created a "chilling effect" on reports of sexual harassment, that Kipnis had "retaliated" against a student she mentioned (though not by name and in an ancillary fashion) in her article, and, of course, that she had created a "hostile environment."

There's no doubt that a hostile environment existed at Northwestern – for Professor Kipnis. She asked if she could have an attorney present during the investigation. This was denied, although she was allowed a "support person." She asked to be given the specific charges against her in writing. This, too, was denied. Instead, two out-of-town attorneys would be assigned to investigate her, and they would tell her the charges immediately before questioning her about them. She finally agreed to a Skype session with the lawyers, which she was denied permission to record. Professor Kipnis never saw any of the evidence against her. Her "support person," who talked in general terms about the case in front of the faculty senate, was slapped with a Title IX complaint for doing so and banned from continuing to be Kipnis's official support person.

With the 60-day "deadline" for making a decision on her case having already passed, Professor Kipnis did the smartest thing she could have done – she blew the whistle on what was happening to her in a second essay in the *Chronicle of Higher Education*: "My Title IX Inquisition." It was only fair. Whereas Professor Kipnis had been asked to keep the proceedings confidential, a student claiming to have highly detailed knowledge of unnamed "factual inaccuracies" in her original article had taken to the pages of the *Huffington Post* to bash her. And as the investigation dragged on with no end in sight, Kipnis's follow-up article had a rapid and profound effect: two days after it was published, Kipnis was informed that she was cleared of all charges.

POWER DIFFERENTIALS AND PEER HARASSMENT

The case against Professor Kipnis, absurd though it was, rested in part on the premise that a professor like Laura Kipnis is a powerful person on campus compared to a student. People are naturally more suspicious of events that can be framed as an abuse of power, and the concept of power differentials is critical to the idea of quid pro quo harassment – after all, you cannot offer someone a promotion in exchange for sex if you have no promotion to give. But most interactions on campuses are among students, who are peers, not between students and professors. In 1999, the Supreme Court took up the issue of the hostile environment doctrine at school and among students in the case of *Davis v. Monroe County Board of Education*. Attorneys for Georgia fifth-grader LaShonda Davis argued that the school district's "deliberate indifference" to the sexual harassment of Davis by a fellow student violated

Title IX by allowing a hostile environment to be created that effectively deprived Davis of an education.

The facts alleged in *Davis* were ugly, especially given the elementary school context. According to the complaint, a student referred to as G.F. "attempted to touch LaShonda's breasts and genital area and made vulgar statements such as 'I want to get in bed with you' and 'I want to feel your boobs.'" Such incidents happened repeatedly over a span of about five months, but the school did nothing effective to stop the behavior until G.F. was ultimately charged with (and pled guilty to) sexual battery.

At issue in the case was the question of whether Title IX applied only to discrimination (including sexual harassment) by the school and its employees, or whether schools could also be held liable for hostile environments created by students, over whom they had far less control. The decision split the Court's liberals and conservatives, with Justice O'Connor joining the liberals in a 5–4 decision that, yes, schools could be liable under Title IX for deliberate indifference to student behavior that created a hostile environment. Schools were now officially on the hook for policing sexual behavior taking place solely among students.

However, the Court went to some pains to limit the scenarios in which a school could be held liable for allowing the creation of a hostile environment – limits much tighter than those permitted in the employment context. At least some degree of free expression is fundamental to the academic enterprise, and schools don't have nearly the control over students that employers have over employees. Therefore, under *Davis*, if schools are to be held responsible for violating Title IX in this context, they must be "deliberately indifferent to sexual harassment, of which they have actual knowledge, that is so severe, pervasive, and objectively offensive that it can be said to deprive the victims of access to the educational opportunities or benefits provided by the school."

It didn't take long at all for OCR to seize on *Davis* to start more closely regulating schools under the aegis of Title IX. On Jan. 19, 2001 – the very last day of the Bill Clinton administration – OCR released a "Revised Sexual Harassment Guidance" document that took advantage of the *Davis* decision to lay out 23 pages of regulations (not counting a whopping 119 footnotes) governing how schools must henceforth treat sexual harassment allegations. Given this regulation's publication on the last day of Clinton's term, one can safely assume that OCR was concerned that the incoming George W. Bush administration would have scrapped the regulation and started over instead of issuing it.

But it *was* sneaked in under the wire, and it *did* go into effect. What could go wrong?

FIVE CONDUCT CHARGES FOR A FOUR-WORD JOKE

Sarah Emerson (not her real name) was a sophomore at the University of Oregon in Eugene. At around 9 P.M. on June 9, 2014 – the first evening of Oregon's week of final exams – Sarah was taking a break and looking out the window of her dormitory. Seeing a man and woman below and figuring, correctly, that they were romantically involved, she jokingly yelled, "I hit it first!" (The phrase is a euphemism for "I had sex with him/her first" or "I hooked up with him/her first," and had been popularized the previous year in a song by R&B singer Ray J.) Sarah did not know either party and obviously meant it as a joke, but the woman below didn't think it was funny, responding, "Fuck you, bitch!" Not satisfied with simply yelling back, the couple marched into Sarah's dorm, identified her by figuring out which window belonged to her, and, in the company of a resident assistant, stormed upstairs to demand an apology. Sarah immediately apologized as demanded, adding that it was a joke and she meant no offense.

In a sane world, that would have been the end of the matter. But the Title IX–driven pressure to police, investigate, and crack down on every reported offense on campus, no matter how frivolous, has resulted in a campus culture that is anything but sane. One or both of the students to whom Sarah had apologized filed complaints with the university's Office of Student Conduct and Community Standards, and on June 13, Sarah was served with notice that she was being charged with not one, not two, but *five* student conduct charges for her joke – one-and-a-quarter charges *per word*. For making a euphemistic, one-off joke about sex that did not even contain any foul language, Sarah was charged with two violations of her university housing contract, disruption of the university, disorderly conduct, and, of course, harassment. She had two choices: an administrative hearing before an administrator who would unilaterally make a judgment about her case that could not be appealed (but in which she could not be expelled), or a formal hearing in which "all University sanctions [were] possible, including suspension, expulsion, and negative notation on the transcript."

Fortunately, faced with two lousy options, Sarah took a third route: she contacted FIRE. In an 11-page letter sent to University of Oregon president Michael Gottfredson on Aug. 1, 2014, FIRE exhaustively pointed out the absurdity of the situation, the inapplicability of each charge, and the unconstitutionality of a public university punishing a student for a joke. While we at FIRE were certain that Oregon would drop the charges after receiving our letter, the university instead chose to remain silent. On Aug. 26, FIRE issued a national press release about the case. The very next day, the University of Oregon notified Sarah that "[t]he charges against you will be removed and you will not have a student conduct record for this incident," though it did "warn" her about this "behavior" in the future. As with Professor Kipnis, Sarah Emerson's Kafkaesque journey through the Title IX disciplinary system ended only when her inquisitors were publicly exposed and ridiculed for their overreach.

THE FEDS CONCOCT A "BLUEPRINT" FOR SPEECH CODES ACROSS THE NATION

Sarah Emerson's absurd and unjust situation can be traced straight back to OCR's Jan. 19, 2001, guidance, which offered a purposely muddled definition of harassment that massively expanded the amount and types of behavior and expression OCR would attempt to regulate. It stated, "Sexual harassment is unwelcome conduct of a sexual nature" and can include "verbal, nonverbal, or physical conduct." (You and I would call "verbal conduct" speech.) This sounds reasonable on first hearing, but it's anything but. Let's take one example OCR and others frequently use: "telling sexual or dirty jokes." Is telling such a joke within earshot of someone who would rather not have heard it sexual harassment? Common sense says no. The law agrees. Simply telling dirty or sexual jokes is a constitutionally protected activity. But in the plain language of OCR's definition, such joke-telling on campus is sexual harassment (although not severe enough to create a "hostile environment").

The genius of redefining constitutionally protected speech as sexual harassment lies in carrying over the impression of moral turpitude that comes from real sexual harassment – like telling your subordinate you'll promote her in exchange for sex – to speech that isn't actually harassment by any sensible definition, such as telling dirty jokes or asking someone on a date who would rather not go out with you. It puts free speech advocates immediately on the defensive by making them either appear to side with "sexual harassment" or spend their time on complicated and often boring wrangling about definitions. It is for this reason that the worst college speech codes have long been enacted under the guise of harassment policies. The 2001 guidance took this deceptive ploy a step further, intentionally putting colleges in a political bind by telling them that they should classify some expression as "sexual harassment" but then should refuse to punish that expression because it did not rise to the level of a "hostile environment."

But it wasn't until 2013 that OCR (joined by the Department of Justice) finally said schools were actually required to use this unconstitutional definition if they wished to be Title IX–compliant. OCR seized on the opportunity of a Title IX settlement with the University of Montana to set forth what it called "a blueprint for colleges and universities throughout the country to protect students from sexual harassment and assault." The University of Montana, which had been embroiled in a nauseating sex scandal involving its football team, was in no real position to protest the fact that the "blueprint" demanded an unconstitutional regime for speech regulation. With the blueprint, OCR and the Department of Justice (DOJ) were tacitly taking the position that both

Sarah Emerson and Laura Kipnis are indeed sexual harassers (though not *necessarily* to the extent that they could be punished).

In fact, the staff members of OCR and DOJ appear to have lost all sense of proportion in their race to use Montana as an opportunity to become a caricature of out-of-control government bureaucrats. Consider this: the resolution agreement with the University of Montana required the school not just to institute mandatory "trainings" to familiarize faculty members with the new, unconstitutional policy and their responsibilities under it, but also to send a list of the names of faculty members who failed or refused to participate *to the Department of Justice.* What in the world did the government plan to do with the list? DOJ never said. As FIRE president Greg Lukianoff put it at the time, with intentionally heavy understatement, "The history of government officials' compiling lists of dissenters is not a happy one." Unsurprisingly, the faculty felt the same way, and the requirement was ultimately dropped.

After FIRE hit the alarm bell as hard as it could and the national media and Congress began to take notice, OCR and DOJ quietly backed away from the blueprint. In a letter to FIRE, OCR head Catherine Lhamon indicated that "the agreement in the Montana case represents the resolution of that particular case and not OCR or DOJ policy," which is pretty much the complete opposite of its earlier declaration that the agreement would be "a blueprint for colleges and universities throughout the country." Yet Lhamon did not see fit to independently inform universities about this change (if she had, perhaps the absurd story of Sarah Emerson would never have happened). This is probably because, like so many government pronouncements on this topic since 2011, it looks like

Lhamon's assertion was actually not true. As recently as April 2016, DOJ informed the University of New Mexico that "[u]nwelcome conduct of a sexual nature" – including "verbal conduct" – is sexual harassment "regardless of whether it causes a hostile environment or is quid pro quo."

Thanks to the First Amendment, though, the blueprint is quite susceptible to a legal challenge. Indeed, FIRE brought just such a challenge in January 2016 on behalf of Teresa Buchanan, an education professor at Louisiana State University who was stripped of tenure and fired for her speech under a policy identical to the one promulgated by the federal government under the "blueprint." Her supposed offense was occasionally using profanity and sexual language as a means of teaching her graduate students, in accordance with her observation that today's K–12 classroom is one in which teachers will inevitably face such situations and have to learn to handle them competently. It is FIRE's hope and belief that the federal courts will strike down LSU's regulation as unconstitutional, therefore demonstrating that the "blueprint" itself cannot withstand constitutional scrutiny, despite its strong backing by the federal government.

OCR's Unlawful Assault on Due Process and Fair Procedures

Matching the blueprint for sheer brazenness is OCR's now-infamous Apr. 4, 2011, "Dear Colleague letter" on sexual misconduct ("the DCL"). This letter has changed the course of so many lives, including that of Dave Weber, whose story opened this broadside. Declaring itself to be a "significant guidance document" – in other words, a clarification of the current law and regulations about sexual misconduct on campus – the DCL created out of whole cloth new regulations that all colleges and universities receiving federal funding had to follow.

This positioning of brand-new regulations as simple clarification of the law was no accident. It was intentional deception. OCR labeled the DCL a "significant guidance document" because such "guidance" does not need to go through the official notice-and-comment process that has been mandated since the New Deal era by the Administrative Procedure Act (APA). To understand what happened and why it is so outrageous, a brief history lesson is necessary.

While few have heard of the APA, it's actually critical to the way our country is governed. With the flood of regulations brought in with the New Deal in the 1930s came the concern that administrative agencies would usurp the role of Congress and effectively make laws without any kind of democratic accountability. The APA was Congress's attempt to put some limits on this activity. It requires that new substantive regulations go through a public "notice and comment" period, during which stakeholders are given a heads-up that a regulation is being considered and are able to submit written comments on those regulations that must be weighed by the regulating agency. Though the agency does not have to agree with comments or make changes because of those comments, the regulators must, at the very least, hear from those it wants to regulate before slapping them with new legal mandates.

Yet the DCL effectively wrote into law two new requirements, to the great surprise of colleges, civil liberties groups, and several U.S. senators, including former secretary of education Lamar Alexander. (In one particularly maddening vignette, OCR managed to tell Senator Alexander in a hearing that the DCL was not legally binding but that OCR expected schools to "comply" with it anyway.) First, it decreed that schools must allow both sides to appeal in a sexual misconduct hearing. In a criminal trial, even for something as minor as a speeding ticket, once you are found not guilty, the process is over. This vital protection against double jeopardy is all that prevents a prosecutor from repeatedly trying to get you convicted of a crime and using up years of your life and all of your money in defense. I had never heard of any college that operated differently until 2011, when OCR decided that accusers in campus cases must be able to appeal even when the accused was found not to have committed the offense. Outrageous though this was, Congress's 2013 reauthorization of the Violence Against Women Act made it the law of the land for now.

The second change, which has proved much more controversial, was the requirement that colleges "must use a preponderance of the evidence standard" (a 50.01 percent certainty of guilt) when determining guilt or innocence in sexual misconduct cases. OCR's contention appears to be that this lowest standard of proof is required by Title IX regulations that mandate that such a hearing be "prompt and equitable," and that a hearing cannot be equitable unless the burden of proof is as close to 50/50 as possible. In contrast, the criminal justice system demands the much higher "beyond a reasonable doubt" standard (a 98–99 percent certainty of guilt), and even civil cases that involve significant reputational damage often require the "clear and convincing evidence" standard (an 80–85 percent level of certainty).

What effect does the preponderance mandate have in the college context? Let's look at some other aspects of the typical college disciplinary system in 2016. First, colleges decide for themselves who will preside over campus hearings and who will serve as jurors. Such panels frequently include college administrators, whose employment prospects may depend in part on their reaching the conclusion most convenient for the college. Some colleges even appoint a single administrator to serve as both judge and jury. Most of the time, neither party to the hearings has a right to active participation of counsel. Cross-examination is limited or even forbidden altogether. There's no guarantee that all the evidence will be shared with both parties – even exculpatory evidence – and the rules of evidence don't apply anyway, with hearsay and other irrelevant "evidence" regularly considered. The parties are usually not placed under oath, and consequences for lying are generally nonexistent. Colleges frequently don't even record the hearing or explain why they came to their decision.

I'd go so far as to say that not a single person at OCR, nor anyone reading this book, would willingly agree to be tried for rape in a system using these rules, run by amateurs, and in which one's guilt or innocence will be determined to a mere coin-toss level of certainty. And the reason neither you nor they would agree to this is precisely because such a system is not, by any stretch of the imagination, just, fair, or equitable. If you require further convincing, imagine a black college student being tried for sexual assault using such rules at the University of Alabama in 1965. Only a madman – or someone utterly blinded by political ideology – would claim that such a system is "equitable." Yet that is precisely the claim OCR makes and that it unlawfully imposes on every college in the country.

There is a remedy for this sort of regulatory abuse under the APA: a lawsuit. While frequently the hardest part of suing the government is proving that you have "standing" to sue – in layman's terms, that the government's actions have specifically damaged you – the students who were found "guilty" of sexual misconduct by campus tribunals under the preponderance standard and who would have been tried under a higher standard before the DCL should have standing to sue. Dave Weber, whose story I opened with, is one of those students.

But Dave isn't interested in suing, and who can blame him? If anything, these "guilty" students have even greater disincentives to sue than do colleges and universities. In the age of Google, nothing is forgotten. Even people ultimately proven innocent of the charges against them, such as the students falsely accused in the infamous Duke lacrosse case, will likely never outrun the notoriety of sexual assault accusations, which are the closest thing to a scarlet letter we have in our society today. It's no wonder, then, that most students are unwilling to challenge OCR in court. Their calculus is simple: What employer, given the choice between two equally qualified candidates, would choose the one who had been found "guilty" of sexual assault by his or her college? What grad school would accept them? Even a student's personal and romantic life is likely to suffer greatly. Who wants to date a possible rapist?

It's the rare student, therefore, who is willing to take on OCR directly and risk his or her name becoming publicly affiliated with the idea of sexual assault. Courts have, rightfully, made this a bit less perilous by frequently allowing students who feel they have been wrongly found guilty on campus to bring lawsuits challenging those findings as "John Doe" plaintiffs – but this is no sure thing, and Doe plaintiffs may be ordered by the court to either proceed under their real name or drop the case. It still requires courage. But such courageous students, though rare, do exist, and, as of June 2016, FIRE has been privileged to find one willing to challenge OCR's unlawful regulation in court, as well as lawyers willing to take on the tough job of slugging it out with a federal agency in a case where a disgraceful public sliming (as "rape apologists," for instance) of those defending due process is nearly inevitable.

There is another obvious group of plaintiffs who could sue in federal court when OCR promulgates unlawful regulations: the colleges themselves. But OCR has an ace up its sleeve that makes using this remedy extremely difficult – the threat of withdrawing all federal funding from a school. Schools live in fear of this power, which so obviously amounts to a death penalty for most schools that it has never been exercised. It doesn't matter much that any school that were to sue would have an excellent chance of winning. Given the slow pace of lawsuits, to do so would require counting on federal bureaucrats who have shown no restraint in violating the law to restrain themselves from retaliating against the school over the years that an APA challenge might take. As a result, it's no surprise that, as of this writing, and after more than 5 years of this patently unlawful regulatory regime, only a single school has been willing to challenge OCR over its obvious APA violation. That school is not the University of Virginia, with its highly publicized rape hoax. It's not the University of Oregon, or even the University of Montana. Out of the more than 4,000 colleges in the U.S., the only school that has proved willing to challenge the DCL in court is the tiny (but bold) Oklahoma Wesleyan University.

Lawsuits can help, but a permanent solution to these problems can only come from a Congress ready to act and a president willing to sign into law reforms of Title IX that will quash OCR's moves to use the law to impose its political will on every school in the country. Although it's unlikely that President Obama, who appointed the OCR heads under whom these abuses took place, would take any specific action to rein in the abuses, it's far from impossible to imagine him signing into law a larger bill that includes reforms to these harmful Title IX interpretations.

Even those unable to get worked up over the fate of students accused of sexual assault need to understand the importance of OCR's regulatory abuse. Perhaps the debate over transgender access to bathrooms will help focus some attention on the problem. In the spring of 2016, the Department of Education decreed that, in the name of Title IX, K–12 public schools must now allow transgender students to use the bathroom and locker room of their choice. (Virtually every parent of K–12 students will likely know about this come the fall.) What they probably don't recognize is that the agency responsible for this decision is OCR and that the mechanism it used to impose this decision was a "Dear Colleague letter" from May 13, 2016, which, even more absurdly than the 2011 letter, it labeled "significant guidance" that "does not add requirements to applicable law." Regardless of your feelings on transgender issues, OCR's argument that a law passed in 1972 requires that students who were born biologically male but who identify as female be allowed to use the girls' locker room at your local public high school – and that this decision is not a change to the law that would, at the very least, require a formal rulemaking process – beggars belief. It is my opinion that the decision to mandate transgender bathrooms in grammar school without going through the normal regulatory progress would simply not have been possible without the supine acquiescence of colleges and universities to the DCL of Apr. 4, 2011.

The substantive due process issues arising from the 2011 DCL are very different from the issue of transgender bathrooms. Yet there is reason for those who care about one issue to follow the other. Culture war considerations frequently warp judicial decisions, especially in an era where courts and judges may act more as mini-legislatures with life tenure than impartial arbiters of the law. But a sufficient number of oxen being gored may have the salutary effect of bringing home to many more people the reality of what can happen when federal agencies like OCR ignore the rule of law in pursuit of social policy. (Apologists for unlawful moves by President Obama's OCR would be well advised to consider that in 2017, this agency may be under the control of Donald Trump.) Ultimately, there's only one thing that will stop the continued conversion of Title IX from a measure against sex discrimination to an all-purpose justification for the preferred policies of whatever bureaucrat happens to be in power at the time: those who care about free speech, the rule of law, and government accountability must come off the sidelines and vigorously resist these abuses as soon as they happen and regardless of the target – not just when their own interests are finally in the feds' crosshairs.

MICHAEL WALSH

THE PEOPLE V. THE DEMOCRATIC PARTY

IT IS ONE of the ironies of American history that the Democratic Party has managed to pass itself off as the champion of the underdog and the crusader for equal rights. The actual history of the Democratic Party – distinct from the history of some individual Democrats – tells a very different story. It is a history in which the lust for power, not a concern for the poor and dispossessed, looms large. This story is seldom told. Indeed, so successful has been the suppression of the true history of the Democratic Party for the sake of the "narrative" that simply laying out the facts appears as a startling forensic exercise, a brief for the prosecution. It might begin like this:

Ladies and gentlemen of the jury: I come not to praise the Accused but to bury him. For too long, he has afflicted our body Politic with vilenesses various, seducing our Youth and employing the Institutions of our Government against the People in a naked Quest for Power. For too long, the Enemy has skulked and lurked under cover of good Intentions, subverting the Principles of Self-Reliance, personal Industry, and limited Government in favor of an alien

Ideology whose maleficent and baleful Presence continues to distress our Nation.

A decent respect to the opinions of mankind, therefore, demands this Indictment. The history of the present Democratic Party is a history of repeated injuries and usurpations, all having in direct object the establishment of an absolute Tyranny over the several States. It is, in fact, a criminal Organization masquerading as a political Party.

To prove this, let Facts be submitted to a candid world:

THE ARGUMENT

The first thing you need to know about the Democratic Party is that its first vice president, the traitor Aaron Burr, shot and killed one of the Founding Fathers, Alexander Hamilton, and then plotted sedition against his own president. Everything else is, as they say, commentary.

Again, let me acknowledge that my indictment of the Democratic Party is not necessarily an indictment of individual Democrats, many of whom throughout our history have been true American patriots who worked hard to better the estate of their fellow man. My brief is against the Democratic Party, which from the inception of the Republic has been a public enemy – an organization antithetical to our nation's traditions, civic virtues, and moral values.

Does that seem overstated? Consider the facts. Whether it has been defending slavery, selling out our secrets, or simply voting "present" so as not to take a stand on the crucial moral issues of both statecraft and soulcraft, the party of slavery, segregation, secularism, and sedition has always been in the forefront of everything inimical to the United States of America.

Its unofficial modern slogan – "by any means necessary" – is indicative of its fundamental amorality. Its will to power, especially since the mid-19th century, is insatiable. It sees greater government as the greater good. It views individual liberty as dangerous and personal choice – always excepting abortion, the only sacrament the atheist left acknowledges and honors – as contrary to the will of the *demos*. It is always in favor of centralized fascism, including but not limited to the power to ban, criminalize, and anathematize speech and ideas with which it does not agree and which threaten its hegemony.

And all of this in disguise – under the cloak of "compassion," of "tolerance," of "fairness." The Tarnhelm beneath which modern "liberalism" (its very name mocks the political origins of the term) lurks, coiled and ready to strike whenever our side lets down its guard. "Come, I think hell's a fable," says Dr. Faustus to Mephistopheles in Marlowe's play. "Ay, think so still, till experience change thy mind," replies the devil. And so in the hell the left has made of America over the past half-century or so we currently dwell.

How did we get here? How have we wandered so far afield from the founding virtues of individualism, self-reliance, bootstrapism, private (as opposed to public) charity, religious belief, religious liberty, personal expression, freedom of both public and private speech, the Judeo-Christian heritage, the right to self-defense? What Mephistophelian toxin has been injected into our body politic, the kind that makes us first doubt, then reject, and then finally mock our own first principles? With America teetering on the brink of collapse for the first time since perhaps the War of 1812, how do we combat, overthrow, and finally eradicate the scourge of "liberalism" – which in its modern incarnation has nothing to do with classical liberalism – from our national dialogue?

The first step is to overcome our innate squeamishness about the nature of the task at hand. In order to defeat existential evil, one must not only give the devil his due but also use his own weapons against him. No doctor seeks accommodation with cancer. No general seeks to give a defeated mortal enemy a sense of self-esteem – not to mention the hope of victory. As we learned during the victorious wars of our national history, "defeat" should not be temporary but permanent: Nazi Germany and Imperial Japan will never again rise, nor the Confederacy. Until the right learns this lesson and acts on its implications – in the words of Ted "Chappaquiddick" Kennedy – "the work goes on, the cause endures, the hope still lives, and the dream shall never die."

Alas, their dream is our nightmare. In order to defeat the left – having now exchanged its carnival mask of "liberalism" for (once more) "progressivism" – we must halt the work, stifle the cause, annihilate the hope, and bury the dream. To do otherwise is to condemn posterity to endless battle.

Observe a current electoral map. The so-called red states (and how did the socialist left saddle the American right with the color of Communism? You can thank the broadcast networks) overwhelmingly represent the flyover heartland. It's the country of the artless hello, of low taxes, low unemployment, and low dependency – the country of unlocked doors, personal honesty, moral standards, and the handshake after which you don't have to count your fingers. The blue states, on the other hand, represent the party of Big Government; high taxes; higher incomes (mostly derived from government, academe, or Hollywood, which is to say from taxpayers or suckers); proud chicanery; public-employees' unions; the corrupt Democratic big-city machines in Chicago, Kansas City,

St. Louis, San Francisco, and elsewhere; flimflam; three-card monte; and a tradition of fleecing the marks – who, after all, have it coming.

Whose side would you rather be on? To answer that question – honestly – is to declare your allegiance in the Cold Civil War. A war in which every man's hand is against every other man's, in which the battle is not being fought over slavery or states' rights but over the most fundamental principles of the Republic:

> *We hold these truths to be self-evident, that all men are created equal, that they are endowed by their Creator with certain unalienable Rights, that among these are Life, Liberty and the pursuit of Happiness. – That to secure these rights, Governments are instituted among Men, deriving their just powers from the consent of the governed, – That whenever any Form of Government becomes destructive of these ends, it is the Right of the People to alter or to abolish it, and to institute new Government, laying its foundation on such principles and organizing its powers in such form, as to them shall seem most likely to effect their Safety and Happiness.*

And yet who knew that less than a decade after the founding, Americans would already be debating the wisdom of the founders? Let the indictment proceed.

Burr, Hamilton, and Original Sin

Aaron Burr, Jr. – the third vice president of the United States – is today a largely misremembered figure, especially on the left, and for good reason. Overshadowed in his treachery by Benedict Arnold (who, like Burr, had been an officer in the Continental Army), the New Jersey-born

Burr avoided the disgraced Arnold's ultimate self-exile to London, spending some years in that city – mostly fleeing creditors – before his return to Manhattan (by tradition, the most seditious city in the Union) and his eventual death in Staten Island, burial in his hometown of Princeton, and resurrection as the revisionist hero of a Gore Vidal novel.

But let's give credit where credit is due. Burr, one of the founders of the Democratic Party – called Democratic-Republicans back then – not only arguably murdered (there is some evidence that Hamilton, who got off the first shot, fired into the ground) the first treasury secretary of the United States but also went on to establish the *fons et origo* of American municipal corruption, Tammany Hall. If one man besides George Washington can be said to have set the American experiment on its future course – in this case not for good but for ill – that man is Burr. Most important, the duel ended with the destruction of the Federalists and ultimately the Whigs, who succeeded the Federalists as the opposition party. It also, in its own lethal way, fixed the notion of the adversarial two-party system in the American psyche – even if it meant that the Democrats literally had to kill off the opposition.

The fatal confrontation of 1804 in Weehawken, N.J., was the culmination of a bitter personal and political animosity between Burr and Hamilton, which included the hotly contested election of 1800, in which Hamilton's vote was crucial in denying Burr the presidency in favor of Thomas Jefferson. But it was more than that. It was the embodiment of the struggle between the Federalists of Washington, Adams, and Hamilton and the Democratic-Republicans of Jefferson and Burr – a struggle that, in one form or another (and with sides changing from time to time), has been going on ever since.

And did Burr suffer any meaningful penalty for killing Hamilton, even though dueling was outlawed in both New York and New Jersey? Of course not – he was, after all, a Democrat. Indicted for murder in both states, he skated in both jurisdictions. In fact, he continued as Jefferson's vice president to the end of the first term. Right from the start, Democrats learned how to game the legal system.

Jefferson was a great president. His fights with the other founders were over means, not ends; they were all patriots who surely would have hanged together had they lost the Revolution. But the party went the way of Burr, not Jefferson. In fact, Burr doubled down on criminality. Tammany Hall evolved into the gold standard in big-city, machine-politics corruption. If slavery was the original sin of the 13 colonies, then Tammany and its imitative ilk in other big cities was the original sin of the Republic: politics as factionalism, special-interest groups, and legalized bribery. During the election of 1828, Tammany threw its support to Andrew Jackson, creating the spoils system and cementing its relationship with the modern Democratic Party to this day.

WHIGS, COPPERHEADS, AND THE GREAT CIVIL WAR

If there's one thing the Democrats hate, it's war – unless, of course, they start one. And if there's one thing they hate even more than war, it's a war fought for bedrock constitutional principles – in other words, a war fought against everything they believe in. And the Civil War, led by the first Republican president, Abraham Lincoln, could not have illustrated that more clearly.

The Republican Party was formed as an explicitly anti-slavery party (as opposed to the slavery party, which was the you-know-whos) in the wake of the Whigs' collapse, as that party was torn asunder over the "peculiar institution." In the election of 1856, the Republican candidate, John C. Frémont, vehemently opposed the expansion of slavery under the Kansas-Nebraska Act, which allowed settlers to vote whether to allow slavery. The party's slogan was "Free Soil, Free Labor, Free Speech, Free Men, and Frémont." Who could be against that?

Naturally, the Democrats were. Frémont lost to Democrat James A. Buchanan, whose party had invented the Kansas-Nebraska Act; the third-party candidate in the race – and the last gasp of the Whigs, who had fractured over the expansion of slavery into the territories – was former President Millard Fillmore, who represented the anti-Catholic Know-Nothing Party. As president, Fillmore had signed the Fugitive Slave Act of 1850, which held that runaway slaves had to be returned to the masters, a law upheld seven years later in the infamous *Dred Scott* decision by the Supreme Court under Democratic (of course) Chief Justice Roger B. Taney. The Democrats' problem with race would only worsen over the years.

During the Civil War, the Army of the Potomac was led by the cautious yet resolutely insubordinate George B. McClellan, who consistently managed to be outmaneuvered by Robert E. Lee, commanding the Army of Northern Virginia, even when McClellan had numerical and tactical superiority – as during the Peninsula Campaign. "If he can't fight himself, he excels in making others ready to fight," said Lincoln, who eventually fired him.

McClellan, who had finished second in his class at West Point and never suffered from a deficit of self-esteem, sought payback in the election of 1864, when he ran against his former commander in chief as a Democrat. His party platform had been written by the antiwar, borderline seditious Copperheads, northern "peace" Democrats who denounced Lincoln as a tyrant and advocated a negotiated settlement with the South. With victory over the Confederacy in sight, Lincoln won with 55 percent of the vote, including the lion's share of the military vote. (Republicans named the Copperheads after the venomous snake; today we would simply call them Democrats but still keep the snake.)

A few months later, President Lincoln was murdered by a Democrat, John Wilkes Booth.

THE SOCIETY OF ST. TAMMANY, GANGLAND, AND THE LITTLE TIN BOX

The Democratic Party has always appealed to the basest instincts of the American people, molting and changing shape as the political winds dictated but solely devoted to its raison d'être: the accumulation and retention of political power. As it evolved over the course of the late 19th century, its chief mechanism became, in essence, bribery – not simply of civil officials but of the public itself.

It's unclear who said, "A Democracy cannot exist as a permanent form of government. It can only last until the citizens discover they can vote themselves largesse out of the public treasury." But that may as well be the party's animating ethos: "social justice" disguised as sympathy or, worse, compassion. Always wrapping itself in the false cloak of righteousness and celebrating the folk wisdom of the *demos*, the Democrats have consistently championed class envy, social division, and often – quite nakedly – racism, if they thought it would buy them votes.

Only the Democrats could reinvent themselves so effortlessly, molting from the party of the Ku Klux Klan to the party of the Civil Rights Act of 1964. From the party of the aggressive atheist Madalyn Murray O'Hair, who destroyed school prayer and helped set the country on its downward moral spiral in 1963, to the party of Bible-toting Baptist presidents (Bill Clinton) and the racist ravings of Obama's pastor, the Rev. Jeremiah Wright. When your only principle is power, it's easy to embrace flexibility and nuance.

This amoral relativism raised to a high art of hypocrisy – for such it is – at the party's core has long posed the most potent threat to its continuing existence; therefore, it is the one aspect of its nature that must be most assiduously concealed and obscured.

And obscure that it has, beginning with the rise of Burr's own Society of St. Tammany, the Democratic Party's political machine in New York City in the mid-19th century. Forget the notorious Boss Tweed, whose reign of blatant corruption finally became too egregious for even New Yorkers to stomach; it was only after his conviction in 1873 that things really got rolling, thanks to the Irish, whom the Tammany nativists had once despised. A series of grand sachems – beginning with "Honest John" Kelly and continuing through the magnificently corrupt reign of Richard "Boss" Croker (who retired to a horse farm in his native Ireland, leaving an estate valued at more than $3 million) and Charles F. Murphy – kept both the votes and the swag flowing. Murphy's private dining room upstairs at the ultra-fashionable Delmonico's restaurant was dubbed the Scarlet Room of Mystery by the New York newspapers, and from it he ruled New York City politics from 1902 to his death in 1924.

In the era of the Little Tin Box, the quiet man was king. Setting the Democrats fully on their strategic path of political tribalism, Tammany assembled a coalition of the dispossessed and the avaricious, of patronage hounds, labor leaders, and various ethnic groups – principally, the newly arrived Irish, Italians, and Jews.

One job open to the toughest gangland chieftains – such as the legendary Monk Eastman, a feared thug who, improbably, later became a war hero – was that of "sheriff" in various bars and dives known as blind pigs or blind tigers. The sheriff controlled crime and violence on his turf (in Eastman's case, part of the Lower East Side) and got out the vote when elections rolled around. His boys pitched in as *shtarkers* – sluggers – who clubbed the opposition's voters into submission at the polls. Meanwhile, other gang members voted two, three, and four times via the simple expedient of shaving off first their side whiskers, then their chin whiskers, and finally their mustaches.

To be fair, Tammany's outreach to the immigrant communities was exemplary. George Washington Plunkitt, a distinguished sachem whose impromptu memoir, *Plunkitt of Tammany Hall* – Plunkitt's wit and wisdom as recorded by William Riordan, a journalist of the day – describes the people skills of your basic Tammany pol:

Big Tom Foley, leader of the Second District, fits in exactly, too. Tom sells whisky, and good whisky, and he is able to take care of himself against a half dozen thugs if he runs up against them on Cherry Hill or in Chatham Square. Pat Ryder and Johnnie Ahearn of the Third and Fourth Districts are just the men for the places. Ahearn's constituents are about half Irishmen and half Jews. He is as popular with one race as with the other. He eats corned beef and kosher meat with equal nonchalance, and it's all the same to him whether he takes off his hat in the church or pulls it down over his ears in the synagogue.

There was a lot to be said for the wigwam's way, and in fact its system of patronage and kickbacks, of favors asked and received, elevated a sizable proportion of the immigrants out of their ghettos and into the middle class. The Irish rabble slowly transformed into the backbone of the city's police force and legal community (William J. Fallon, the most flamboyant defense attorney of his day, was known as the Great Mouthpiece – he never lost a homicide beef); the Jews, who briefly dominated violent crime in the 1920s and early '30s, overcame institutional discrimination and sent their kids to Harvard and other Ivy League schools; the Italians, last off the boat, were electing mayors and governors within a couple of generations.

Indeed, the Roaring '20s and the Depression '30s were probably the closest the modern Democratic Party has come to doing well by doing good. Tammany and its big-city machine imitators in Chicago, Kansas City, and elsewhere brazenly opposed the GOP "goo-goo" (good government) types. As the unapologetic Alderman Paddy Bauler famously said in 1955, "Chicago ain't ready for reform," and after generations of mayors named Daley, it still ain't.

Indeed, the Roosevelt years were probably as close as the Democrats ever came to a workable electoral model. The country rallied around FDR twice, first during the Depression and later during the war. Roosevelt got elected four times for a reason, and not simply because the nation had rejected Hoover and the GOP. FDR gave the country hope in the worst of economic times – even if his Big Government nostrums largely continued the failed philosophy of the previous administration and his statist inclinations recalled Wilson's – and promised ultimate, unconditional-surrender victory over the Axis. It was a promise he delivered on, even if he did not live to actually see it.

But the introduction of Big Labor into the Tammany/

gangland mix would prove exceedingly harmful to the party's moral center. Although they are less well known today than their more flamboyant colleagues such as Lucky Luciano and Dutch Schultz, two pivotal figures in the transformation of the modern Democratic Party into a full-blown criminal enterprise were the murderous Louis "Lepke" Buchalter and his muscle partner, Jacob "Gurrah" Shapiro, who not only were instrumental in the founding of Murder, Inc. (a Brooklyn-based alliance of Italian and Jewish gunsels) but also took over the garment-district unions. The legalized shakedown rackets we call the public sector unions today, such as the Service Employees International Union (SEIU), are the spiritual sons and heirs of Lepke and Gurrah, except it is the public they now bleed, not just private employers.

Gangland's code of coercion was a system that worked in its own way, but it came with a soul-corroding price. Even as Hollywood films of the period – especially those from Warner Bros., which are practically gangland documentaries (particularly *The Roaring Twenties* with James Cagney and Humphrey Bogart) – always ended with the moral that crime doesn't pay, real life spoke differently. And not just Boss Croker, hying himself back to the Ould Sod with the contents of his Little Tin Box, but a veritable rogue's gallery of corrupt cops, judges, politicians, mayors, and governors. Everybody, it seems, was either on the take or on the lam.

Let a couple of examples suffice. The first is Aaron J. Levy, a lifelong Tammany hack who was first the Democratic majority leader of the New York State Assembly and then state Supreme Court judge, who protected gambling clubs belonging to Arnold Rothstein and then, after "The Brain's" untimely demise in 1928, continued to shield prominent gangland figures from the bench.

Prominent among them was Owney Madden, a British-born Irish immigrant who was king of Prohibition New York: brewer of Madden's No. 1 beer; Mae West's lover and Broadway angel; owner of five heavyweight champions of the world, including Primo Carnera and James J. Braddock; and the founder of the Cotton Club, which employed Duke Ellington, Harold Arlen, and Lena Horne. Madden "retired" in Bill Clinton's hometown of Hot Springs, Ark., and died in 1965, having run the spa city known affectionately as Bubbles as his personal fiefdom for 30 years.

It's Madden who leads directly to a more famous figure, Herbert H. Lehman, the former governor of New York and, later, a U.S. senator. Lehman succeeded Franklin Roosevelt in Albany after FDR defeated Hoover, so he was well acquainted with the cozy relationship between the New York underworld and the upstate bonzes in Albany. Lehman himself had a squeaky-clean reputation – and yet when Madden needed a huge favor, he paid off like a slot machine.

When Madden's brother Martin, a British subject who, unlike Owney, had never bothered to get himself naturalized, was threatened with deportation in 1954, Lehman joined Arkansas Senator John McClellan to co-sponsor a Senate bill, S. 541, which was ratified in June 1955. Favors given and favor received. As Thomas E. Dewey, then the Lehman-appointed special prosecutor in charge of busting up gangland, said of Democrat-dominated Hot Springs in the 1930s, "The whole crowd are a complete ring: the chief of police, the chief of detectives, the mayor and the city attorney." No wonder they called Hot Springs "Tammany South."

Eight decades later, Dewey might make the same observation about the United States of America.

SPIES, MARXISTS, AND BARACK HUSSEIN OBAMA

With the waning of Tammany power in the 1950s and the beginning of the Cold War, the price of Democratic corruption suddenly ratcheted up as national security came into play. During World War II, the Soviet Union had been busily placing penetration agents at high levels in the American government. Under a top-secret initiative run from Moscow called the Illegals Program, the Soviets managed to infiltrate American-born agents into the war effort and the administration during the Democrats' long reign from 1933 to 1953.

One such agent was George Koval, an Iowa-born scientist who was perhaps the Soviet Union's most effective atomic spy. Koval's radical Russian-born Jewish parents had come to Sioux City from a shtetl near Minsk but returned to the USSR in 1932, to Stalin's "Jewish Autonomous Region" of Birobidzhan. Recruited by the GRU (Soviet military intelligence), Koval was sent back to the U.S., where he looted secrets from the Manhattan Project labs in Oak Ridge and Dayton. The year after his leisurely 1948 return to Moscow, during the Truman administration, the Soviets exploded their first bomb. Koval's existence wasn't revealed until 2006, the year he died in obscurity at age 92.

Even more important was the Soviet agent Harry Dexter White, a senior Treasury Department official under FDR, whose perfidy was exposed by the Venona cables – intercepted Soviet transmissions that revealed the extent of Communist penetration. What seems today a cavalier disregard for security was the result of our wartime alliance with Stalin, but it had significant repercussions for American foreign policy under Truman (the Alger Hiss case), Eisenhower, and Kennedy. Senator Joseph McCarthy wasn't crazy after all: There really were spies in the State Department. Lots of them. Even today, State remains the most consistently left-wing, at times anti-American, entity in the executive branch.

Take the case of "Agent 202," Walter Kendall Myers, a State Department analyst who in 2010 received a life sentence for spying on behalf of Cuba for 30 years. Unrepentant to the end, Myers and his wife, Gwendolyn (who had once been a legislative aide to former Democratic Senator James Abourezk in her native South Dakota), told U.S. District Court Judge Reggie Walton that "we acted as we did because of our ideals and beliefs. We did not act out of anger – or out of any anti-Americanism. Our overriding objective was to help the Cuban people defend their revolution."

The Myerses sold out their country for love: the worst and most dangerous kind of spies. But the fact is, a significant segment of the left sees absolutely nothing wrong with what they did. Traitors like the Myerses and the Rosenbergs can justify their treachery by appealing to what the left likes to call a "higher morality." An unearned, bogus moral superiority justifies, in their minds, any actions they take against their own country – which, after all, is to blame for the parlous state of the world.

And that's because on the left, there has always been considerable sympathy for Marxist ideas and ideals. Koval came by his naturally; others, like Hiss, gravitated to them; and the Myerses went looking for them. But something in Marxism, Communism, and – especially, I would argue – totalitarianism fires the imagination of the "peaceful and tolerant" left, which can't wait to seize power and impose its will on the citizens of the United States – for their own good, naturally.

And yet many, particularly on the left, play down intelligence operations directed against the U.S. Writing in *The Wall Street Journal* in April 2012, Michelle Van Cleave, the chief of U.S. counterintelligence under George W. Bush, noted Vice President Joe Biden's flippant attitude toward ongoing Russian espionage, then remarked, "The vice president may be surprised to learn that there are as many Russian intelligence officers operating in the U.S. today as during the height of the Cold War – it is arrests and criminal proceedings that have fallen off." For the former Soviets, the Principal Enemy remains, well, the Principal Enemy – and the Obama administration remains willfully blind. Even when in 2010 it actually caught some illegals – including the 10-member ring of the fetching Anna Chapman – it hustled them back to Russia before any useful intelligence could be extracted from them.

But then that's to be expected under a Democratic administration, especially one as socialist-friendly as Barack Obama's. For Obama is the ne plus ultra of the twin strains of anti-American leftist thought, the spawn of the gangster ethos of the 1920s and '30s and the fashionable Marxism of the "revolutionary" year of 1968, which gave birth to the George McGovern candidacy in 1972 and has been waiting – like the Shiites for the Twelfth Imam – for its next messiah ever since. All the strains of modern "progressivism" are present in the president: the hostility toward the country as founded ("fundamental change") and the mad desire to hobble the country's future via taxation, regulation, and executive order. The Columbia-educated Obama is the living embodiment of the Columbia-born Cloward-Piven strategy, the word made flesh and dwelling among us, practicing a "progressive," American form of *taqiyya* in order to conceal his real, ideologically inimical intentions.

Michael Walsh

EACH DAWN I DIE,
Jake Lingle, and the Way Forward

Despite – or perhaps because of – their great triumph in 2008, the Democrats are today faced with a new dilemma: how to hang onto their gains. For the modern left, electoral victories are now subject to an American version of the old Brezhnev Doctrine. That relic of the Soviet Union decreed that once a country went Communist, it could never return to the old ways. (The same is true of territories conquered by Islam, which may be one reason why the totalitarian left is so fond of the Mohammedans, ideologically speaking.)

And so they redouble their dance with the thing what brung them: Tammany Hall and its proud history of voter fraud. Note how fiercely the Democrats fight laws requiring citizens to produce some form of government-issued identification in order to vote. Without the crucial element of inner-city voting "irregularities" in places like Philadelphia, St. Louis, and Seattle, their holds on Pennsylvania, Missouri, and even Washington State would be seriously weakened.

Thus – by any means necessary – they continue to steal elections, discovering new ballots (Seattle, 2004); simply printing as many new ballots as needed to make up a deficit (Bridgeport, Conn., 2010); or getting pet judges to keep polling places open after hours (St. Louis, 2000).

Lefties like to claim – based on zero evidence – that there's no proof of actual voter fraud, as opposed to registration fraud, which even they can't pretend doesn't exist. But it goes beyond merely voting. In April 2012, four Democratic officials in Indiana were charged with felonies for allegedly faking petition signatures for Obama and Hillary Clinton – enough to put them on the ballot.

Obama went on to squeak out a November win in Indiana, but it's an open question whether he ever should have been on the ballot in the first place.

Didn't know that? That's because, despite the rise of the Internet and talk radio, most Americans still get what passes for news from the MSM (the mainstream media, AKA the "legacy media"). Although printed newspapers will soon be a thing of the past, they still survive, along with their visual counterparts, the dinosaur broadcast networks.

And despite their pro forma denials, the American media remain resolutely "progressive" and Democratic – more so now than at any time in the past half-century. The reasons are not conspiratorial. Just as liberals have taken over academe and Hollywood, so also have they commandeered the media, because – unlike conservatives – they naturally gravitate toward those professions. Like the civil-rights movement in the decade before it, the Watergate scandal of 1972–74 energized journalism, attracting those amateur evangelists who wanted to "make a difference" and who might otherwise have gone into, say, the law.

The problem is, reporters are supposed to report – not make a difference. The American news business now more closely resembles the frankly partisan European media than it does, say, the old *New York Times* of Mike Berger, Abe Rosenthal, and Harold C. Schonberg. Today, however, reporters conceal more than they report. It is, for example, something of a parlor game on the right to play "Name That Party," an amusement that spontaneously occurs whenever a Democratic politician or public figure is caught with his hand in the cookie jar: Almost never will the left-leaning media provide his party affiliation in their accounts.

Worse, reporters have uncritically adopted the Marxist tone and vocabulary of the left ("social justice," "gender inequality"). They've been steeped in the brew of leftism, if not from birth, then certainly from education, so it's no wonder that Obama in 2008 was the beneficiary of the most adoring, uncritical press in American political history. It wasn't that the reporters didn't want to know about the president's obscure past: his parents, his upbringing, his college years, his grades, his employment history, all the stuff of normal "human interest" stories. It's just that the signal aspect of his candidacy – that he would be the First Black President – outweighed their fiduciary duty toward their employers and the American public.

Today's journalists are only too happy to protect a compromised pol – think Teddy Kennedy – as long as he's on the "right" side of the issues. For them, the struggle between ends and means always results in favor of the ends. (In a pair of 2012 blog posts, two prominent writers for *The New York Times*, Stanley Fish and Andrew Rosenthal, more or less said this openly.) Favored targets are businessmen, not Democratic government officials; with Obama in office, all Washington is a skating rink on which characters like Barney Frank and Chris Dodd turn triple lutzes while their media cronies applaud like the Harvard-trained seals many of them are.

Today, following the lead of David Axelrod, the former *Chicago Tribune* reporter turned wealthy Democratic campaign consultant and adviser to President Obama, reporters play both sides of the street in the hopes of striking it rich. Like the fence Mr. Peachum in *The Beggar's Opera*, they act "both against Rogues and for 'em." With a little luck, they can hope to escape the demeaning drudgery of journalism and become the White House press secretary, the head of the Aspen Institute, or a deputy secretary of state.

In other words, they've all become Jake Lingle, the corrupt *Tribune* legman who made an illicit fortune covering the Capone mob for Colonel McCormick's broadsheet while at the same time working for Scarface Al himself. One day in 1930, while crossing under Michigan Avenue on his way to the train and the racetrack down in Homewood, a gunman put a Colt Detective Special .38 – gangland's weapon of choice – behind his ear and pulled the trigger. Jake died with his cigar still smoldering in his mouth, which ought to be a cautionary tale but hasn't been.

Locked in an unholy ideological alliance with a criminal organization masquerading as a political party, the media need not wonder how they – representing the American public, on whose behalf they're supposed to operate – got here. All they need to do is keep doing it. Once the ends justify the means, anything goes. When "by any means necessary" is not just a revolution slogan but a philosophy of life, when emotion is prized over reason, and when the icons of the left are Che Guevara and Mao instead of Jefferson and FDR, then all power really does flow from the barrel of the gun of electoral-power politics.

In Conclusion

For more than two centuries, the Democratic Party has done its best to disguise its real aims. It preached tolerance even as it oppressed immigrants and lynched black people. It spoke of compassion even as it condemned three generations of African Americans to a plantation existence and destroyed their cultural institutions. It "celebrated diversity" not by defining deviancy down (in the late Daniel Patrick Moynihan's memorable phrase) but by elevating and mainstreaming, via journalism and Hollywood, the worst cultural pathologies of the underclass. It constantly agitates for society to drop its squaresville morality and worship at the altar of the only god leftism really honors: the God of Self-Gratification.

In Milton's *Paradise Lost*, Books V and VI, we read the almost throwaway story of the seraph Abdiel who, swayed by Lucifer's tongue, at first dawdles with the insurgents and then realizes his folly and returns to the light. Abdiel is perhaps the most sympathetic character in the poem, a stand-in for weak humanity (though angelic). Listening to Satan, Abdiel rebukes the demon's monstrous lies:

> *So spake the Seraph Abdiel faithful found,*
> *Among the faithless, faithful only hee;*
> *Among innumerable false, unmov'd,*
> *Unshak'n, unseduc'd, unterrifi'd*
> *His Loyaltie he kept, his Love, his Zeale;*
> *Nor number, nor example with him wrought*
> *To swerve from truth, or change his constant mind*
> *Though single. From amidst them forth he passd,*
> *Long way through hostile scorn, which he susteind*
> *Superior, nor of violence fear'd aught;*
> *And with retorted scorn his back he turn'd*
> *On those proud Towrs to swift destruction doom'd.*

After nearly two and half centuries of Democratic political perfidy, cultural malevolence, and, when necessary, sedition and outright treason – and however imperfect the political alternative – is it not time for us to emulate Abdiel and call them what they are? To no longer be seduced by their sweet nothings of tolerance and compassion and fairness and social justice and to instead apply the hard-won realism of our forefathers, who, like Milton, understood man's fallen nature?

The days of patriotic, centrist Democrats like the late

Washington State Senator Henry "Scoop" Jackson have been over since the McGovern revolution. Once upon a time, conservative Democrats were in the vanguard of the fight against Communism. Today, a "Scoop Jackson Democrat" – socially liberal but strong on defense – is as extinct as his namesake. Instead the radical left, following their guru, Saul Alinsky (who famously acknowledged Lucifer in his manifesto, *Rules for Radicals*), continues to insist that conservatives are their enemy and that we can be broken by the application of his rule No. 4: "Make the enemy live up to their own book of rules." That any deviation from what the leftist media insists are conservative standards is proof of hypocrisy. Like the aliens in *Independence Day*, they're using our satellites – our institutions and our moral code – against us, and for decades their ethos and their arguments carried the day.

No longer. It's time to make them live up to *their* rule book and their moral code, which is to say, no rule book or moral code at all. To expose them for the power-hungry nihilists they have become – the true sons and daughters of Aaron Burr. The minute the American people fully grasp that the modern Democratic Party has become the reductio ad absurdum of itself, the inevitable result of its cynical nihilism, the Democrats' long war against the United States will finally end.

After more than two centuries, it's time to send the Democrats the way of the Federalists, the Whigs, the Know-Nothings, the Dixiecrats, and the other splinter parties and factions that litter American political history. No law says a given political party is eternal. And yet as long as the party of Burr continues to thrive, its loaded gun is no longer pointing at a man but at a whole nation.

Is there a place in the American political system for a truly loyal opposition – one that does not seek "fundamental transformation" of our constitutional Republic but rather its betterment and continuance? Of course there is.

But is there a place for a criminal organization masquerading as a political party?

If our nation is to survive, not any more.

KEVIN D. WILLIAMSON

WHAT DOOMED DETROIT

*The dynastic character of American politics is distasteful at best —
the 2016 election might very well have been a contest between
another Clinton and another Bush, and so might the 2036 presidential race — but some dynasties are worse than others. In his
twenty incompetent, corrupt years in office, Mayor Coleman Young
damaged Detroit in ways that it has not yet recovered from, and
may never. The 2017 mayoral election is a contest between the
reformer Mike Duggan, who saw Detroit through its modest post-
bankruptcy bounce, and . . . the California-raised illegitimate son
of Coleman Young, who goes by the name Coleman Young II. The
younger Young ran for mayor of Detroit before but had to settle for
a seat in the state senate, to which he was elected with a Third
World–style margin: 93.3 percent of the vote. Before his entry into
office, he had worked as a political intern and at a Subway sand-
wich shop. He recently appeared in a rap video titled "We Be
Winning."*

*The FBI still ranks Detroit as America's most violent city, with
a population of only a little more than a hundred thousand. The
local police chief says he has software that indicates otherwise.
That must be comforting.*

*Detroit's municipal institutions remain unable to perform the
most basic tasks. After the water-pollution scandal in Flint, Michigan, Detroit decided to take a look at its own water infrastructure.
To no one's surprise, elevated lead and copper levels were discovered at seventeen schools. (Two already had been identified as*

*having a heavy metal problem.) That's the sort of thing that rou-
tine oversight would have turned up; that is, if there were any
competently executed routine oversight.*

*The mayoral contest will be an interesting test for Detroit's
politics. Mayor Duggan is white, Coleman Young II is black, and
Detroit's local politics have been overwhelmingly racial in character for generations. Duggan's modest successes have by no means
been the stuff of profiles in courage, but embracing Coleman Young II
would represent a symbolic and literal regression. Duggan led the
polls as of this writing. Maybe Detroit finally has had enough.*

"Better to reign in Hell than serve in Heaven."
JOHN MILTON, *Paradise Lost*

IN THE SPACE of a single generation, Detroit managed
to ruin itself. Some of the factors that led to the immola-
tion of Detroit are unique to the city and its politics, but
some are not. As the nation watches the city descend into
insolvency and chaos, the question is: Is Detroit an outlier,
or is it just ahead of the curve?

The proximate cause of Detroit's bankruptcy is its
inability to make good on debts owed to the funds paying
out pensions and health care benefits to current and
retired city workers. Those obligations make up the great
majority of Detroit's $20 billion or so in outstanding debt.
While the city's population has been plummeting since the
1950s, its public sector has continued to grow relative to
the size of its population. In 2011, it maintained nearly
13,000 city employees, or one municipal employee for
every 55 residents, twice the number of larger cities such
as Charlotte and Fort Worth. (That one may write "larger

cities such as Charlotte and Fort Worth" speaks volumes about what has become of Detroit.) When staffing reductions have been proposed, both the unions and city officials resisted. When modest reductions were proposed in 2011, city Finance Director Tom Lijana protested, "You can't do this in one year.... I'm going to be picking up your garbage once a month. I'm only going to turn on power to your house every once in a while. You just can't do that." Yet the city of Austin, hardly a Spartan outpost of small-government skinflintery, manages to provide what are generally conceded to be very good municipal services with far fewer city employees per resident than Detroit. San Jose does so with *half* the per capita municipal workforce that Detroit maintains.

Detroit is an extreme example of the fact that public-sector employment has become in effect a supplementary welfare state, with salaries and benefits – and, above all, pensions – entirely disconnected from legitimate municipal purposes. Unionized public-sector employees with a high degree of political discipline fortified by narrow financial self-interest become an unstoppable constituency, and the government becomes its own special-interest group. But while salaries more or less have to be paid out of current revenue and therefore impose at least a measure of pain on taxpayers, promised future benefits need not be backed by anything more than good intentions. While there were areas in which the city proceeded responsibly – as late as 2011, its police and firefighter pension fund was being adequately provided for – many future obligations were not funded at all, or funded to only a tiny degree of the liabilities accruing. A 2012 Kennedy School study found that Detroit had set aside less than half of what it would need to fund its pensions and was attempting to fund its health-insurance and life-insurance plans on a pay-as-you-go basis, resulting in unfunded liabilities amounting to a massive $5 billion.

In spite of these growing liabilities, Detroit's public-sector workers consistently managed to increase their share of the city's workforce while stopping dead any and all efforts at meaningful reform.

They have been empowered to resist reform by a particularly nasty form of racialist politics that has reached its fullest expression in Detroit but is by no means limited to that unhappy city. When the mayor of Philadelphia boasts that "the brothers and sisters are in charge," when the mayor of Washington declares the nation's capital a "chocolate city," they are cultivating the same sort of tribalism that has helped make Detroit what it is. The tolerance for black racism in American politics is striking. When Representative Joe Mitchell, an Alabama Democrat, was challenged by a constituent about a question related to gun rights, Mitchell responded that he was elected to represent the interests of blacks and maintained that he could care less about the interests of his white correspondent and those of his "slave-holding, murdering, adulterous, baby-raping, incestuous, snaggle-toothed, backward-assed, inbreed [*sic*], imported, criminal-minded kin folk." The anti-Semitic remarks of the Rev. Jesse Jackson and the Rev. Al Sharpton are of course well documented, as is the habit of mostly Democratic black politicians of consorting with such openly racist demagogues as Louis Farrakhan. It is an irony of our history that the political home of black racism in American politics is also the historical political home of white racism: the Democratic Party.

The end point of such politics is Detroit. As late as 1960, Detroit was the most affluent city in the United States – and perhaps the most affluent industrial city in the world – with a per capita income exceeding that of any other U.S.

city, according to the U.S. Census Bureau. In 1961, it elected
as its mayor Jerome Cavanagh, a 33-year-old Democrat
whose youth and idealism brought immediate and inevitable comparisons to John F. Kennedy. Cavanagh's triumph
was a surprise, and he was borne to victory on the strength
of an African-American vote whose power had not yet
been fully appreciated. Added to the Democratic alle-
giances of Catholic white ethnics, the subordination of the
conservative-voting autoworkers to their left-leaning union
bosses, and the growing sympathy for Kennedy–Johnson-
style progressivism among the professional classes, the
attachment of the black vote to the Democratic cause
meant the end of Republicans in Detroit and the establishment of a de facto one-party government.

The effects would prove catastrophic in a remarkably
short period of time.

But Cavanagh entered office on a wave of optimism.
He promised reform, and reform was needed – and seemed
within reach. Already in the 1950s and early 1960s, Detroit
had troubles, but they were not insurmountable. Detroit,
like many similar cities, had a problem: the concentration
of poverty and related social dysfunction in its inner city –
in no small part a legacy of the explosion of the city's black
population during the Great Migration, soaring from
6,000 in 1910 to 120,000 in 1929 and from 1.2 percent of
the population in 1910 to about 30 percent of the population by the election of Cavanagh. It is one of the great
tragedies of American history that wherever black Americans go, from the Jim Crow South to the great industrial
cities, they are persecuted by the Democratic Party, then
help entrench the power of that party.

The black workers arriving to fill industrial jobs in
Detroit found discrimination very similar to what they had
endured in the South, with Democratic politicians such as

Representative Rudolph G. Tenerowicz leading efforts on behalf of their white-ethnic working-class constituents to prevent desegregation, especially when it came to housing. The segregation of housing would prove to be the flashpoint for the periods of civil unrest that give Detroit the distinction of being the only U.S. city to have been occupied by federal troops on three occasions.

Tenerowicz was among the key political figures who fought the 1943 effort of the Detroit Housing Commission – then under the leadership of Republican Mayor Edward Jeffries and his reform-minded director-secretary, 25-year-old George Clifton Edwards, Jr., – to build a housing project for black defense workers in a largely Polish section of the city. The backlash against this plan resulted in, among other dispiriting displays, the insalubrious spectacle of a mob of pale-faced Polish Americans holding up signs reading "We Want White Tenants in Our Community" in front of a housing project named after Sojourner Truth. The Rev. Charles Hill, a prominent civil-rights activist, wryly observed at the time that his opponents were under the mistaken impression that Sojourner Truth was a Polish woman.

Tenerowicz was joined in his effort by the unholy leadership of Father Constantine Dzink, whose sermons highlighted the danger of "the Jews and niggers making a combination" in local politics. (The theory that Protestant Republicans and Jews colluded to place black housing projects in Catholic areas in order to break up Democratic voting blocs is absolutely deathless, still with us in the work of the Catholic polemicist E. Michael Jones and others of his ilk.) The Ku Klux Klan was not unheard-of in Michigan, but more common were organizations such as the Fenelon-Seven Mile Road Development Association, Detroit's version of the South's white citizens' councils. Facing pressure from white Democratic constituencies, Franklin Roosevelt's Federal Housing Administration (FHA) decided that the Sojourner Truth project would be a whites-only development, while a blacks-only project would be built elsewhere – outside the city limits. After sustained protest, the FHA again reversed itself, and eventually a number of black families – who already had paid rent and signed leases in anticipation of moving into their new homes – began to relocate into the project, doing so in the face of an armed mob and by the light of a burning cross. Some 1,600 National Guard troops and 1,100 police officers had to be dispatched to prevent their being lynched.

Those racial tensions were further exacerbated when 25,000 white autoworkers at Packard walked off the job to protest the hiring of three black men to work on the assembly line. Three weeks later, Detroit erupted into a full-fledged race riot. Mayor Jeffries begged the federal government for help, which was not immediately forthcoming – not until the Germans began using Detroit's bloodshed in their propaganda efforts. After having his advisers cook up a legal rationale that would save his having to formally declare martial law, President Roosevelt dispatched federal troops to occupy Detroit. Some 6,000 soldiers would be needed to restore peace in the city.

It was the beginning of the end of Republican power in Detroit, which had elected a good deal many more Whigs to its mayoralty than Democrats. Before Jeffries's time, the Democrats had won election to the mayor's office only five times in the 20th century, as opposed to 14 times for the Republicans. Jeffries was the fifth of five back-to-back Republican mayors preceded by the Democratic reformer Frank Murphy – who was himself preceded by five back-to-back Republican mayors. The Democrats had not won consecutive mayoralties since the 19th century.

But the riots badly damaged Jeffries's standing. His political machine kept him in power until 1948, when Democrat Eugene Van Antwerp sent him back to the city council. The 1949 election saw Jeffries's young housing director, now aligned with the Democrats, running on a civil-rights platform in a racially charged election against Republican Albert Cobo. The Republican won, but the GOP was increasingly alienated from the black vote. Cobo was succeeded by Republican Louis Miriani, a corrupt party-machine man who would later serve time in prison for tax fraud – but not before losing the election to the charismatic young Jerome Cavanagh, the first of Detroit's Democrats to figure out how to marry the black vote to the union vote. Detroit would never elect another Republican mayor, at least as of this writing.

Cavanagh's administration came out like gangbusters, and for years he could do no wrong as far as Democrats were concerned – which now meant, as a practical matter, as far as political Detroit was concerned. Having run as a civil-rights man, he marched in the streets of Detroit with the Rev. Martin Luther King, Jr., and 100,000 constituents. He appointed a reform-minded police chief and instituted affirmative-action programs. He proved to be an expert at wringing money out of the federal government. President Lyndon Johnson was an admirer and an ally, and his Model Cities Program showered money on Detroit – and made Mayor Cavanagh the only sitting elected official to serve on its board. The riots of 1943, all the well-informed people said, were a distant memory. We were to have a Great Society, with Detroit as its model city. For a time, it seemed likely that the progressive vision of urban renewal under an expert technocratic administration would be realized. The *National Observer* wrote during Cavanagh's first term:

The evidence, both statistical and visual, is everywhere. Retail sales are up dramatically. Earnings are higher. Unemployment is lower. People are putting new aluminum sidings on their homes, new carpets on the floor, new cars in the garage.

Some people are forsaking the suburbs and returning to the city. Physically Detroit has acquired freshness and vitality. Acres of slums have been razed, and steel and glass apartments, angular and lonely in the vacated landscape, have sprung up in their place. In the central business district, hard by the Detroit River, severely rectangular skyscrapers – none more than 5 years old – jostle uncomfortably with the gilded behemoths of another age.

Accustomed to years of adversity, to decades of drabness and civil immobility, Detroiters are naturally exhilarated. They note with particular pride that Detroit has been removed from the Federal Bureau of Employment Security's classification of "an area with substantial and persistent unemployment."

But there was a problem. In 1962, the city had faced a serious fiscal deficit – $28 million, back when that meant something – but the young mayor was not about to back away from his ambitious agenda. That meant more money, and that meant new taxes and higher taxes. Among them were a city income tax and a city commuter tax, which Cavanagh was empowered to establish after a fight with the state legislature. Armed with his new revenue-reaping tools, Cavanagh set about building his urban utopia, and he made the same unpleasant discovery that has, slowly and painfully, dawned upon central planners, reformers, and utopians of all stripes over the ages: nobody wanted to live in his model city.

Contrary to the *National Observer*'s observations, Detroit's population had peaked in the 1950 census. It soon was losing more than 20,000 residents a year on net. But that does not begin to tell the whole story. From 1960 to 1970, Detroit lost 158,662 people on net – some 22,000 in 1966 alone. But it lost nearly twice that many white residents: 344,093 of them from 1960 to 1970. In 1950, there were 1.5 million whites living in Detroit, virtually all of whom – all but 75,000 – would leave by 2010. Throughout the 1960s and beyond, the combination of higher taxes, crime, civil disorder (especially the 1967 riots), and the declining quality of schools and other government institutions created enormous pressure for people and businesses to relocate outside the city limits. The new plants serving the increasingly decentralized automobile industry moved outside the city, and the workers – also the taxpayers – followed them. The white residents, being generally better off and more able to secure jobs and housing elsewhere, led the way.

Ironically, it was Detroit's signature product – the automobile – that hastened the city's dissolution. Under the leadership of President Dwight D. Eisenhower, the United States had begun in the postwar period the country's greatest experiment with economic central planning: the federal highway system. Cities such as New York and Boston (and, to a lesser extent, Philadelphia) had geographic and social forces that helped preserve their urban cores, whereas truly postwar cities such as Houston were simply organized around the automobile and incorporated outlying areas as the population shifted. Detroit, like many Rust Belt cities, had neither factor to reinforce its municipal integrity. While sprawling, automobile-centric Los Angeles saw its population double from 1940 to 1980, despite the decline of key industries such as furniture making and steel, Detroit continued to trickle away. The federal government paved the way to the suburbs, and the city of Detroit gave its people ever more powerful incentives to take those roads and never look back.

Like the rest of the country, Detroit missed a critical opportunity in the immediate postwar era. The United States was in an unprecedented position: it was the sole surviving major industrial power that had not been ravaged by the war. In the immediate postwar era, the United States was home to at least half – and possibly more – of the world's manufacturing capacity, a not insignificant chunk of it in Detroit. And those factories were humming. The United States was producing 60 percent of the entire world's manufacturing output. The nation alone constituted 61 percent of the total economic output of the countries that now make up the OECD. The Eisenhower administration had success wringing the postwar inflation out of the economy with a conservative monetary policy, which contributed to a series of small recessions that had little effect on employment or wages, which were robust, especially as wartime wage and price controls were rescinded. Detroit's working men enjoyed undreamed-of prosperity, and the city had a thriving black middle class. It is disheartening to consider the counterfactual case of what the United States and its industrial capital might have done had our political and economic leadership fully appreciated the uniqueness of our economic position and, most important, the inescapably transitory nature of that position. Instead, we set about building the welfare state. Government grew at all levels, and unions in the private sector – notably Detroit's autoworkers – set about creating unsustainable workplace practices and compensation structures that would eventually put them out of jobs, while their counterparts in the public sector set about looting the fiscs. The model of government at the federal, state, and local level that emerged in the late 1950s and 1960s was built on a defective foundation: the belief that the postwar economic boom would last forever. While Vietnam and desegregation were the headline issues of the 1960s, much of the real domestic politics of the period consisted of infighting over the money from the postwar economic boom, with little or no attention given to the fact that the money would someday run out.

And it has run out spectacularly in Detroit.

The textbook example of postwar shortsightedness was the debacle of Cavanagh's attempt to implement the Model Cities program. The Johnson administration was generous with the money, but Detroit was divided over what to do with it. Local business interests – back when Detroit had local business interests – wanted the money to be invested in the downtown commercial district, creating an urban anchor for the city, but they gave little thought to the question of who, exactly, would inhabit the skyscrapers they envisioned at a time when the city's population was in steep decline. The Detroit left – the community organizers, if you will – wanted the money to be invested in housing projects and other affordable-housing developments, along with the usual array of antipoverty programs, the unstated purpose of which is to provide comfortable employment for the politically connected. As in other Model Cities such as Newark, Camden, and Atlanta, Detroit's efforts to shore up its city center went up in flames with the riots of the 1960s.

The 1967 Detroit race riot was the largest civil disturbance since the Civil War and the New York City draft riots. Some 2,000 buildings were burned to the ground; 7,200 people were arrested; 1,189 injured; and 43 left dead – killed by snipers, beaten by mobs, immolated alive in burning buildings. Firefighters were gunned down while trying to put out the flames of the city. Cavanagh, a Democrat, hesitated to seek assistance from Governor George Romney, while President Johnson hesitated to deploy troops at the request of Governor Romney, who was expected to be his opponent in the 1968 presidential election. As the politics were sorted out, the city burned. Eventually, Johnson invoked the Insurrection Act of 1807 and deployed 4,700 troops from the 82nd Airborne, while Romney sent in the National Guard. *Newsweek* described the aftermath:

> *The trouble burst on Detroit like a firestorm and turned the nation's fifth biggest city into a theater of war. Whole streets lay ravaged by looters, whole blocks immolated by flames. Federal troops – the first sent into racial battle outside the South in a quarter of a century – occupied American streets at bayonet point. Patton tanks – machine guns ablaze – and Huey helicopters patrolled a cityscape of blackened brick chimneys poking out of gutted basements. And suddenly Harlem 1964 and Watts 1965 and Newark only three weeks ago fell into the shadows of memory. Detroit was the new benchmark, its rubble a monument to the most devastating race riot in U.S. history – and a symbol of domestic crisis grown graver than any since the Civil War.*

It is worth noting that while Detroit already was in decline in the 1960s, the position of its black middle class was very strong. As the economist Thomas Sowell notes, "Before the ghetto riot of 1967, Detroit's black population had the highest rate of home-ownership of any black urban population in the country, and their unemployment rate was just 3.4 percent. It was not despair that fueled the riot."

What was it?

Mohandas K. Gandhi famously told representatives of the British Raj that India, like any self-respecting country, would prefer bad government under its own people to good government under a foreign power. A similar notion has held sway in Detroit, but its motivating factor is racism rather than nationalism. Detroit is a city in which black identity politics has trumped, and continues to trump, every other consideration, from basic finances to public safety. In 1974, Detroit's racial politics would come to full fruition with the election of Mayor Coleman Young, an incompetent administrator, a friend of corruption – two of his closest political allies, who happened to be serving as police chief and deputy police chief, managed to loot $2.6 million from city funds between the two of them – and a practitioner of poisonous racial politics who nonetheless managed to keep himself in the mayor's office for 20 years, thereby foreclosing any opportunity the city might have had to reverse its course. As James Q. Wilson put it, "Mayor Coleman Young rejected the integrationist goal in favor of a flamboyant, black-power style that won him loyal followers, but he left the city a fiscal and social wreck." Young's stock-in-trade was blaming whites for the problems of an increasingly whites-free city, charging that, in his words, "the money was carried out in the pockets of the businesses and the white people."

As Nolan Finley notes in the *Detroit News*, Mayor Young's spirit is very much alive in "the black nationalism that is now the dominant ideology of the council." Finley reported on the city council's debate regarding the expansion of a city convention center. Many of those backing the project, and many of the union members who would be employed to work on it, were white, which infuriated both the council members and the residents who showed up to denounce the project. The assembled crowd shouted that whites addressing the issue should "go home," while council president Monica Conyers dismissed the case of a white union representative with these words: "Those workers look like you – they don't look like me." But race was not Conyers's sole concern in matters of municipal finance: she was subsequently convicted on bribery charges related to city contracts. Other members of the city council have proposed the creation of blacks-only city contracts and a blacks-only enterprise zone. The city has considered restricting some grant money to black-owned businesses under the rubric of "minority" economic development – in a city that is 80 percent black.

From Cavanagh to Young to the current dispute over the city's bankruptcy, the combination of racial politics and union financial interests has undermined every public institution in Detroit. And while the black-power style may be the most remarkable feature of Detroit's poisonous political coalition, the unions have the upper hand. As life for blacks – and everybody else – in Detroit deteriorated, the ever more deeply entrenched unions installed political candidates who rewarded them with ever more extravagant promises of compensation, benefits, and retirement pensions. That the city was in no way positioned to make good on those benefits apparently mattered little to Detroit's ruling class, which has been happy to trade promises of future payouts in exchange for immediate power and financial rewards. Their actions have ranged from the negligent to the outright criminal. Mayor Kwame Kilpatrick resigned after being convicted of felony perjury and obstruction of justice. In 2010, he was returned to prison for violating his parole, and in 2013, he was convicted of 24 additional felonies ranging from extortion to bribery and fraud.

Against that background, Detroit's decision to seek protection in bankruptcy court is almost anticlimactic. Union power ensured the growth of the public sector; racial hostility and municipal incompetence drove first the white middle class and then the black middle class out of the city and ensured that as Detroit's signature industry struggled, no new centers of economic activity emerged to replace it. It had always been a matter of time – indeed, the main interest of the sorry case of Detroit is to learn how long it takes to entirely ruin a prosperous city. The answer is less than one generation in the worst-case scenario, but possibly longer for cities that suffer the same kind of problems as Detroit to a lesser degree.

Detroit's decline is related to the decline of the automobile industry but was not an inevitable outcome of it. Many cities have seen their key industries shrink or evaporate without descending into similar chaos. But the autoworkers' unions bear a special responsibility for Detroit's cultural and economic troubles inasmuch as they undermined their industry and the institutions related to it at the very moment Detroit most needed them. In addition to simply being greedy, they were also caught up in the same countercultural nihilism as the rest of the country in the 1960s and 1970s. John Lippert, who worked to build Cadillacs at the Fleetwood plant during those years, tells the story: "Our militancy at GM drew on the youthful rebellion that was gripping the U.S. Hundreds of us at Fleetwood, black and white, grew our hair long, fueled by antiestablishment fervor that helped end the Vietnam War and sweep Richard Nixon out of the White House. During our 30-minute lunch breaks, we sat in our cars and listened to Jimi Hendrix as we smoked marijuana, drank beer, and took Desoxyn and other methamphetamines before returning to the line. Our quality levels and absenteeism rates were among GM's worst. We didn't care."

GM's bailout by the federal government was an exercise in lawlessness, but at least this much can be said for it: GM produces actual goods. It has assets, products, facilities, and production capacity. Detroit already is sniffing around for a federal bailout, too, but there is, practically speaking, nothing to save. One-third of the city's land is vacant or derelict. Half its streetlights have been rendered inoperable by thieves stripping the copper wiring. It has more than 120,000 vacant homes and empty lots. It is closing its schools and police stations and discontinuing some public transport, in part because it cannot afford to operate the buses and in part because their drivers are too afraid to drive them on the city's lawless streets. Its notional unemployment rate was 16 percent in April 2013; its real unemployment rate is probably closer to 50 percent. Its murder rate is about 11 times that of New York City. The median value of a home in the city is $9,000. When the Cold War classic *Red Dawn* was remade in 2012, the producers saved themselves some of the cost of creating a postapocalyptic United States by filming in Detroit, though filming had to be stopped when councilwoman JoAnn Watson, in a car with municipal plates, parked in the middle of a scene and refused to leave.

Detroit has at least $20 billion in debts that it cannot pay. Its unfunded liabilities related to union pensions and benefits may prove greater still. The bankruptcy is playing out according to Detroit rules, which means a combination of racialist politics and union self-dealing. Rick Snyder, the Republican governor of Michigan, was denounced as a racist for appointing an emergency financial manager to oversee the city's insolvency. The manager, Kevyn Orr, is a black man who was denounced as an "Uncle Tom" by the Rev. Charles Williams II, the head of the Michigan division of the Rev. Al Sharpton's National

Action Network. A crowd marched on the governor's private residence, chanting, "Detroit won't go to the back of the bus. No EFMs. No racist cuts." The unions, which are threatened with losing pension payments worth billions of dollars, challenged in court the city's very legal right to seek bankruptcy protection, though federal law explicitly provides for it, and a local judge attempted to throw the bankruptcy out unilaterally, much to the amusement of the federal courts, which have jurisdiction in the matter. Detroit has, at this counting, more than 100,000 creditors making claims against its empty purse. Simply cataloging those claims and beginning the process of adjudicating them may take years.

Mayor Young, of all people, was insightful about the effects of the riot and its aftermath. "Detroit's losses went a hell of a lot deeper than the immediate toll of lives and buildings," he wrote in his autobiography. "The riot put Detroit on the fast track to economic desolation, mugging the city and making off with incalculable value in jobs, earnings taxes, corporate taxes, retail dollars, sales taxes, mortgages, interest, property taxes, development dollars, investment dollars, tourism dollars, and plain damn money."

Detroit is not alone in its situation. Other cities – and large states such as California – face similar problems. It is worth noting that Detroit's heavy pension liabilities, amounting to about $19,000 per household, still are only the fifth worst in the country, according to the Kennedy School study, with Chicago leading the way and New York City, San Francisco, and Boston in worse shape than Detroit. The difference is that none of those other cities, even Chicago, is an obvious economic basket case. Indeed, San Francisco and New York are the centers of two of the nation's most productive economic sectors: technology and finance. A highly productive economy can carry the weight of a lot of political misdeeds before it collapses under the burden.

But there are limits. Detroit is a case of the parasite having outgrown the host. Whether that will be the case in cities such as San Francisco or in states such as California remains to be seen. Indeed, the main challenge for reformers at the state and local – and national – level for the coming generation is: Don't become Detroit. But reform is neither politically easy nor necessarily popular. And if the Age of Obama has taught us anything, it is that shouting "Racist!" while looting the treasury is a viable political strategy beyond Detroit.

ABOUT THE AUTHORS

JAY COST has been a top political analyst for a decade. He is the author of *A Republic No More: Big Government and the Rise of American Political Corruption* and *Spoiled Rotten*. He currently writes for the *Weekly Standard*, and his work has been featured in the *Wall Street Journal*, the *New York Post*, *National Review*, the FOX News website, the RealClearPolitics site, *National Affairs*, and *Policy Review*.

PHILIP HAMBURGER is the Maurice and Hilda Friedman Professor of Law at Columbia Law School. He writes on constitutional law, including religious liberty, freedom of speech and the press, administrative power, and unconstitutional conditions. His previous books are *Separation of Church and State* (Harvard, 2002); *Law and Judicial Duty* (Harvard, 2008); and *Is Administrative Law Unlawful?* (Chicago, 2014). He received a BA from Princeton and a JD from Yale. Hamburger is a member of the American Academy of Arts and Sciences, and has been awarded the Sutherland Prize twice, the Henry Paolucci/Walter Bagehot Book Award, the Hayek Book Prize, and the Bradley Prize.

MOLLIE ZIEGLER HEMINGWAY is a senior editor at the *Federalist*. A longtime journalist, her work has appeared in the *Wall Street Journal*, *USA Today*, the *Los Angeles Times*, the *Guardian*, the *Washington Post*, CNN, *National Review*, *Federal Times*, and many other publications. She is a frequent guest on FOX News, CNN, and National Public

Radio. Hemingway is a 2004 recipient of the Robert Novak Journalism Fellowship and a 2014 recipient of the Claremont Institute Lincoln Fellowship.

DAVID B. KOPEL is an associate policy analyst at the Cato Institute, the research director of the Independence Institute, and an adjunct professor of advanced constitutional law at Denver University, Sturm College of Law.

GREG LUKIANOFF is an attorney and the president of the Foundation for Individual Rights in Education (FIRE). His writings on campus free speech have appeared in the *Wall Street Journal*, the *New York Times*, and the *Washington Post*, in addition to dozens of other publications. He is a regular columnist for *HuffPost* and the author of *Unlearning Liberty: Campus Censorship and the End of American Debate* (Encounter, 2014).

ANDREW C. MCCARTHY, a former top federal prosecutor, is a senior fellow at the National Review Institute, a contributing editor at *National Review*, and a columnist for PJ Media. He is author of the best sellers *Willful Blindness: A Memoir of the Jihad* (Encounter, 2010) and *The Grand Jihad: How Islam and the Left Sabotage America* (Encounter, 2012). His most recent book is *Faithless Execution: Building the Political Case for Obama's Impeachment* (Encounter, 2014).

JARED MEYER is a senior research fellow at the Foundation for Government Accountability. He is the coauthor of *Disinherited: How Washington Is Betraying America's Young* (Encounter, 2015) and the author of *Uber-Positive: Why Americans Love the Sharing Economy* (Encounter, 2016). He is included on *Forbes*'s "30 under 30" list and has testified before various congressional committees on regulatory reform. In addition to publishing hundreds of opinion articles, Meyer has discussed his research on many radio and television shows broadcast by the BBC, FOX, and NPR.

JAMES PIERESON is a senior fellow at the Manhattan Institute and president of the William E. Simon Foundation. He is a contributor to the *New Criterion*, the *Wall Street Journal*, *Commentary*, the *Weekly Standard*, and the *Washington Post*. He is also the author *Shattered Consensus: The Rise and Decline of America's Postwar Political Order* (Encounter, 2015).

CLAUDIA ROSETT, a prize-winning journalist for her reporting on the United Nations and a former editorial writer and foreign correspondent for the *Wall Street Journal*, is currently a foreign policy fellow with the Independent Women's Forum.

AVIK ROY is the president of the Foundation for Research on Equal Opportunity, a nonpartisan, nonprofit think tank that conducts research on market-based ideas that can expand opportunity to those who least have it. He has advised three presidential candidates on policy: Mitt Romney in 2012, and Rick Perry and Marco Rubio in 2016. Roy is opinion editor at *Forbes* and runs *The Apothecary*, the influential *Forbes* health care blog. He has also written for the *Wall Street Journal*, the *New York Times*, the *Washington Post*, the *Atlantic*, and *National Affairs*, among others, and is a frequent guest on national news programs. Roy lives in Austin, Texas.

ROBERT L. SHIBLEY is executive director of the Foundation for Individual Rights in Education (FIRE). He is a graduate of Duke University and Duke University School of Law. Robert and his wife, Araz, live in North Carolina with their two daughters.

About the Authors

MICHAEL WALSH, a former associate editor of *TIME* magazine, is the author of six novels and six works of non-fiction as well as a columnist for the *New York Post* and a contributor to *National Review* and PJ Media. He was a winner of the 2004 American Book Award for his novel *And All the Saints* (Warner, 2004).

KEVIN D. WILLIAMSON writes for *National Review*, and his work has appeared in publications including *POLITICO* and the *New York Post*. He was the 2015 Pulliam fellow at Hillsdale College in Michigan, and he is the author of *The End Is Near and It's Going to Be Awesome* (Broadside Books, 2013); *The Politically Incorrect Guide to Socialism* (Regnery, 2011); and the Broadside *The Dependency Agenda* (Encounter, 2012).

INDEX

Index

Index

Index

Index

Index

Index

Index